Upward Panic

Choreography and Dance Studies

A series of books edited by Robert P. Cohan, C.B.E.

This book is part of a series. The publisher will accept continuation orders which may be cancelled at any time and which provide for automatic billing and shipping of each title in the series upon publication. Please write for details.

Upward Panic.

The Autobiography of Eva Palmer-Sikelianos, E.

Edited, with an Introduction and Notes
by

John P. Anton

University of South Florida, Tampa, USA

harwood academic publishers
Switzerland • Australia • Belgium • France • Germany • Gt. Britain •
India • Japan • Malaysia • Netherlands • Russia • Singapore • USA

NN309
P182
A3u
c.3

Harwood Academic Publishers

Poststrasse 22
Chur 7000
Switzerland

Post Office Box 90
Reading, Berkshire RG1 8JL
Great Britain

Private Bag 8
Camberwell, Victoria 3124
Australia

3-14-9, Okubo
Shinjuku-ku, Tokyo 169
Japan

58, rue Lhomond
75005 Paris
France

Emmaplein 5
1075 AW Amsterdam
Netherlands

Glinkastrasse 13-15
O-1086 Berlin
Germany

5301 Tacony Street, Drawer 330
Philadelphia, Pennsylvania 19137
United States of America

Library of Congress Cataloging-in-Publication Data

Sikelianos, Eva Palmer, 1874–1952.
    Upward panic : the autobiography of Eva Palmer Sikelianos / edited with an introduction by John P. Anton.
      p.   cm. -- (Choreography and dance studies ; v. 2)
    ISBN 3-7186-5264-1 (hard) ISBN 3-7186-5310-9 (soft)
    1. Sikelianos, Eva Palmer, 1874–1952. 2. Dancers--United States--Biography. 3. Dancing--Greece--History--20th century. I. Anton, John Peter, 1920– . II. Title. III. Series.
GV1785.S5543A3   1991
792.8'028'092--dc20
[B]
                                                92-4461
                                                CIP

add 1/04

Contents

Introduction to the Series

Choreography and Dance Studies is a book series of special interest to dancers, dance teachers and choreographers. Focusing on dance composition, its techniques and training, the series will also cover the relationship of choreography to other components of dance performance such as music, lighting and the training of dancers.

In addition, *Choreography and Dance Studies* will seek to publish new works and provide translations of works not previously published in English, as well as publish reprints of currently unavailable books of outstanding value to the dance community.

ACKNOWLEDGEMENTS

A University of South Florida Research Grant enabled me to visit Greece in the summer of 1985 to begin the collection of materials related to the editorial work on the manuscript. I owe a note of gratitude to The Angelo and Sophia Tsakopoulos Fund for a grant to prepare the notes of the manuscript and obtain related materials; and to the Pan-Arcadian Federation of America and its officers, Dr. P. Gouzoulis, Dr. C. Sarantopoulos, Mr. Manny Giannakakos and Mr. G. Sourounis for financial assistance to complete the English edition during its final stage.

I want now to express my gratitude for the initial help I have received in securing information and copies. Mr. Nearchou, former Director of the European Center for Delphic Studies, and his then associates Mr. George Zacharopoulos, Mr. A. Apostolopoulos and Mr. Nikos Levendis; to Mr. Angelos Delivorias, the Director of the Benakis Museum, for granting me the copyright to the English edition of the manuscript, giving generously of his time to provide me with the needed information and making available the files of the Sikelianos Collection; I am also grateful to his staff and to Mrs. G. Tselika in particular for her assistance in preparing photocopies of the text of both A1 and A2 as well as a number of documents pertaining to biographical information; Ms. Theresa Sellers has been invaluable as a source of information and for introducing me to Mrs. Joan Vanderpool, of Athens, who kindly provided me with copies of a number of letters Eva wrote to her in 1935, all of which are related to the production of classical tragedies at Smith College and Bryn Mawr; to Ms. Vivette Tsarlamba-Kaklamanis for her advice and the materials from of her own archives, especially the photographs printed in this edition. The late K. A. Papageorgiou, publisher of the periodical IOS, had kindly provided me with a copy of the two-volume special issue of this publication he had dedicated to Eva. Mr. Athan Karras of California, was most supportive throughout this undertaking. Special thanks go to Glafkos Sikelianos for granting me an interview at his residence in California. The index is the work of my assistant, Ms. Nancy Stanlick, whose expert help in preparing the typescript of this edition rendered it free of many an error I had inadvertently allowed to go unnoticed.

John P. Anton

INTRODUCTION

Eva Palmer-Sikelianos (1874-1952) wrote her autobiography at the suggestion of her former husband and celebrated Greek poet, Anghelos Sikelianos.[1] One must therefore read the text, printed here for the first time, in the spirit in which she wrote it. We do not know whether Eva would have written it had Sikelianos not urged her to do so, nor do we know whether her husband's motives and her own concerns coincided. Anghelos was too confident in the value of his poetic work to have depended on Eva or anyone else, for that matter, to enhance his reputation as a poet, thinker and visionary of the Delphic Idea. Nor did he expect Eva to provide a narrative of their personal lives together or state in it her perception of his creative development. The real motive seems to have been his interest in preserving her side of the story of an idea and the work they accomplished together: Anghelos' conception of the Delphic Idea and its practical application to contemporary conditions as Eva's contribution. Seen from this point of view, Eva's autobiography emerges as a story of how an idea that is rooted in the Greek soil, matures and communicates the expectation of founding a new world of universal peace and culture. Thus the autobiography appears to have been conceived and then written as an explanation of the attitude toward life she calls *upward panic*, intended to challenge the current yet dubious blends of alleged Apollonian and Dionysian traditions.

Being neither the narrative of a personal history nor a literary *opus* stringing together episodes to construct plot with culmination and resolution, the actions and experiences *Upward Panic* records are intended as having transcended the boundaries of personal relevance in the effort to share a universal and inclusive vision that gave meaning and direction to the subjective dimension of her life. This is the reason that the emotional elements that determine the unfolding of the narrative are kept under control. Their

---

[1] She began to write in 1938 and stopped adding chapters referring to specific events sometime in 1942. The twenty-eight chapters fall into two parts: the "historical" consisting of chapters 1-18, and the "theoretical," chapters 19-28. Although the second part treats a number of significant develpments, mainly the encounter with Ted Shawn and their cooperation, the narrative is intentionally subordinate to the theoretical concern. Additions to part two were made in 1948 when she thought of submitting the manuscript of *Upward Panic* to a publisher. Eva viewed the second part mainly as a set of essays to convey her convictions and criticisms of ideas that had become influential among intellectual and artistic circles before the war, but mainly to put forth her own ideas on the nature and practice of the arts, music, dance, theater and architecture. Her contribution to art theory has not received the attention it deserves. The main reason must be sought in the unfortunate circumstances that prevented the publishing of her autobiography. There is no available collection of her lectures and essays, her choreographical compositions, her musical pieces (some of them in Byzantine notation) for the performance of Greek tragedies, and her extensive correspondence with directors, performers and intellectuals.

significance derives from the value of the idea she embraced and persistently sought to embody in her conduct.

Ultimately, *Upward Panic* is more the biography of an idea than the autobiography of a person, of an idea that swept the person in a steady course toward self-realization. This perspective is exactly what explains the style, sometimes innocent, clearly unpretentious at the start, complex in the last chapters, trusted to reveal a gradual and unswerving movement from the particular to the universal. If the reader is in a hurry to come to the latter, the theoretical and critical distillation of the idea, it would be advisable to ignore the early chapters where the narrative indulges the events of childhood and adolescence before moving on to the more serious ones of Eva's first maturity. Such a reading, however, would simply obstruct the preparation for the full appreciation of the only drama in the life of the author: how this particular person in this century won the good fight of the spirit while striving to understand an elusive ideal with ancient roots.

Upward Panic reports a brilliant episode in the long history of an idea that has lasted through the centuries of civilized life. Arcadian in its conception and Delphic in its fulfillment, at once uplifting and ennobling, it was given new life in the course of its history when it was chosen to serve as the focal point of Anghelos Sikelianos' poetry. It became the seeding concept for his *"Alafroiskiotos"* (The Visionary), a poem that made him known overnight when he was still in his early twenties. He shared it with Eva who waited, a visitor in his island, for his return from the shores of Northern Africa, expecting his decision to marry her. He brought back both the poem and the proposal to wed.[2] She promptly accepted both, turning them into preparatory stages of what was to be the mission and purpose of her life. In her own way, she sought to undertake the task of projecting and extending the Delphic Idea to permeate the lives of her contemporaries, beyond the boundaries of Europe, confident it will effect the cultural salvation that could put an end to the evil omens of the advancing technocracy. The onslaught of the machine age, obliterating every traditional value it met on its ominous march, was introducing in its wake new ways to oppress the spirit of its own makers. The sirens of the modish trends and the fascination of the material goods threatened to replace with different goods every healthy offshoot of the great myths of the past.

The more clearly she perceived the threats of the approaching storm, the more

---

[2] Anghelos Sikelianos (1884-1951) dedicated the poem to Eva, "who has the wisdom and the eyes of Athena." It was published in its entirety in 1909.

determinately she became to exchange personal comforts for the imperative of a universal vision. This transition fills the account of the events that shaped her mature years. There the idea becomes judge and inspiration until finally she finds it natural enough to end the last page of her book by citing the verses of her beloved mentor. It should come as no surprise that the last chapter does not recount any events preceding her death. The autobiography is left incomplete, as it should, leaving out of the narrative the last years of her life. What mattered was the life of the idea that gave meaning to her existence, not the chronicle of her career. The latter belongs to biography.

The parts of the autobiography parallel the main phases of Eva's life. Each chapter is composed with deliberate selection of pertinent events. At the very opening we see her expressing the first signs of restlessness, a curiosity looking for a cherished vista, a ray of light to come from the exit out of the cave. The embrace of her father's views anticipates the idea of Upward Panic. The dominant element in the early chapters, aside from the idiosyncracies of the precocious child, remains the impressive and magnanimous figure of the father: protector, pioneer, reformer, humanist, progressive citizen, innovative educator, missionary of peace, visionary utopian devoted to his idealistic conception of social justice.[3] From her mother she inherited the sensitivity and love of the arts, together with the awareness of the importance of music and the place of the dance in human civilization.

The cultural opportunities and early experiences in the family environment and social relations tied Eva to parents and siblings, especially to her brother, Courtlandt, for the rest of her life. In fact, her brother proved supportive of her values despite Eva's eccentricities and dreamy tendencies to support such causes as the regeneration of lost institutions in the deepest layers of Greek mythology. She was fully aware of his reservations, indeed his disapproval of her marriage. Courtlandt's and Anghelos' paths crossed only twice in their lives, without ever discovering what they had in common, the one being a musician and the other a poet. Eva's faith in the unity of the arts was not enough to remove temperamental differences. Both were Eva's great loves, yet fate did not favor the building of a bridge across the chasm that divided the two men. No compromise was ever reached. She overcame the dilemma by making Anghelos her final choice. In return he shared with her the promise that the ancient message of the Delphic Idea held for the future.

---

[3] Eva's father, Courtlandt Palmer (1843-1888), was the founder of the Nineteenth Century Club of New York. Among the friends of the family were James Blaine, Andrew Carnegie, Moncure D. Conway, Thomas Davison, Edgar Fawcett, W. D. Howell, R. Ingersoll, William Loyd, Felix Mendelsshon, John Sherwood and others.

Her father's death when she was fourteen wounded her deeply and left a permanent scar. The search for a mission waxed stronger and became a quest for a replacement to fill the vacuum that the loss of the father created. Later, after reaching maturity, she met again with her father's values but in a different cultural environment, this time in the presence of a beloved person destined to become her husband, Anghelos Sikelianos. Despite being her junior, he rose before her as the timeless carrier of tested and radiant ideals beckoning the return to her own father's spirit at a new level of activity. When the first encounter occurred in Kopanas, Eva knew immediately she was in the presence of a leader, visionary and cultural reformer.

She felt the power of irresistible grace. She wanted to trust him, and took the first step, priestess in a Dionysian rite, surrendering to the call of the Upward Panic. Together, they widened their surrounding space for a symbolic encounter between the New World and eternal Greece. The power of art and poetry, in particular, acted as intermediaries between myth and the living present. Eventually the upward movement brought both closer to the essence of the tragic, beyond and above the initial expectations of the young lyric poet. With the passing of time, the crystallized message provided the tangible bonding to reunite tragedy and the art of dance, a project that proved decisive for Eva's development in response to her father's call for action. From then on, the experience of Upward Panic was seen as the great gift to mankind and the new uplifting savior.

Panic, the sacred fear, became the positive force to sustain a continuous process. The first chapters of the book are best read as the intended incidents that prepared the writer to seal the union of the person and the idea that was destined to transform her being. The first three decades of her life fall in place like the well hued drums of a rising doric column with the suitable capital already selected. The crowning event occurred soon after her arrival in Greece, when in the company of Raymond and Penelope Duncan, the trio took up residence at the "House of Agamemnon." Isadora had built it years before on an arid slope of Mt. Hemyttus. Thus the voyage that started in New York, and after delays in Paris where Eva indulged her acting talent in futile experiments,[4] ended one mild evening in Attika. Goats

---

[4] In Paris she became an intimate member of the circle of literati that included a great number of personalities, among them Sarah Bernhardt, Ph. Berthelot, Isadora Duncan, James Frazer, James Joyce, Pierre Louÿs, M. Maeterlinck, A. Rodin, Paul Valéry, and also the couple, Raymond and Penelope Duncan. The latter, a young dancer, singer, and instrumentalist from the island of Lefkas, was Anghelos' sister whom Raymond had met and married in 1901 in Athens. Eva while still living in Paris, went to England to study theater with Beerbohm Tree and the actress, Mrs. Patrick Campbell. Isadora Duncan makes ample reference to Penelope Duncan in her autobiography, *My Life*.

were still grazing freely the scarce vegetation on the countryside in 1906.

It was an auspicious beginning. The dream of the wide-eyed child, precious heirloom from a noble father, more valuable than the wealth she had inherited, was being suddenly transformed into an exciting plan for a meaningful life. The search entered its final stage when she and Anghelos met in Kopanas, and only the right opportunity and final consent remained to be secured before it could be put into action. It is perhaps best to read chapters seven to thirteen as the deciphered smiles of Fate.

A number of events contrived to bring Eva inside the temple of the Greek spirit. Anghelos took her by her hand and guided her first steps until she felt confident enough to let Upward Panic carry her to whatever length her own strength could bear. The restless spirits of the couple merged into a solid desire to conjoin the vitality of the New World and the universal vision of Greek humanism. Having shut off the screams and shouts of the modernist intoxication, their union threw deep roots into the soil hopeful to produce the fruits of a creative conception of art committed to the brotherhood of humanity. The meaning became increasingly inclusive as it enriched its symbols in the effort to revitalize the essence of the tragic dance and the function of the chorus. Toward the end of the third decade of the century, the original intent of the art of tragedy radiated for a short while its social and religious function. As though driven by a relentless logic of their own came the decisions and the energies that actualized the dream to institute the Delphic Festivals. The chronicle Eva left us constitutes a moving testimony of the events that stirred the hearts of the artists and the intellectuals who were waiting for an idea that would resurrect the forgotten god.

Ridicule proved unavoidable then as it still does today, more from ignorance than lack of faith in the great undertaking. Some found the events pretentious, groundless, even sterile, unrelated to the current realities. Whether the reservations of the critics were right only time could tell. Yet for a brief moment at Delphi the god opened his arms and received the prayer. Once the celebrations were over, it went with the wind on a voyage to the unknown. Nevertheless memory took notice and the events at Delphi were duly recorded. The people who gathered at Delphi in 1927 understood.

The flame of Upward Panic was still alive and it filled Eva's heart and mind. She decided to travel to her native America and stay there for a while to carry out a double mission. She was determined to bring the great message to her own country and win the needed support to meet at least part of the heavy expenses the First Delphic Festival had incurred. The difficulties continued to multiply beyond the initial estimates. Her efforts were met with only limited success.[5] She returned to Greece after a brief stay in Paris. The wealthy Mr. Benakis persuaded her to undertake and organize the Second Delphic Festivals. The year 1930 was one of triumph, calmness, and saw the birth of the Idea of the Delphic University. However, debts had piled up beyond her estimations, and she finally decided to return to America. August 1933 signaled her permanent separation from Greece.

After the second return to the United States, her understanding of the meaning of the Delphic mission entered a new and unexpected phase. Eva had added a new catholicity to the idea of tragedy: the purposiveness of the progressive process of humanity reborn. She formulated her view with aspirations that went beyond the limits of the technique of the theatre. Perhaps this is the place to say that the new phase in her life remained unnoticed to this day. It was relegated to the marginalia of cultural events. The originality of her insight has been ignored for more than a half century just like the manuscript of her autobiography that was to remain unedited in the archives of the Benaki Museum.

I am not certain whether anything has been written about her critical genius. The text of her autobiography permits a relevant identification. Based on the experience of the Delphic Festivals and the Commands of the Delphic Idea Anghelos had worked out, Eva proceeded to evaluate the intellectual currents that had taken a dynamic turn after the end of the First World War. She assumed a powerful stance against the established trends on the whole that dominated the attitude of her fellow Americans toward art and culture.

Behind the prevailing cultural movements she suspected the long shadow of the great figure of Emerson, whose oration before the Phi Beta Kappa Society of Harvard on August 31, 1837 declared the intellectual independence of the American scholars. The idealistic optimism of Emerson's idyllic pragmatism filled the souls of the young men with dreams of new and endless conquests.   The wind of innovation began to blow, powerful and uncontrolled, but for that matter also fraught with dangers. She criticized the premises of Emerson' message and found them wanting. The same argument was used to judge and castigate Nietzsche and Schopenhauer, and indirectly to express her reservations toward the musical puritanism of her brother, the innocent follower of aestheticism that he was. It brought back her childhood's bitterness over Oscar Wilde's sarcastic remark about her father's well intended speech in London. Her distrust of art for art's sake had its beginning there. Eva

---

[5]   What is not known about this period of her stay in the United States is that she was offered a professorship in the Department of Drama at Yale University. She declined the offer in order to use all her time and leisure to promote her views on the role of the arts and the place of aesthetics in life. The frustrations and disappointments she experienced while working toward this end and while trying to persuade others to accept them, make a very moving part of her story, told as it is with unusual calmness.

rarely forgave impertinence.

In the same uncompromising manner she objected to what she believed were Isadora Duncan's distorted and pretentious imitations of the ancient dances. From Eva's point of view, the appropriation of the traditions of ancient Greek culture as done in the radical choreographies of Isadora Duncan inevitably were seen as corruptions of the very idea they sought to express. She disagreed precisely because she believed that Isadora distorted the art that alone possessed the unique means left to us for the recreation of a genuine humanism. It is worth noting that she never condemned Isadora for engaging in invidious projections of her art. Yet she thought it her duty to state her reservations about the effects that attend the pillaging of the Greek genius, even if inadvertent.

Eva found such practices wanting in aesthetic worth and polluting the lives of her contemporaries as well as menacing the coming generations. In the special chapter she wrote on Isadora the great dancer, she describes with deep emotion the accidental drowning of Isadora's two children. In that and the chapters that follow she sketched the impasse to which the relentless effects of technocracy have brought us. She held her own generation accountable for having yielded to the lures of material gains by accepting without protest the spread of consumerism.

To a certain degree her fears seem excessive yet the critique did not altogether end in negation. Suddenly there surfaces a synthetic idea at the center of which converge two strong components, the father's social effectiveness and the husband's vision: both beloved persons, the former representing the vitality of the New World, the latter the resourcefulness of the Greek myths. She was convinced that Greece was carrying in its primordial currents the true substance of culture that had survived the vicissitudes of time. It could be found in the richness of Byzantine music, the domestic crafts of the villagers and the authentic ritual of celebrations. At this point, Eva's narrative is transformed into a luminous vision of love and energy. Her best moment of epiphany came along with another encounter at the fount of the art of dance.

The last phase began on the day of her cooperation with the great American dancer, Ted Shawn, and the decision to create an all-male chorus. Yet, at the very moment that a meeting of minds was about to forge an identity, at that critical moment came their disagreement and conflict about a topic that could easily be seen as secondary. It was a disagreement about the appropriateness of Shawn's mid-western pronunciation of English to render authentically the subtle nuances of meaning as the tragic art of Shakespeare and other dramatists demanded. Shawn's male sensitivity and pride of the dancer rose in opposition to the uncompromising absoluteness of Eva's vision of the future. Behind the discord on the theme of linguistic sounds were waiting in ambush the passions for the great revolution in art, fired by the unrequited expectations for the emergence of a new form of civilization. The unfulfilled prophesy, the glorious marriage of Helen and Faust, as Goethe envisaged the event, seemed for a while destined to take place on the other side of the Atlantic. Eva had redesigned the new marriage to be the union of the Delphic Idea of the tragic with the creative genius of America. Their offspring was expected to be the incarnation of the Upward Panic, the new manifestation of tragedy. Eva understood the new expressive instrument to be the exceptionally sensitive English language in all its pure oral perfection, repeating the same glory that classical Greek reaped in the greatness of Aeschylus' poetry. New tragedy meant a new phase in Western civilization: fulfillment of poetic genius in articulate speech and rhythmic dance.

Ted Shawn, dancer, artist, choreographer, proceeded at his own pace and rhythm, on a course running parallel to Isadora's own. He did not respond to the opportunity his historic encounter with Eva presented. The long awaited miracle shattered into pieces in the small town of Eustis, Florida. The sacred fire Anghelos and Eva Sikelianos had lit at Delphi was now but the weak flame of a small candle in an abandoned church on the countryside. The gentle hands of a handful of pupils in Greece, who had remained loyal to Eva, were determined to kept the flame alive. The worse was yet to come. About the same time instead of the spreading of peace in accordance with the imperatives of the Delphic Idea, a horrible world war broke out. It all happened in the opening days of September 1939.

The war years coincide with the last phase of Eva's life. Death and destruction in Greece caused deep pain and agony to Eva, living far from her beloved land and mate. She raised a voice of protest and worked day and night for aid to be sent to the suffering Greek people who were gallantly resisting the conquerors. She sided with the freedom-fighters and prayed for the return of the day when the Delphic Idea would herald the arrival of peace. And one day she heard, along with countless others, the news that Anghelos recited a defiant message built into a heroic elegy, while leaning on the coffin of Kostis Palamas before it was lowered into the grave. While Anghelos issued his call to liberty, the German machine guns had readied their aim toward the thousands of mourners gathered at the Cemetery. For a brief moment his voice shattered the heavy cast of gloom:

> Trumpets resound ... Church bells thunder!
> Shake the whole body of our land..
> All of Greece rests on this coffin!
> The name "Palamas" reverberates across the world.

. . . .
Unfold the terrible banners of liberty.[6]

In the United States, Eva was summoning all her strength to arouse the public to support the indomitable Greeks. The war was hardly over when she found herself misunderstood, isolated, with only few friends left at her side. Yet proud in her poverty, strong in her faith, unyielding as she was optimistic, always inspired and inspiring, drawing strength from the truth of Upward Panic, free in her expressions, honest in her views, she bravely withstood the verbal attacks of those who resented her ideas.

The writing of her autobiography stopped before the end of the war. It would seem as if she found it impossible to record the withering of the Delphic Idea. Civil strife broke in Athens in December 1944. The specter of hatred and divisiveness continued to haunt the people of Greece. Aging and sickness, together with the way post-war political attitudes developed in the United States, conspired to prevent Eva's return to Greece.

Until the very end Eva could still dream and plan the continuation of the great Delphic Idea. On April 21, 1950, she wrote a long letter to Angelos outlining how to proceed with the Third Delphic Festival. She wrote:

> In 1930, the whole of Greece was aflame to carry on the work...because it involved the whole people, and each one knew it. After a quarter of century of preliminary work by two people, the stage was set, and Greece could have gone on to a kind of advancement which would have developed her age-old genius and, incidentally, brought prosperity to the country, and money with Government offers, more than the Minister of Education dreamed of...

> For the first year I shall not be needed. I should like this much time to bring to a head several matters that I have worked on here for seventeen years ever since I left Greece. These matters are now approaching a hoped for conclusion, and I would feel sorry to have my effort of all these years go to waste...Then, a year from now, I will come over and start work on the plays, which would be ready in the Spring of 1953...

> There is one more personal consideration. At present, in New York, I am provided for by my brother. He has been very generous toward me. But he was not present at our festivals, and knows nothing about the whole Delphic program. He has no sympathy with my work in Greece which left me almost penniless, and, on my return there, it is unlikely that he will do anything for me. Therefore, arriving in Greece, I shall be without any means of livelihood... (Signed) Eva Palmer-Sikelianos[7]

Eva never broke the spiritual ties with Anghelos nor did she ever stop feeling deep

---

[6] Translation by T. Maskaleris in his *Kostis Palamas* (Twayne Publishers, Inc., New York, 1972), p. 137.

[7] The original in the Peggy Murray file, Smith College Archives.

affection for Anghelos and his new wife, the former Anna Karamanis.[8] Instead she maintained touch with the couple, even offered financial support when she could, and kept the surname "Sikelianos." Her frequent and long letters to him reflect her undying admiration for his poetic genius. What Eva did for her husband is a separate story. What really surfaces in the autobiography is how deeply she respected and admired his poetry, how dedicated she was to the ideas he stood for, ideas she recognized as being close to her father's philosophy of life and social ideals.[9] In most cases of the translations of Anghelos' poems into English one suspects Eva's hand. She always put her own name last when the work was one of collaboration. We also know that Ted Shawn paid for the publication of Sikelianos' *Dithyramb of the Rose* and that its translation into English was done by Eva and Frances Walton, Glafkos' wife.[10]

Anghelos Sikelianos, after several heart attacks, died on June 19, 1951. He was suffering from ill health and political disfavor. Eva, upon hearing the news, made her decision.

"I must die in that sacred land," she told her friends.

The prospect of dying and being buried at Delphi gave her courage and determination, after so many years, to return to Greece and breathe her last breath there, and let her body rest forever under the Grecian sky. It was her last wish. Things eventually turned for the better, and along came the epilogue of her life. A group of intimate friends bid her farewell one evening in the Spring of 1952; we danced and read poetry in her honor. Two close friends, the sculptor Michael Lekakis and the dancer Athan Karras accompanied her to Greece. They were with her when the last event came like the distant beat of a solemn march

---

[8] In her letter to Anghelos Sikelianos, dated Friday, April 21, 1950 (Original in Peggy Murray File, Smith College Archives), she wrote: "No doubt Mr. Christie knows that our marriage has been annulled. This was an emergency measure, with which I was in agreement, during a sudden and very serious illness which struck you at the beginning of the civil war. I felt at the time, and I still feel, that it was largely Anna's care that saved you. Therefore, I was and I am grateful to her. Besides, she is an old friend of mine. So my coming will change nothing in our present relations. But this will necessitate a separate place for me to live." The divorce took place in 1934. In 1939 Anghelos wrote to Eva asking for her blessing to marry Anna Karamanis. The couple married in June 18, 1940, months before the invasion of Greece. The civil war to which Eva refers is difficult to identify. She may have confused the date with a later event in the WW II, when the Italian army invaded Greece in October 1940. Even so, neither 1934 nor 1940 are dates associated with Greek civil wars.

[9] See especially her article "Anghelos Sikelianos," *Athene*, IV, No. 9 (December 1943): 23-35, 67-8. Aside from being a document written from a personal point of view on Sikelianos' development and the scope of his conception of the Delphic Idea, the article has utilized portions of her autobiography in several places, notably material in pp. 29-30 correspond almost verbatim with pages found in *Upward Panic*, Chapter 15.

[10] See Chapter 13, "My Son".

up to the Sanctuary of Apollo, where the spirit of her dead husband was awaiting to greet her at the gate of eternity. The twin rocks of the Phaidriades had nodded approvingly.

Good fortune had it for Eva to end her life at Delphi. Two weeks after her arrival there, she died.[11] Death came like a soft whisper at the hour she was attending as honored guest for the last time the performance of a tragic drama, her beloved *Prometheus Bound.* There at Delphi closed another chapter in the book of the history of Upward Panic, a non-repeatable episode of our turbulent century.

Mortal we are and ignorant of what the loom of history has in store for the future of persons and their ideas. But it would not be proper to claim that our century failed to bless us with flashes of cultural greatness. One such brilliant outburst of light was the life of Eva Palmer-Sikelianos, notwithstanding the modesty that pervades the pages of her *Upward Panic.* Eva disdained self-praise. She stayed in the background of her own account, like a priestess humble before the command of the divinities she believed guided her spirit. Her strength to tell her story came from the dignity and self-respect Anghelos perceived when he made the decision to ask Eva to join him in the quest that renders life meaningful and poetry the record of its significance.

John P. Anton

Appendix: The Manuscript of *Upward Panic.*

The original of an outline of Eva's plan for an autobiography is in the Library of Performing Arts, Dance Collection at the New York Public Library, General Library and Museum of the Performing Arts in New York City. After several tries she decided in favor of the title *Upward Panic.* Eva's plan, which she followed in general outline, had divided the book into two major parts, preceded by a Preface, Part I: *Autobiographical,* and Part II: *Music.* She followed the division in the final script but with certain changes and additions.[12]

---

[11] The opening paragraph of the obituary that appeared in the New York *Times* (June 4, 1952) wrote: "Athens, June 4-- Mrs. Eva Palmer-Sikelianos, credited with having inspired the revival of the Delphic Festival in modern times, died in Evangelismos Hospital here today. Her age was 77. American widow of one of Greece's best known modern poets, Angelos Sikelianos, Mrs. Sikelianos suffered a stroke a week ago while attending dramatic performances in the Classic Theatre at Delphi. According to her expressed wishes, the body will be buried in Delphi."

[12] The original titles of the Chapters were: Part I: 1. My Father; 2. My Brother; 3. School; 4. My Mother; 5. Paris; 6. Penelope; 7. Kopanos (spelled correctly "Kopanas" in page 4); 8. Angelo Sikelianos; 9. The Delphic Idea; 10.Lefkas; 11. Weaving; 12. America; 13. Greek Music; 14. My Son; 15 The First Delphic Festival; 16 America; 17. The Second Delphic Festival; 18. Five Years More. In the outline of the Notes, p. 4, Chapter 18 is listed as Chapter 19, a typographical error, no doubt; the description of the planned contents reflects

Thus the final manuscript consists of two parts: The first part, chapters 1-18 recount her own story, starting with her family and ending where the Second World War began. The second part, chapters 19-28, consist of semi-biographical material cast mainly in the essay form with occasional shifts in style. On the whole, the second part is a series of essays on cultural and aesthetic problems.

The writing of *Upward Panic* began on January 13, 1938, at Anghelos' suggestion. In 1939 she tried to have it published, probably in the shape it took according to the original plan of 25 chapters.[13] It may be doubted that Eva submitted in 1939 the ms. to Macmillan for publication and that Harold Ober rejected it.[14] Anyway, if a publisher actually saw an early version, it could not have contained all 28 chapters. For instance, the Chapter titled "Ted Shawn" was written after 1939, at a time when she was collaborating with Shawn in Eustis, Florida. It was actually in 1941 when she wrote the account about her disagreement and parting with Shawn. The last chapter refers to the Italian invasion of Greece, an event that took place in October 1940. In 1948 Eva revised the finished last version. After Eva's death the original was finally deposited in the Benakis Museum in Athens.

The manuscript Eva left, written in English, is published here complete and for the first time. I was aware of the existence of the manuscript of her autobiography but had not read it in its original form. I knew that after her death the manuscript had passed from private hands to the archives of a museum. By a happy coincidence, in July 1984 the European Center for Delphic Studies informed me of its plan to hold an International Symposium on the Greek national poet Angelos Sikelianos in the Spring of 1985, and asked me if I would accept their invitation to deliver one of the main addresses on the poet's philosophy of the Delphic Idea in his prose writings. The Director of the Center at that time, Mr. Pericles Nearchou, kindly also asked me if I would be willing to write the preface for a commissioned Greek translation of Eva's autobiography. That the translation project did not materialize is another story. We also exchanged views about the future of the English text, after which Mr. Nearchou asked me to consider the possibility of editing and

---

correctly the contents of the final chapter 18. Part II: 1. Thing in itself; 2. Trilogy: Ancient Greece, Science, The Male Word; 3. Satyrs; 4. Emerson and Apollo; 5. Contemporary Impression of Greece; 6. Is Music dead; 7. Krishna and Apollo. Part II must have been revised a number of times before chapters 19-28 were given their final shape and order in the manuscript.

[13] Evidently, the chapters titled "Isadora," "Ted Shawn," and "American Dream" were added later, along with new materials and editorial changes in other chapters of Part II.

[14] There seems to be confusion here. What is certain is that Macmillan did not accept for publication the translation of Anghelos Sikelianos tragedy *Sibylla*, on the ground that it was not commercially suitable.

preparing it for publication. To this effect, he arranged with a member of his staff, Mr. George Zacharopoulos, to have photocopies made of two existing typescript versions of *Upward Panic* in the archives of the Benaki Museum, and forwarded to me. These copies arrived between November and December 1984, respectively. I labelled them A1 and A2.

The conference on the poetry of Angelos Sikelianos took place at Delphi on March 30 to April 2, 1985. Mr. Nearchou inquired at the end of the conference if I had reached my decision to undertake the edition and publication of the original English text of *Upward Panic*. I was happy to accept and agreed to proceed with a definite plan as soon as I was assured of transference of the copyright to my name.

Photocopy A1 of the typescript consisted of 358 double spaced typewritten pages. It soon became evident to me that the copy I had labelled A1 was Eva's own, since all the corrections, additions and deletions had been done in her own handwriting. It was in fairly good condition except for three missing pages (281, 310 and 359) that were either not photocopied or had been removed by accident. Except for the missing three pages, A1 was superior in every respect, and I decided to use it as the basic version of Eva's text in preparing the final copy. Photocopy A2, flawed and imperfectly produced, consisted of 338 typewritten pages; it was done on three different typewriters and in a mixed style of line spacing. It became obvious that this was a later typescript and was based on A1, but it contained the missing pages. In general A2 proved to be an inferior typescript—the typist had missed numerous whole lines from the text of A1 and had to be inserted by hand. It was of little value for editing purposes except when confirming some point in the text of A1 deemed necessary. Comparing typescripts became a tedious and time consuming task, but it was necessary in order to make certain that a perfect typescript could be prepared for a prospective publisher. The final text, as printed here, is in fact the result of editing A1 with occasional comparing of the two copies, A1 and A2. In a few places, where words or phrases were missing, I had to use my own judgment to fill the gaps, minor though they were.

On a sheet of paper and in her own handwriting Eva left a table of contents in Greek but only for the first twenty chapters. At the head on the first line, again in her own handwriting, is her name: Eva Sikelianos. In the second line she had scribbled the title in Greek <u>Ζήτω ὁ πανικός!</u>, and in the third line the word "Περιεχόμενα" (contents), followed by the titles for each of the first twenty chapters. Chapter 22 in copy A1, titled "Greek Influence Today," consisted of pages 258-83. This was divided in copy A2 to form two separate chapters. Thus pp. 258-67 of A1 became Chapter 22 in A2, keeping the original title: "Greek Influence Today" (pp. 234-43); and pp. 268-83 were used in A2 to make Chapter 23, with another title: "Isadora" (pp. 243-59). Whoever typed A2, presumably following Eva's directions to divide chapter 22 into two, neglected to renumber the chapters that came after the newly created Chapter 23. The oversight explains why "Chapter 23" is used twice in A2, and why both A1 and A2 follow the same numbering of chapters after chapter 23, for a total of 27 rather than 28. The discrepancy was readily removed.

By May 1987 I had produced a final and satisfactory text. In July 1987, when I visited Greece to collect additional materials for my introduction and notes, Mr. P. Vlachoyannis of Athens, Greece, informed me that the owner of a bookstore, Mr. John Ghoudelis, had in his possession another copy of *Upward Panic*. I was grateful to have this information. Mr. Ghoudelis kindly offered to have a copy made for my use. Upon my return to the United States, when I examined the copy, which I labelled B, I realized that it was an exact *replica*, including flaws and typos, of photocopy A2 from the Benaki Museum. Since B was in certain respects a better photocopy than A2, already in my possession, I decided again to make occasional use of it, mainly for settling doubts concerning the confirmation of several passages. I was now finally confident that after almost fifty years from the day the autobiography was written, the time had come to plan for its publication.

In preparing the present edition, I found it necessary to introduce a system of paragraphing to accommodate logical units of thought and narrative where the text in most cases was lacking. I also thought it necessary to depart from the continuous typing as found in Eva's text, where dialogue was invariably imbedded in surrounding text and with nothing to indicate dialogue except through the marks of single or double quotes. By setting dialogue apart according to printing conventions, the reading was now greatly facilitated. There has been no interference with the text except for the removal of typographical errors. Footnotes have been added where needed and indicated as the work of the editor.

The title is Eva Palmer's own and refers to the sacred terror, panic, that lifts human beings in a sacred movement to the heights of experience. The Arcadian divinity Pan, the half-human and half-goat god of fertility, occupied a special place in Greek mythology and in the rituals of Dionysian worship. The special fear of Pan—the root of our word 'panic'— was a source of uplifting inspiration as well as one that elicits profound respect for the power of the god. An early title she had considered was in Greek: "*Zito o Panikos*." It was inserted as an afterthought when she revised the table of contents, but was finally abandoned in favor of the present one. The expression "upward panic" aside from serving as the final title, occurs in a number of passages in the text:

(i). *Foreword*:

> [Upward panic] contains a suggestion of a technique which can start and sustain *panic moving upwards*, unlike the terror that rushes men swiftly down a steep place to destruction, as pictured in the story of the herd of the Gaderene swine in the *New Testament.*[15]

(ii). Chapter 17, *The Second Delphic Festival*:

> We were struggling again, as we had after the first Festival, for the completion of the Delphic Plan. The performance of great drama had done its work and done it well. Again it had set moving the spirit of Upward Panic. Again the artistic success of the second Festival, much greater than it had been the first time, made the next Delphic step more than ever important. (A1 p. 201).

(iii). Chapter 27, *Architecture*, where upward panic is identified with the Aristotelian "catharsis" or purgation:

> There is in fact no apparent effort, over the whole United States, to produce even an example of this admirable architectural achievement which can, as Nietzsche said, liberate simultaneously all the faculties of man. And without it, our hands are tied. Not all choruses, or the dancing and singing and acting we could dream of, not the ancient Greeks themselves if we were to put them on a modern stage, could accomplish the miracle which is nevertheless a normal consequence of the mere shape of a Greek theatre. Something happens in this great magnetic circle which does not and cannot happen anywhere else: something which is the very be-all and end-all of Theatre: a sweeping emotion which does overcome enmities and misunderstandings, which makes hatred and fear fall inert in the great rotating wind of beauty which Aristotle called Purgation, and which actually is Upward Panic. (A1 p. 337).

(iv). Chapter 28, *Greece* (last pages), referring to "man's love of God: man's love of man":

> This is UPWARD PANIC, which alone can carry men beyond their own fear, into the heart of their love for each other. (A1 p. 355).

(v). Chapter 23, *Isadora*. Here Eva undertakes to criticize Isadora's claim that her dances have tapped the Greek origins of dance, and has occasion to draw attention to a major difference between the ancient and the modern. The key is the idea of the *upward* thrust of the Greek dance:

> It was fatal that her outward expression resembles a Greek bas-relief, and not an Irish jig, because Greek dancing is the upward dancing of the world; and because the Greeks alone made dancing not the specialty of a few but the universal accomplishment of a nation. (A1 p. 280).

---

[15] The Note of the original outline of the book has the following as a blueprint for the general theme, in the form of a Preface: "the possibility of transmuting downward panic into its own opposite. Fear is now everyone's master. But, just as there exists a technique for loosening or tightening men's sinews through terror, so the opposite consciousness which could liberate them from this obsession also has its technique...less well known and not practiced at all." (page 1) Next come three words: "human solidarity, world peace, music." Evidently, what is meant as the opposite of the downward panic is the upward panic.

FOREWORD

With terror to guide them, men, like the herd of Gadarene swine*, now are rushing swiftly down a steep place to destruction. The infusion of this terror into men is an ancient technique, well-known and widely practiced today. But the opposite technique, which can start and sustain panic moving upwards, is less well-known and is not practised at all. This book contains a suggestion of what that other technique is.

* [Ed. The allusion is to the *New Testament*, Mark 5, 13. -JPA]

1

Prologue

In fatuous nineteenth-century optimism I was raised: human sympathy, world peace, music. The concept of these as essentially one was perhaps wished on me in my cradle. Certainly they are closely linked in my earliest memories and cataclysms of world wars have only brought them closer.

CHAPTER 1

My Father

Among these earliest memories are the meetings of the Nineteenth Century Club. Leaning over the banisters from our third storey vantage ground, we three red-heads, all carefully dressed for the occasion, used to watch the grand ladies coming up to my mother's sitting-room, and the gentlemen to my father's bedroom, to leave their coats. Edging down a little on the stairs we would sometimes greet the people we knew; and then, when all were seated in the drawing-room and the library, we would slip down as far as the lower landing on the stairs to hear my father's voice; and afterwards the speaker of the evening; then the opponent of the speaker; then rebuttals from each; and finally an open discussion.

I suppose, at that time, we three were too young to have followed the intricacies of the many subjects which were discussed; but at each of these meetings there was a diffused excitement, a sort of lurking danger which held our interest, and kept us keyed up at hours when we should normally have been asleep. At the end of the speeches we children must have been allowed to come in; for I remember mingling with the guests when the time came for punch, ice-cream and cake.

Probably, even then, my father's reason for taking all this trouble was not strange to me. In a society which had raised impassible barriers between differing forms of religious dogma or political belief, and where each believer was listening only to his own interpreters, he wanted to make people listen to what their opponents had to say. There were many kinds of dogma, and many kinds of opposition.

My father made it his life-work to see to it that the most distinguished representatives of opposite sides of various questions meet, and that they listen to each other in a spirit of courtesy. To me he was a heroic figure. I loved to follow his brilliancy in discussion, with people who were constantly dropping in to lunch or dinner in the dear old Gramercy Park house. And how varied they were!

I remember the commanding figure of Robert Ingersoll, the atheist, in a procession of Protestant ministers, Catholic priests, Hindu swamis, Jewish rabbis, anarchists, painters, politicians, poets, journalists, musicians, novelists. My father would go to any trouble to obtain key people for his Nineteenth Century Club meetings. When the Russian Douma was founded he brought one of the founders from Russia to speak about it. No doubt there was something heroic in his choice of a mission, and in the directness of his attack in carrying it out. Today we can judge of the difficulties he must have encountered by the fact that at first he was ostracized from New York society for daring to bring opponents on any subject together. But he went right on; and the thing became so interesting that gradually those who had turned a cold shoulder to it would filter in to listen, somewhat on the sly; then these disapprovers would see each other there, and so the ice would be broken. Later on, requests for invitations became far greater than the capacity of our house, and it was decided to move the Club to Sherry's ballroom; and so the original charm was lost.

But he himself wished it to grow. It was not for him an intellectual play-thing for the benefit of a small circle of clever New Yorkers. "Are we furthering charities, art, culture, independent thought," he wrote to Mrs. John Sherwood, "or are we simply amusing ourselves?" In fact, in founding his club, he probably was indifferent about the adherence of these people except as a means to an end: a small starting-point toward a mighty goal. He hoped to bring about mutual understanding among small hostile groups: between denominational Christians, then between world religions;   between political parties, then between nations. I think that he really believed that open discussion, joined with true kindness, would be enough to regenerate the world.

And so, when the Nineteenth Century Club outgrew the old house, he felt it was strong enough to take care of itself in New York; and his next idea was to sow the good seed in London and, after that, in other capitals of Europe. He obtained letters to many distinguished Englishmen; and the whole Palmer family went abroad on the City of Rome, then the largest ship on the ocean, on the 9th of May 1885. I was then nine years old.

In London, men of letters, diplomats, musicians, gathered in the studio of Felix Mendelssohn Moscheles to hear my father speak. He expounded his plan to them with his charming ease of manner, and no notes in his hand. Several of those present arose afterwards and answered him at some length, and with apparent seriousness. From different points of view they all said practically the same thing: that his plan was no doubt excellent for America, where much clannishness was apparent between members of different sects; but that in England, and on the Continent, such conditions did not obtain; and that what he wished to establish existed already in the natural breadth of outlook common to Englishmen.

Among others who spoke was Oscar Wilde, whose ship, at that time, had not yet foundered on the reefs of scandal. His words were slow, and somewhat impressive; and afterwards, thinking back, I realized that the quality of his voice probably was beautiful. At the time, however, during his short speech, only my own mounting fury was real to me; and only his final sentence has remained in my mind:

"I do not think very much," he said, "of Mr. Courtlandt Palmer's ideas: but his style is wonderful!"

I could have killed him. All the people who had discussed my father's speech with a show of respect had not awakened my anger, even though their conclusions were mostly unfavorable; but to have someone make light of his ideas, and then talk admiringly of his "style" seemed to me the height of insolence. Yet, in looking back, I have sometimes wondered if perhaps Oscar Wilde was right. For certainly none of us would imagine, today, that open discussion, however courteous, would be enough to regenerate the world. We have seen enough of it in our time to know that this, by itself, has not the magic which my father attributed to it. And no doubt there was something a little childish in his going abroad as he did, to bring this panacea to Englishmen and Frenchmen, who rightly answered that to them it was not so new as it had appeared to be in America.

"But his style is wonderful!"

This phrase, which had seemed so outrageous to me as a child, now stands out with peculiar interest. I can see him, quite thin, middling height, auburn hair, standing there in that London studio speaking; and also at home in the dear old house, presiding, with his incredible knack of drawing the best out of people who were itching to spit out their worst. Courtesy, always the essence of his outward manner, went so deep with him that it became something else, very akin to love. "Style" which was "wonderful!" Well, it was.

Kilgraston is also a vivid memory. It was the first year that Mr. Andrew Carnegie had returned to Scotland after his long successful years in America. He had hired for that summer, an old Scottish manor-house, and had invited as his guests the whole family of James G. Blaine, the whole Palmer family, and Walter Damrosch, who, during that summer, became engaged to Margaret Blaine. We used to go off on long drives with a coach-and-four, and a bugle standing up at the back of the coach, announcing our departures and arrivals, and blaring out our passage through the villages, with the four fine horses clattering through the streets. It was very gay. And there was also a bagpiper, who swaggered up and down the terrace in front of the house as the coach returned, his Scotch kilts and bright tartan swaying like a pendulum as he moved. Then, when we were all dressed for dinner, the piper would start up his Scotch tunes again, strutting around in the central hall. We would gather behind him in single file, and start strutting too, until all had arrived; then, with the piper leading the way, we marched into the dining room, circled once around the whole table, and finally sat down.

The conversation at these dinners was monopolized almost entirely by the three older men, and centered largely on the possibility which my father and Mr. Blaine saw in the distribution of Mr. Carnegie's wealth for objectives other than those he had so far favored with donations. Up to that time, Mr. Carnegie had limited his gifts to buildings for public libraries in many American cities. Mr. Blaine and my father both thought this an excellent objective, but they were both aiming at bigger game. Why not establish a World Court where the differences between nations could be handled peacefully instead of always resorting to arms? I do not know, after so many years, which of these two men first launched this idea. No doubt it is well in line with my father's passionate belief in discussion as a panacea for world problems, and with his whole life effort to foster "sweet reasonableness" in the human race through a broader knowledge of the opponent's point of view. But we also know that Mr. Blaine's vision reached beyond national boundaries and prejudices; and his work later, in founding the Pan-American Union, is only one of the proofs of his universality of spirit. Both were brilliant talkers; and certain it is that, up to that time, Mr. Carnegie had not considered using his wealth for any other cause than to supply the public with buildings for libraries; and it is also certain that, before that time, no World Court had been founded.

After that summer in Kilgraston and other parts of Scotland, we came back to Gramercy Park. The Nineteenth Century Club was then large and ugly, but still animated by my father's spirit. This may have been the year when he went to Chicago to try to save the lives of the six anarchists who had been condemned to be hanged. He did this not because he was an anarchist: he was not: but simply because of his sense of justice. He felt that these men were innocent; and he threw himself into the breach to obtain a retrial. William Dean Howells was, I think, the only other New Yorker who did this. Of course, this again caused a temporary eclipse of my father's social authority. He was called all the names which were considered insulting: anarchist because he stood up for men who seemed to have been unfairly condemned: atheist because Robert Ingersoll was his friend. He was none of these things. He called himself an agnostic and he gave to this word its true meaning: one who does not know.

Three stories I will record which seem to me characteristic of my father. The first one I know only through hearsay.

His own father loved him more dearly than his other children, and so made a will leaving the bulk of his fortune to this son, and smaller portions to the other three. But when my grandfather was dying, my father secretly drew up another will, leaving share and share alike to all; this he took to the bed-side, saying casually that he needed a signature, without saying for what. My grandfather, because he had always trusted him signed the paper without knowing what it was.

The second story falls within my own recollection. He went one day to my mother and said to her:

"You call yourself a Christian, and Christ said: 'Sell all you have, and give to the poor.' Are you willing to obey this command? If you are, I will follow it to the letter: not for the sake of Christ, but because I feel that wealth is unfair."

My mother took days to think this over, and finally stated her belief:

"Destiny places us" she said, "in the circumstances in which we can do the most good." She felt that he himself, and the children, would do greater good with the portion which had been given us than the very inadequate distribution which his sacrifice might accomplish. Both of them, I believe, were completely sincere.

The third story is about myself. I was about seven years old when he said to me:

"Listen to everyone. Read everything. Accept only what appeals to you personally as true."

I took this seriously, as I did everything he said. But the responsibility and anxiety it placed on me were certainly beyond my years.

Lake Dunmore, in Vermont, was the last place where my father saw the summer. It was far from cities, or even towns. He was happy rowing on the lake, especially round the edge, under the birch trees, with the water lapping quietly; or riding horse-back with us on the nice dirt roads. The far-awayness of it all delighted him, and the freshness. It was perhaps this very isolation which caused his death. There was no telegraph. Days passed before the surgeons from New York could reach us. And so an attack of appendicitis had become general peritonitis before they arrived. He lived through the operation, and his brain was perfectly clear in the end. But it was only to say good-bye to us very quietly.

After his death, the objective for which he had lived, to find a common ground for human beings, above and below and beyond their creeds and dogmas, seemed to have gained a momentum of its own. Just as, during his life, he had brought earnest and intelligent minds together, so his passing seemed to weld them closer in their common devotion to him. As one reads today the funeral orations of Robert Ingersoll and Dr. Heber Newton, something more seems to emerge than the usual heightening of the virtues and accomplishments of the dead. These two men, one an atheist, the other an Episcopalian minister, must each have reached out beyond the impetus of his own life-movement in thus presiding together over the funeral rites of a friend. The antithesis of disbelief and belief in a life after death throws a light on the compelling force which, at such a time, and for such a duty, brought them there, and lends to what each one said a solemnity out-measuring the half century which has intervened. Thus the impressive periods of Robert Ingersoll seem not merely rather fine oratory, but somehow make one believe that there had been a man "to whom majorities meant nothing...who gave better than he received." And when Dr. Newton tells us of the intellectual narrowness of New York before my father's time; of the complete isolation of the sexes in social and intellectual pursuit; and of how, for the first time, a rich man had given to the poor something better than charity, one believes that what he says is true, and that these gatherings of men and women in the old Gramercy Park house did bequeath to New York certain permanent legacies, notably Town Hall.

So also, at the Memorial Meeting, in the speeches of Dwight H. Olmstead, Alfred R. Conkling, Edgar Fawcett, Rev. William Lloyd, Rev. Charles H. Eaton, the Rabbi Gottheil and others; in letters from London of H. R. Harweis and O. B. Frothingham; in these records and many others reverently collected by Raymond St. James Perrin after my father's death, it seems as if the personality of a single man who realized in action this goal of human understanding beyond creeds and races had been itself sufficient to establish a bond between men of conflicting beliefs, which had been his declared mission in life. He evidently had created a region of agreement in which, without lessening their own strength and originality, the exponents and advocates of the most widely differing beliefs were completely at home in each other's company. Thus, the Rev. Charles H. Eaton seems to have spoken truly when he quoted a eulogy, once addressed, he said, to a brilliant prime minister of France: "Sir, you have labored for ten years to make yourself useless." And indeed, after my father's death, his own ideal seemed, as it were, to have taken his place, and rendered "useless" his own enthusiasm for the kindlier forces he was constantly evoking. In the many testimonies concerning him one often meets the equivalent of Professor Thomas Davidson's statement: "Although I differed from him widely on many and fundamental questions of theological and ethical thought, I was always exhilarated and encouraged by contact with a mind so honest, sincere and fearless.

They all "differed from him widely" for one reason or another, but they all considered "The Club" their own. There is a recurring refrain about "our Club" affectionately spoken by people who certainly could not have met each other anywhere else: because Courtlandt Palmer did succeed, in spite of marked beliefs of his own, in exercising what Edgar Fawcett, in his Elegy, called "clarion hospitality." "It was the genuineness of Palmer" said the Rabbi

Gottheil, in describing what he called 'the First Church of the Nineteenth Century Dispensation', "that drew differing minds around him, and held them there. He must have been conscious of the strength of his position in our Club as its founder and trusted leader, yet he was always open to advice, even remonstrance; and often I have wondered at the deference he showed to the views of the members, both in private and public deliberations. The reason for this lay in the fact that the welfare of the Club was dearer to him than his own opinion; he loved his child better than himself."

"They may keep their theories" he said to Moncure D. Conway, "and their theologies; but they must abandon their bigotries."

That was all he cared about: to get the best side of people on top, and to make it expressive. He brought out the eagerness and the enthusiasm of others with what they spoke of as his intellectual avidity, or his sacred fire, or his kindness.

"His zeal" said H. R. Harweis, "sometimes outran his discretion; but in an age when discretion abounds and zeal is scarce, that was certainly a fault on the right side,...few people could resist the charm of his personal influence."

Again what they are all agreed about is the openness of his heart and his hand.

"A brave soul" said Andrew Carnegie, "intense and impulsive, . . . reared in luxury, he longed to throw away all the pecuniary advantages which he possessed over the meanest of his fellows; distressed, conscience-smitten that he should have and enjoy what others lacked . . . He saw the want, the misery, the unequal distribution of desirable things, and he would like to plunge forward, Buddha-like, to remedy all wrongs, to make all right by drastic change at a stroke, . . . his soul on fire for the good of humanity."

But Mr. Carnegie rather amusingly deplored this anxiety to accomplish in a day what would normally require a thousand years.

"His wealth and position he felt more as obstacles than helps," said Jennie Cunningham Croly, "and he wished above all things to be enrolled in the rank of the workers, the indispensable workers, those who are counted among the faithful."

But of all these tributes, there is one that is finest: it is that of Mrs. Charles Adams Coombs. She quotes as a motto words from I do not know whom.

"The reward of one duty is the power to fulfill another."

This I take to be the true measure of my father: the performance of one right action with no other end in view than added capacity to fulfil another. I believe that really was the inner motive of his life.

CHAPTER 2

My Brother

Again in the neighborhood of Gramercy Park, but many years before the events already recorded, an old German musician peeked through the open window of a basement room to see who was playing the piano. He saw a little girl, so small that false pedals had been arranged for her feet. He listened again, examined the front door of the house, and found that it was a girl's boarding school. He rang the bell, and asked the name and the home address of the little girl who was playing. He went to her father and offered to take the child to Germany, to have her play there in concerts immediately, and afterwards to continue her education as a musician. But my grandfather refused this offer. This little girl was my mother.

About fifteen years after this, two people were often seen together sitting very near each other, on a long piano-stool covered with electric-blue velvet, in front of a Steinway grand. The room was almost empty. An inlaid wood floor, mahogany book-cases, a long sofa, a deep chair. The elder of the two was my mother, playing Mozart, Haydn, Gluck, Beethoven. The younger was a very tiny boy, so little his feet stuck straight out in front of him as he sat. This was my brother, Courtlandt Palmer Jr. He would watch my mother's hands very attentively as she played, and, when she got up, he would take her place, and play from memory what she had been playing. A little later he was taken to operas and concerts, and it turned out that he could retain whole programs with hardly any differences, and reproduce them on the piano when he returned home. He was nine years old when the first Wagner troop that ever crossed the ocean came to New York. Materna, trained by Wagner himself, sang Brunnhilde and Isolde. The Wagnerian harmonies, strange then to everybody, must have been particularly so to a child who had heard more of Mozart and Haydn than anything else. Nevertheless, his musical memory was as keen as before. At that time he had a high soprano voice, and, in spite of the frequent lack in Wagner operas of any evident similarity between the orchestral accompaniment and the solo parts, he would come home after these performances and sing the Liebestod, or Brunnhilde's last scene with Wotan, or the Waldersrauschen from <u>Siegfried</u>, while his hands seemed to render all the instruments of the orchestra on the piano. His excitement in playing the Walkurenritt or the Feuerzaube when he first heard the <u>Walküre</u> is unforgettable. It seemed as if all these things came directly out of him through inspired creation, instead of being, as they were, an incredible feat

13

of memory. One day he and I were taken to see Materna. She listened ecstatically while he played and sang to her own roles. Then she caught him up on her lap and embraced him; and he seemed to me to disappear entirely within the huge hug of her enormous arms.

Yet he still could not read music at all. Every day my mother would force him to decipher simple four-hand duets with her. He hated it; and tears of disgust would stream down his face while he hammered out: do, re, mi, fa, sol, fa, mi, re, do, with all ten fingers, first in the treble and then in the base, while my mother played variations above or below.

"Why should I learn to read music" he would say, "when I can play anything I hear?"

It was at about this time that an offer came to my father from the impresarios, Abbey, Schoeffel and Graw to take Courtlandt all over Europe and America as an infant prodigy. But my father refused, just as my grandfather had on a similar occasion. He felt that a concert career was too much of a strain for so young a child; and that he should wait for perhaps ten years.

About a year or two after this, the same impresarios brought out Josef Hoffman as an infant prodigy. I remember very well his first concerts in New York and London, with his white sailor-suit and light blue collar. After a short and brilliant career as a child, he was taken off the concert stage by Mr. Higginson, founder of the Boston Symphony Orchestra, who thought he ought to study until he was eighteen. Quite recently, at his own great jubilee, commemorating fifty years of varied and distinguished work as a musician, Mr. Hoffman made the statement that probably this intervention had been a mistake, and that gifted children should be allowed to go ahead and work out their own salvation, if the public wants to hear them, and if they themselves want to play. And this raises again a question I have often thought of: was my father wise in refusing this impresario's offer to bring Courtlandt out when he was about nine, or was he over-cautious? When the allotted time was over, Courtlandt had added many years of serious study to the art which came to him so easily. He had worked with Leschtitsky in Vienna, with Breitner, Paderewski and others in Paris. There must have been very few compositions for piano, or for piano and orchestra which he did not know by heart. His repertory was enormous. But he had acquired by that time a positive hatred of the concert stage. He almost ceased to go to concerts and operas to hear other people play, feeling that the atmosphere created by the buying and selling of seats was completely hostile to the production and enjoyment of music.

During these years of his boyhood he also had moments of revolt, not only against the whole set-up of concert activity, but against the piano itself. These storms that sometimes swept over him were caused by nothing in his outward surroundings. They were inexplicable to all of us because the piano was so obviously what one might call his own pre-natal choice. He was born with an astonishing technique in that one thing, and no apparent leaning toward anything else. In spite of his uncanny musical memory, he did not seem to remember other things any more easily than the rest of us; and sometimes, when we produced amateur theatricals, he would struggle to get his words by heart, while the other children learned them easily. Except in the matter of deciphering written music, which did not take very long, he had never been forced to practice, but rather implored to get up and go out, lest the constant playing injure his health. He was in a way his own master; and he and the piano seemed bound up together as one living and inseparable organism. Yet these storms would sweep over him; and every once in a while, perhaps every year or two, he would order men from Steinway's, or from Erard's, or from Bechstein's, according to the country where we happened to be at the time, to come with a truck and take away his piano. On these occasions the whole family was shaken; and I remember the agony in his voice: "How can one produce true sounds on such an instrument? The intervals are all false."

No one of us knew what he meant. His suffering was intense, and so was ours. But even when after days or weeks as the case might be, rapture returned to us, through his hands again touching the key-board, the conflict did not seem to be deeply settled in his own inner being. It appeared to be the emptiness which ensued when he was without his instrument which made him bring it back, rather than any psychic reconciliation with the instrument itself. So in his younger days, in spite of outward triumphs, there seemed to be, within himself, a problem which was obscure to us all. A predestination if ever there was one, toward a special form of artistic expression; and a latent, sometimes dominant revolt against his own ineluctable medium.

Years later than this, long after my brother's ship had weathered and passed beyond the range of these musical hurricanes, it sometimes seemed as if I myself had unconsciously absorbed this anxiety about musical intervals which his intensely musical nature had led him to long for instinctively as a boy. At all events, by following a path altogether different, I came once to a cross-roads where I seemed to know why he had been tortured as a child, and why he had passed beyond this agony and forgotten it, and how in both instances he had been right. In short it became clear to me that there are two great fields of music,[1] in one of which he was born, and whose highest ideals he has served steadily through his whole life; and that those intuitions which seemed to call him temporarily away from his own true

---

[1] This statement will be clarified further on.

medium as a boy were signals from the other great field which he was touching then, as it were, at a tangent. And it was nothing at that time in our surroundings which could have made their meaning clear; and without this necessary clarity: this understanding of the different functions of these two types of music, it is possible for one to destroy the other: whereas both are needed, and both should be preserved.

During the late Gramercy Park period, my mother used to lead an orchestra of her own every Saturday night. She had brought together all the musicians she knew, young and old, to play the early symphonies, especially Haydn. She herself was happy on these evenings, and she used to say that her idea of paradise was to have an orchestra to lead. But we never got very far. It was so much more pleasant to sit quietly and listen to Courtlandt play than to go to so much trouble to obtain a half-way result. Little by little we all gave it up. I stopped playing the violin; my sister stopped playing the cello; even my mother gave up playing except for an occasional orchestral arrangement on a second piano of whatever concerto Courtlandt happened to be studying. She also preferred to listen. And our quiet evenings were the best; with father stretched out on the long sofa; and the rest of us, and anyone else who happened to come, sitting anywhere, completely happy, and speaking only to prevent Courtlandt's getting up from the piano, no matter what the hour of the night.

Abroad it became more circumscribed, and his dislike of audiences, even of his own devoted friends, seemed to increase. It reached the point where he would stay in one city till his friends discovered him, and then move on to another: London, Paris, Rome, New York. Yet he always had a potential audience lurking in his wake. In hotel corridors, below his window in the street, crowds would gather. One time, while crossing the ocean, he sat down at the ship's piano and started to play. Gradually all the passengers, the stewards and stewardesses and the cooks were present. It seemed as if the captain on the bridge and the stokers in the hold were not there only because they had not heard him from so far. Finally he stopped playing and went out, and another pianist who was on board took his place. But before he had come to the end of one piece, the room was empty. Courtlandt was a born pied-piper. No one has ever had audiences so easily, and no one has ever avoided them so much.

But this avoidance, as years have passed, has taken on another character. The pure beauty that flows through his touch on the keys, his creative inspiration in composition, and the almost religious unison of his whole nature have seemed to carry him, beyond all negative elements, into a realm of true harmony where one has almost ceased to regret that more people cannot hear him; for his life itself has become one with his music, and he has created something completely his own. His wonderful playing has not ceased. But today, from a distance beyond oceans and continents which have long separated us, his audience seems to be one person only: my sister May. Like Ludwig of Bavaria, for years, she has had a rare musician entirely to herself. And, in a way, perhaps she is like our brother. For she keeps her own pictures hidden away in closets: and few people know that she is a gifted painter.

CHAPTER 3

School

I have spoken of the Palmer children as if we were three. And so we seemed to be, and actually are; but originally we were five; and, as we all had red hair, and my parents also, people used to call us the torch-light procession. My eldest sister Rose died when I was quite young, and I remember her best as I watched her through the window when she went out to play in Gramercy Park, wearing a black and white check coat, with her flaming hair lifting from her shoulders at each step. She always had her little dog Silky on a chain, and she would loose him after opening the locked gate of the Park, and then they would tear around together in mad glee. My mother used to say that she was the most gifted of her children. I do not know why, except that she could draw easily, and could cut out long procession in paper, of men and women, horses and carriages, children and dogs, and so amused the rest of us.

Rose died when she was fourteen; and then Silky, a silver Skye, with a coal-black nose and large brilliant eyes, became very precious. One day he was stolen. Mother offered a thousand dollars' reward, but a year passed with no news. One day, preparing for some journey, she happened to send the second man to a railway station to buy tickets. This servant had been in the family for about three months, and heard of the lost dog, but never had seen it. Suddenly, while walking through the crowded station, a dog jumped up on him in wild delight.

The dog's master drew him angrily back by his chain, and tried to quiet him, but it was of no use; the animal became frantic in spite of his chain, and was entirely unmanageable. The footman, skeptical, yet thinking it might be our dog, followed the man until he could call a policeman, told the story, and the man and dog were led to our house. Did Silky feel the smell of our house, or is there no normal explanation of his instant recognition of a servant whom he had never seen?

Silky died at Lake Dunmore, a short time before my father's death. We buried him on a tiny island in the middle of the lake, in a grove of slender birch-trees. And we put up a marble tombstone inscribed: "Silky. 1888."

My brother Bob was different from all of us. He was rather fat, pleasantly sociable, could play the violin and several other instruments quite badly; he disagreed with my father when he was still a boy; left home, and became a midshipmate on an old-fashioned sailing-vessel; then a cowboy while the West still deserved the epithet of Wild; a planter in South America; and finally a retired gentleman in Hawaii where he died a few years ago.

He was rarely at home when I was little; but on these occasions he would take me up, on the sly, to his big attic room; and there he taught me to smoke cigarettes and to play poker. I was very fond of him and am still; and although for a number of years he went in rather heavily for gambling and drinking, my memory of his is very warm and glowing, and I know that he loved me.

Then came May, who turned all my early years into a fairy-tale. Probably no one else at that time, and certainly no one since, has had any idea of her extraordinary gift for telling stories. Others did not know because never, I think, did she put herself out to enchant anyone but me in this way. Incredible as it may seem to those who knew her later, May was at that time a tom-boy. Among the boys and girls of Gramercy Park she was a leader in all the games which were then popular: and in running she could beat any boy in the Park except Richmond Fearing who was much taller than the other children, and who afterwards, I heard, became the champion runner of America.

This success in outdoor games, and her popularity among the children, make it the more remarkable that she spent so much time with me. Whenever I was taken into the Park by my nurse she would run from her "prisoner's base," or any other game, with her golden hair flying, to walk quietly around the Park with me, and continue our story. Or in the house we would go off into a corner; and sometimes, in the evening, we would sit between the heavy inside curtains and the windows facing the Park, and curl up in this space, so "the Story" might go on in a whisper, while the others talked in the drawing-room, beyond the barrier of our curtains. Sometimes Mother would call out: "What in the world are you two talking about?"

But that was our secret. We never told anyone that these stories, sometimes entirely fantastic, sometimes with known characters, ourselves included, as protagonists, were what held us both spell-bound, one story often going on for months; or that, when one came to an end, another would begin immediately.

During all this time I literally lived to hear what was coming next. And this fascination kept up for years. I do not even know when it ceased. But it was perhaps when my mother was very ill with pleurisy in Paris, and May devoted herself to her, while I stayed at school in Neuilly. And after that we may have gone to different schools; or perhaps May "came out" in society, and we were not always on the same side of the ocean.

And so, because she never told stories to anyone but me, this gift became obscured, and probably by her forgotten. And her life seems to have turned inwardly and somewhat secretly toward an instinctive interest in color and form, and outwardly to an unfailing courtesy and generosity toward others. But under both of these aspects, however unknown as much, there is still her early athletic strength. And this raised the question: is there ever, can there be, any true delicacy without strength beneath? Thinking of May, I believe that this is impossible.

Then after May, came Courtlandt, the musician.

These four children I have spoken of were all very healthy. They went in for riding, swimming, sailing, rowing, and, especially when we were in Stonington, for all the activities of country life. My uncle, Charlie Palmer, owned a place there called Walnut Grove. There he had private race-course and large stables, orchards and vineyards, brooks and millponds, sail-boats, and row-boats, green-houses, vegetable gardens, flower gardens, tennis courts, herds of cows, and barnyards full of pigs and chickens.

All these things remain in my memory as more or less of a torment; for inexplicably, and differing from all the others, I, the youngest, was not strong at all.

At first I was not expected to live. In fact this conviction was so positive in the minds of my parents that they did not hide it; and my earliest memory is that I must not do this or that "lest I die." Before we first went abroad, a portrait was painted of me by John W. Alexander. This portrait was not an order, but was done by Alec, as we called him, because he also thought I was going to die; so he painted this picture for himself, to have as a remembrance, when I should have "gone." I was surrounded with the utmost care; and I had a dear Irish nurse, old Mamie, attached to my person, whose whole time was occupied in taking care of me.

My next memory is a carefully reasoned decision which I probably came to quite slowly: "Why," I said to myself, "since I am going to die anyway, should I not do this thing I want to do, and so die a few days sooner?" I do not remember at all that I ever minded the idea of dying: but I do remember my surprise that, except for temporary exhaustion, which everyone was used to, nothing unusual happened; and also that no one knew anything about what I had done.

I also do not remember what it was that occasioned my first trial; but this is natural enough, because, for a long time, my inner life was a series of trials, each more difficult than the last, and so always equally dangerous, according to the vision of my own incapacity which had been imprinted on my mind.

The first actual occasion which I do remember, and that is probably because it was the first when this secret game of mine was discovered, was in regard to learning to read. I had not been allowed anything in the way of lessons; but my mother used to read aloud to me, especially from Kingsley's *The Heroes* and Hawthorne's *Tanglewood Tales*. Years later I found one of these old books with a dedication in my mother's writing: "To my little Myth, Eva, from Mother" and the date, "1881." I was then seven years old. Did she imagine, I wonder, what Greece was to mean to me later on?

As she read, I often sat on her lap, or on the arm of her chair; and, without her realizing it, I would follow the letters on the page, as her voice sounded the words. One day I found a story-book, printed with large letters for children. I managed to get upstairs with it alone; and sitting down on the floor of an empty room with my treasure, I started pronouncing the words aloud, delighted that they made sense. I was so absorbed in my discovery that I did not notice a servant who had come to find me, and was standing in the door-way listening. As I looked up, she suddenly fled down the hall screaming:

"Eva's reading! Eva's reading!"

Probably as a result of this incident I was allowed to go, at about this time, as a sort of visitor, to the Van Taube School. This was a venture in education which my father had undertaken, and my sister and brother were regular pupils. It was also on Gramercy Park, and had been a girl's school, kept by some old maid sisters, who, on retiring, had sold it to my father. He immediately instituted, beside the ordinary curriculum, a gymnasium, a printing-press, a scroll-saw, and lessons in wood-carving, drawing, sculpture, photography and fencing. He also wanted a garden to start lessons in agriculture; but for this there was no room. He entrusted the direction of this school to Mr. and Mrs. Van Taube, probably because they alone, at that time, believed in technical education.

Mr. Van Taube was a Russian, or rather a Tartar, enormously tall and very thin, with gaunt features, coal black shaggy hair, and heavy black eyebrows. He spoke about ten languages, and suffered from occasional fainting fits from the effects of a bullet, lodged, it was said, near his heart, in one of his many duels. He was a remarkable fencer, and he used to arm five or six children with foils, and allow them all to attack him at once; but no one ever hit him. His wife was French, very kind, but the picture of slovenliness. Her hair fell away from the hairpins in gray wisps and she always wore a black dress, or rather, from the waist down, a piece of black stuff, drawn together with large white safety-pins over a white petticoat which showed through the intervening spaces; but the petticoat was always clean. They had a little boy named Narouche who, as a baby, had been used to sleep, in Russia, they said, quite naked, under the snow; and Mrs. Van Taube used to insist that this is a very warm way to sleep. Such treatment would make one either a giant or a corpse, and Narouche probably became a giant: even as a child he looked like a Norse Viking, rugged and blond.

This school was run on such pleasant principles that when the children got tired of studying arithmetic, or any other dull task, they were at liberty to go and exercise with the fascinating equipment in the gymnasium, or to carve out patterns with the magic scroll-saw, or dig out designs in relief with their wood-carving tools, or to draw, or sculpt, or do anything else they pleased. In fact my father also believed in the innate reasonableness of children. And, on the whole these children justified his faith, and probably made as much progress in their lessons as they would have in an ordinary school. But the old-fashioned teachers who had followed the new regime, and the parents who were used to more conservative institutions had too many new methods thrust on them at once: co-education, technical training, lack of strict discipline in classes, and a startling departure from type in the directors of the school. It was a wonder that the thing held together at all; and the fact that it did last a few years was probably due to the real interest which the children themselves felt in the new sort of chances they found there.

I believe that this school did not continue for long after our first departure for Europe in 1883; but however short-lived, and however imperfect, it was the first technical and, perhaps after the Quakers, the first co-educational school in New York. And although I was not an active pupil, and was allowed to go there only as an observer of what the others were doing, I feel that I owe to this rather crazy school my instinct for making things rather than buying them, whenever it is humanly possible.

This venture of sending me to school unofficially evidently worked: perhaps my own inner game of taking risks was gradually assuming the proportions of a theory. I began to see that temporary weakness caused by any effort seemed to leave me not worse but better; and probably my mother felt that I was stronger; and so, after our trip to London, and a tour round the cathedral towns and the English Lakes, when Courtlandt went to a school in Vevey, I was also sent with my sister to another school near Paris.

I was still nine years old. To my family, used to coddling me, I had seemed too young to be left in a boarding school even though I was with my sister. But once in I was considerably older than any of the other little girls in the baby class. It followed that at other schools I went to afterwards, in Germany, in America, and in France, (never staying two consecutive years at any one of them), I was older than the others all along the line. When I "came out" in New York, I was older than the other debutantes, and older afterwards than my classmates, when I went to college. In the beginning this appeared to me a disadvantage.

It seemed so smart to be the youngest in one's class. But the habit stuck to me; and, as time went on, it became unexpectedly pleasant. As I grew older, long past the ages of schools and colleges, I was still surrounded by people younger than myself; and at present, when I would normally meet with people in their[1] seventies, actually almost all my friends are between twenty and thirty. But I no longer regret this discrepancy.

After about seven different ventures in boarding-schools and day schools in France, Germany and America, and considerable traveling in between, my mother gave me what was called a "coming out reception" in New York. Then, for two years, the thing which I probably enjoyed most, in the constant round of gaiety among people whom I hardly knew was to watch the magnificent turn-outs, as I drove with or without my sister to endless tea-parties, where one met the same people everywhere, but could talk to no one anywhere. I loved the prancing horses, and the smart carriages on Fifth Avenue. And evenings, at the opera, I used to be fascinated when the house was darkened, by watching the rainbow colors darting from Mrs. Astor's diamonds as she breathed. Her box, on the left of the house, was not far from the stage, so that her jewels caught upward reflections from the foot-lights. She was usually simply dressed in black velvet; and she seemed, with her glancing rivers of diamonds, which she wore so well, the very essence of gay New York. But I liked to look at her from a distance, in a darkened opera-house, while others were attending only to the people on the stage.

In the same way, the ball I enjoyed most was the very first one I ever went to. Courtlandt and I were together, and we knew no one. We occasionally danced together, and otherwise sat and watched the couples moving rhythmically in a grand old wainscoted room. The effect was quite fine; and again, as a spectacle I enjoyed it. But later on, as I came nearer to the people producing these glamorous effects, the glamour seemed to diminish, and a prolonged monotony to increase. After about two years of dinners, lunches, balls and tea-parties, the monotony seemed eternally established, and the glamour had disappeared. I began to consider activities outside of this kaleidoscope in which the colored glasses fell back always into known patterns. I decided in the spring of 1896 that I would find out what a college education was like; and that I would enter Bryn Mawr the following October.

On a first visit to the college, to feel my way toward this new objective, I met the amazing Martha Carey Thomas, President of Bryn Mawr. She told me bluntly that my plan of entering in October was out of the question because I had none of the requirements for the

---

[1][Ed. "The" instead of "their" appears in the MS. -J.P.A.]

entrance examinations except a little French and less German. I perhaps owe my success in carrying out this plan to Miss Thomas' uncompromising assurance that it was impossible. If she had said that it was easy I should probably have failed. For up to that time I had taken advantage of my parents' unconquerable inhibition about me that I was a weakling who must not be forced to study. With this grand excuse, in one after another of my various schools, I had, rather consistently, avoided those things which I ought to have done, and done those things which I ought not to have done: which meant that I liked to learn Shakespeare and a few other English poets by heart.

One time, when I was twelve, in the school of Thavenet and Taylor, in Neuilly, Miss Taylor pounced on me like a cat where I was hidden behind some bushes in the garden, and confiscated a tiny pocket edition of the *Winter's Tale* which I happened to be learning. She wrote to my mother in high dudgeon, and said that Shakespeare was an improper author for children of my age to read, and that, unless I were given an expurgated edition, I should be expelled from the school. Mother answered that they could expel me if they wanted to, but that my books must be returned to me, for which I am still grateful. Of course the result of this was that they kept me in the school with carte blanche to do as I liked.

So there, and later everywhere else, I steered clear of arithmetic and algebra and other uncongenial lessons, with only occasional punishments of a hundred lines of Racine to learn by heart, which I did not mind at all. But because of all this, when I drew up before the closed ramparts of Bryn Mawr, I found myself empty of arms and ammunition. The difficulty spurred me on, and I actually did enter that October. Only, as this feat required about eighteen hours' work a day for six months, I took the way of least resistance and chose Latin, of which I knew a little, reserving the excitement of a first approach to Greek until I had passed beyond the outer barrier, and could study it with Mortimer Lamsen Earle.

I was no sooner actually in Bryn Mawr than I discovered why I had taken so much trouble to get there. There was at that time in the college a sort of cult for the English language, which centered largely in a course of lectures by Miss Gwinn, afterwards Mrs. Hodder. The subject of one of her courses was "Arnold, Pater and Swinburne" (the latter as critic); and through the essays of these three a range was afforded which brought one in contact with many great writers, and gave an ever widening vision of literature and art. In this class were gathered a number of gifted people: Helen Thomas, sister of the President; Lucy Martin Donnelly, Mary Richie, classicist, beautiful and gifted, afterwards killed in a runaway accident; Helen Hoyt, now teaching English in Santa Barbara.

Among these learned people I was an outsider, but Mrs. Hodder used to allow me to listen in, and her own charm and wit created a sort of higher heaven of attainment which made Bryn Mawr remarkable. Somewhat outside of this circle there was also the poet Grace Constant Lounsbery, who then, as now, has stood apart. But, continuing this characteristic atmosphere of Bryn Mawr in the nineties, one of this group has been chiefly remarkable: Lucy Donnelly. After years of keen and inspiring criticism of English literature in the college, she is now one of the silent phalanx of free and balanced minds in a contorted world. Near her one finds again the virtues which we so ardently cultivated in the nineties, only grown, blossomed, perfected; justifying attainments which have passed, and also our own enthusiasm of long ago. Arnold's ideal of "sweetness and light": what it meant to him, and what the rest of us added to it. Lucy Donnelly is all this, but she is more: because she is not dated. In the world of today she is as easily at home as the youngest; only she makes them seem old-fashioned and dull.

Along side of this inner heaven, or rather underneath it and supporting it were Miss Thomas' own lectures in her General English course. I had probably read before going there most of the things which she taught; but that made me more appreciative of the originality with which she presented such a vast field to so many novices. And she had also a knack of sensing and encouraging one toward one's own strong but still unexpressed leanings. One day she said to me, after I had produced *As You Like It* as the Freshman class play:

"Miss Palmer, next year, I hope you will consider *Hamlet* as your class play."

I did not do this, but I am still pleased that she wanted me to.

From my first interview with her, when she told me flatly that I could not get into Bryn Mawr because I knew nothing, I admired Miss Thomas exceedingly. Her quick decisions, her incisive way of expressing them, her great vitality which had over-ridden all the obstacles put in the way of her own education, and her boundless ambition for scholarly accomplishment among women, made the college, in its young days, a sort of challenge to the age-old accomplishments of men. One day someone asked her if she believed in co-education.

"I will believe in it" she said, "when men knock at the doors of Bryn Mawr."

But only many years after these college days did I really appreciate her. I was directing a Greek play for the Senior Class. She was no longer President. She was living in Philadelphia and came out twice to see me, although she had long given up any active collaboration with the college, and we talked over the general arrangements of the play, and chose together a site on the campus for the erection of my temporary theatre. And one day she came to the deanery to hear a lecture. It was just a matter of entering the room walking through the aisle, and sitting down. There were many people present. She alone was alive. I tried afterwards to analyze the technique of it, and find out just how she did it; how she walked; how slow, how fast; whether her slight lameness added in any way to her extraordinary dignity; what were the almost imperceptible gestures of her hands; how she greeted a few friends. But there was no technique. It was just pure magnificence.

Nevertheless, when I was a student at Bryn Mawr, neither the ambitious striving toward excellence in scholarship which Miss Thomas had created, nor her great energy and latent grandeur, not even her complimentary judgment of my acting was sufficient to hold me for long. After two years I felt that I had gained that for which I went: somehow to bridge the chasm between my life up to that time and those who had had a more regular sort of schooling. "What have they which I have not?" was the question which made me go there. But after this initiation into the possibilities of college life I said, "It would take me a lifetime to acquire all the learning which all the professors of Bryn Mawr possess. If I were to choose those subjects which I prefer, I could master them more easily and quietly at home. If, for the sake of variety and all-round mental training, I were to choose those which are less interesting to me, how, among so many subjects, could I select one or two, in order to obtain a degree?" But I did not care whether I got a degree or not. It seemed a choice, logically, between living in Bryn Mawr for the rest of my life, to gain a smattering of varied and unrelated subjects, or of leaving as quickly as possible.

It was spring again. My brother was starting for Rome, and he invited me to go with him. I did not hesitate.

I have never regretted this choice.

That year, in Rome, I was alone with Courtlandt, and, for that brief period, it was I who had a rare musician entirely to myself.

CHAPTER 4

My Mother

After my year spent in Rome my life had become different. This was due partly to the fact that my mother's life had become different. A few years before this she had married Dr. Robert Abbe, Chief Surgeon of St. Luke's Hospital in New York. This marriage had its romance. Many years before, when she was still a girl, my mother was keeping watch by her father's death-bed at St. Luke's Hospital. My grand-father, by the way, had been kept alive, awaiting her coming, by the attending physician who knew of his patient's love of ancient Greek. Being himself a classicist, when he saw his patient sinking into the last lethargy, he started reciting a Pindaric Ode. My grand-father recovered consciousness and finished the passage.

At that time Dr. Abbe, who had recently graduated from a medical school, was an intern in the hospital and happened to have been placed on duty in my grandfather's room. Those days and hours when he observed the old man's daughter were enough to give direction to his life. He fell in love with her. After the death of her father, my mother ordered presents to be sent to all those who had taken care of him, and, along with the others, the young intern also received his present, which happened to be a water-color painting of a young girl sitting on a bench in a forest. Years passed. My mother had married and had five growing children; and it happened that in midsummer she and my father were in New York for a short time, and that he had an attack of one of his violent headaches which usually kept him in agony for three days. The family physician was out of town on vacation. Several others were called but were also absent. Then a servant went out to look for any doctor's sign in the neighborhood. He saw Dr. R. S. Weir and Dr. Robert Abbe. Dr. Weir, the senior partner, was also out of town, and Dr. Abbe was called in. He proved to be a good doctor, and, calling him in from time to time, he gradually became our family physician.

One day my mother was in his office, and he asked her if she remembered the water color over his desk. Of course, she did not. She had probably never seen it. But is was only after my father's death that she learned why this picture had occupied so central a position in the doctor's house for so many years.

We children did not oppose the marriage. Yet, in looking back, I suppose it was the cause of a number of changes. The old house on Gramercy Park had been sold; and we had moved into a much smaller one next door to Dr. Abbe's at 11 West 50th Street. These two small houses were thrown into one on the second floor, and made a pleasant music room with two Steinway grands. This gave one the illusion of being at home. Courtlandt lived there whenever he was in America, as we all did. But there was an atmosphere, beyond the adjoining entrance, of nurses in uniform, of smells of ether and iodoform, of sick people waiting in rows, which made it seem foreign to all of us.

Dr. Abbe was a great surgeon and a good man. He was so successful in making his patients live that he acquired the nickname, much to his own chagrin, of "the lucky surgeon." "There is no luck in it" he used to say, "there is nothing but forethought and skill." Nevertheless, the name stuck to him. He was absolutely quixotic in his devotion to poor people who could not pay him a cent; and he was adamant in his rule of making rich patients wait their turn in his office, no matter what their wealth and social standing might be. If two patients called him out simultaneously he would give preference to the poorer one; and one day my mother said to him laughingly:

"I do not ask you to prefer the rich; but you are positively unfair to them."

One evening at dinner he said:

"Tonight I could become a millionaire."

We all looked at him quizzically:

"Yes," he said, "all the other surgeons, and everybody else, think that Mr. _____ is going to die; and the stocks have fallen to zero. But I know that he is going to live; and in three days from now, everything will go soaring up again. If I were to buy stocks as they are now," he continued, "and sell them again when Mr._____ will have passed the crisis, I could make any amount of money."

"I would understand," said I, "your unwillingness to profit by your knowledge if the case were the other way round; but as long as the profit would depend, not on the death of your patient, but on your skill in keeping him alive, and on your experience which makes you sure that you can do this, where is the harm to anyone concerned?"

"Ah!" said he, "that is true today; but another time, profit in the stock market might depend on a patient's death; and the success of the first instance might initiate a tempting habit. No good physician ever dabbles in stocks."

He read one day in the *New York Herald* of Madame Curie's discovery of radium. He was very much excited and said that he was going to cable a thousand dollars to get some of it immediately. Mother said: "But why not wait to see if the story is true? It may be a newspaper invention." He listened, but afterwards went out and cabled the money. Within a week, the French Government had forbidden all export of radium out of France. But his promptness had gotten in his order ahead of the embargo; and so it happened, that for quite a while, Dr. Abbe was the only scientist in America who possessed any of this bright glowing powder. He had half a dozen or more little tubes, each about half full, which he kept in a small velvet-covered leaden box, which he and I made together. At first he carried this box around in his vest pocket. And shortly (because another sympathetic characteristic of the doctor was his habit of experimenting on himself, whenever possible, rather than on animals), he tied one of these tubes, for I do not know how many minutes, to his shin bone. On taking it off, nothing seemed to have happened; so, for a number of days running, he tied it again to the same place, with no apparent result. Finally he gave up this game, believing that radium had no effect whatever on the human body. But, in two or three weeks, a burn appeared on his leg, which continued to grow deeper and more inflamed, and had considerable difficulty in healing it.

Dr. Abbe was the first physician who tried to cure cancer with radium. After many experiments, he told me that he believed that it does positively cure external cancer, owing to the difficulty of isolating rays from the surrounding tissue. Among other things, he experimented with growing seeds, and with cocoons, and obtained interesting results. But no doubt he had recorded them all in the scientific journals of the period. He also had one of the very early X-ray machines in his office and he used to entertain us with exhibitions of our own bones. He was eminently an experimentalist. But, with these early acquisitions of radium and X-rays, he was traveling on uncertain ground; for no one, at that time, realized the power of these new discoveries. And when he later died of pernicious anaemia, it was thought that his early carelessness in handling these new scientific toys was the cause of his fatal illness.

During all this period my mother was, as I have said, somewhat different from the way I remember her in the early days. She had not quite abandoned her piano, and used to have friends come on regular evenings to play trios or quintettes with her. One day I told her that I missed hearing her play by herself. She looked at me rather sadly, and said she thought I was the only person who ever had. It was true that I loved her playing. Her hands were so small that it was impossible for her to play a series of octaves on the white notes with her hands above the keys. This made large sonorous effects impossible for her; but she never tried to do what she could not. She had a way of her own of playing the old masters and was at her best with Mozart. Her musical manner was a little like dear Wanda Landowska's, not when Wanda plays the piano, but when she sits down at one of her nice old-time instruments. In fact, with mother, the piano sounded like a spinet; whereas with

Courtlandt, it was a whole orchestra.

Musicians still continued to come to our house; Kreisler once played for us. The Kneisel Quartette were Courtlandt's and our friends; Melba, Nordica, Emma Eames, Sembrich, and especially the beloved Emma Calvé, were near our hearts. But to Mother these things were becoming secondary.

She started to think more about social problems, and especially about the controversy then raging for Woman's Suffrage. She had long believed in it ardently. She was perfectly certain that if women could only gain political equality with men, there would be no more war, no more social injustice. I think she really believed that all the most terrible evils in the world would right themselves automatically through the superior purity and self-sacrifice of women if only they could once get the vote. So, for a few years, round the turn of the century, she was in the front line of battle to fight for the suffrage of women.

She was also very much preoccupied with the problem of immigration. At that time about five thousand immigrants from all parts of Europe used to arrive in the port of New York every day.

"How," she kept asking, "will all these foreigners ever become Americans? How will they become conscious of America's traditions and the deeds of our great men?"

Finally she thought she had found the solution:

"If I had a child," she said, "who had a distinguished ancestor, the first thing I would do to make him conscious of that ancestor would not only be to tell him of great former accomplishments, but also to take him around, and show him the places and the objects which had been in one way or another connected with his ancestor's deeds. In the same way, " she continued, "both for American children, and for the foreigners arriving on our shores in such hordes, the teaching of history should be local and familiar at first: for to children, and to unschooled foreigners, historic characters become real when they can actually see the places where great men lived or where they fought. Then," she went on, "when the island of Manhattan will have become rife with historic memories, the study of American history in general should be pursued, always suggesting questions which would awaken a child's curiosity. As, for instance, why do we speak English, rather than French, or Dutch, or Spanish? any of which languages was in the run to prevail. Then later, the histories of other countries connected with America should be taught; and finally the history of the world."

"But," objected her friends, "New York has no history. It has never been anything but a commercial town."

So people thought at that time. But Mother, following on the heels of her theory, started delving into the history of New York. The picturesque period of Peter Minuet and Peter Stuyvesant came to life again. Few people then knew that Canal Street had really been a canal, built by the Dutch, because they were used to having canals at home. And few knew that the Bowery was so named because that whole quarter was once a colony of summer homes of the well-to-do citizens, whose winter houses were below Wall Street; or that where Wall Street is now there was once a wooden wall, built to protect the citizens from wolves, from the Indians, and from the English who might come down from New England and attack them.

Presently mother's interest in the forgotten records of our local heroes made her organize a history class which she taught herself. Eventually these pupils were called on to become teachers in various College Settlements or Church Settlements, and all those who were teaching or studying were finally welded together into what mother called the City History Club of New York, which, after a few years, counted some fifteen thousand members. The classes used to visit all the historic sites in and near New York. Prizes were given for essays, for maps, and for the writing and producing of plays connected with the history of New York which, incidentally, was a way of discovering considerable local talent. One of their ambitions was the placing of bronze tablets to mark historic sites; and there is now one in Central Park, commemorating the boy who saved Washington's army, which was donated in penny subscription by the whole City History Club.

Recently I was pleased to learn from one of the very early members of the Club, Miss Ellen Hill, now Director of the School for Girls at Great Barrington, Massachusetts, that the activity of the Club has never ceased. There are still about twenty-five centers in New York, with groups studying the history of the City, and that the present membership of the Club is about fifteen thousand.

Later on my mother realized that neither she nor anyone else [in her group][1] knew anything about the Constitution of the United States, nor the general laws under which we live. She invited five of her friends to come regularly to her house to study these matters. The meetings were led by Mrs. Runkle, and the other four were Mrs. Ben Ali Haggin, Dr. Mary Putnam Jacobi, Mrs. Sanders and Miss Adele Field. These six women afterwards became the nucleus for the League for Political Education, of which Mrs. Sanders became first president; and later, through the generosity of Mrs. Sanders, this League became the nucleus of Town Hall. So that Town Hall also, in a way, started at our house.

---

[1][Ed. The bracketed expression "in her group" does not appear in the MS. -J.P.A.]

CHAPTER 5

Paris

When my mother spoke so gravely to me about the danger of ignoring conventions, I think, in spite of the rapidity of my answer, that her meaning was not quite clear to me. I am sure that it is not now. What is the society from which she thought I would be excluded, and what was she afraid of? In consequence of certain deeds or attitudes of my father's I had often heard that he had been violently disapproved of, even ostracized, by certain people, as a sort of punishment for not agreeing with, for instance, the parishioners of the old Dutch Reformed Church from which he had seceded; and later from other such groups. But this disapprobation did not seem, usually, to be connected with living people; or, whenever it was, they were rather stiff and rusty old ladies, whose indignation did not, so far as one knows, pierce the suavity of my father's social armor. The impression which has actually remained with me concerning his relation to society is that he was constantly surrounded by fascinating people who were all doing something interesting; that they were natural and contented in his company and that neither he nor they ever were preoccupied by the obstructive opinions of absentees: except, perhaps, as a subject of momentary amusement whenever these came back into the fold.

My brother was also surrounded more than he wanted; and Mother, although she always stood up for traditions, seemed to consider social functions as a burden rather than a pleasure, and she was very much happier when she was playing the piano or leading her small amateur orchestra. So what was it she feared? Who were the people who mattered to her and, in general, in America, who are they? In England, where social values are concentrated in the person of the King, one can see that an ascent or a descent on the social ladder might have a serious meaning, that those who are used to English court life, or to the glamour of its edges, might have no resources within themselves to withstand or conquer adversity. In such a country social bankruptcy, joined to inner emptiness, might border on tragedy. But in New York, where the center and the circumference of the four hundred have always been vague, and have not reached the vanishing point, are we not essentially free from these delights and dangers?

I settled in Paris, or rather near Paris, in Neuilly, in one of the pleasant little <u>pavilions</u> which were easier to find then than they are now. It was small, but it had a large garden and fine old trees.

Soon I started to take lessons with Madame le Bargy of the Comédie Française. She was very exacting, and took great pains to correct what she called my "American accent."[1] She would make me recite whole scenes from Molière with my voice pitched extremely high, in a key which had no relation to any sound either natural or agreeable to me. For a long time I tried to please her, but finally either she got tired of me or I of her, I do not now remember which, and I dropped these lessons. I then went to Marguerite Moréno, also of the Comédie Française, to ask for advice. I told her that Madame le Bargy had found it impossible to correct my American accent, in spite of much labor spent on it both by her and by me, and was it worth while to go on trying? Moréno asked me to recite for her, and I went through several of the scenes from Molière which I had learned with Madame le Bargy. Moréno made no comment, but after I had performed several of these parlour tricks, she said:

"Now recite something for me which you learned by yourself before you went to study with Madame le Bargy."

Accordingly I recited *Le Balcon* by Baudelaire. When I had finished, Moréno's rather beautiful pallor was lit by her strange upward smile:

"You have no foreign accent," she said; "what you have is a kind of voice which is not French at all. If you wish to change it you can spoil what you have, but you will never gain a French intonation. Remember, however," she went on, "that Sarah Bernhardt also has a kind of intonation which is not French. At one time she was ridiculed for this, then she imposed herself by her gift for acting, and finally people came to adore her voice. You may be laughed at, if you go on the French stage, or you may be adored, but the quality of your voice will never be French".

Shortly after this I met Sarah. I was taken by a friend to her theatre and to her dressing-room. On entering, my attention was arrested by three enormous mirrors arranged as a triptych, so that the outer ones could move on their hinges and reflect from all angles a person standing in their midst. And there was Sarah, triply reflected and re-reflected, in such a way that one saw many Sarahs: back, front and sides, moving in all directions into eternity. And suddenly I heard Sarah's voice:

"Oh! Quels grands yeux!"

No one, before or since, has ever spoken about my eyes. I had had my hair talked about until that had come to seem the inevitable form of greeting from strangers, and I was

---

[1][Ed. Quotations are not in the original MS. -J.P.A.]

grateful to Sarah for saying something unexpected. But, afterwards, when she heard I was studying for the stage, she also became interested in my hair. She took it down to see the length of it, and immediately imagined herself as Pelléas, with such hair to climb by, to the balcony of Mélisande.

She asked me if I had studied the part. I said I had, and she told me to come to her house and rehearse with her. Of course I was delighted; and, after that I saw her quite often. When she felt that the play was ready, she said that she would produce it on her next American tour, which was to begin shortly. One day she asked me to go over to New York before her, to see Mr. Frohman, who was then her manager, and announce, in the American papers, that I was to act with her in Maeterlinck's play. So I came to New York, quite proud of my mission, but with unforseen results. It seems that Sarah, in allowing me to act with her, had taken it for granted that I was as unconnected with New York as I had seemed to be[2] with Paris. All she cared about was that I had hair long enough and strong enough to really pull her up to the balcony of Mélisande with my braids. She therefore did not foresee that, when I carried out her order, the New York papers would evince more interest in me as my father's daughter than she considered fitting for anyone who was to act with her. The result of this was that no sooner had these newspapers reached Paris, than a cable came from her canceling her American engagement. I never was consoled about this episode until years later, when I read Yvette's adorable *Chanson de ma Vie* and saw how her nobility had triumphed against another example of Sarah's foibles. "If she could act so to Yvette Guilbert" I thought to myself, "what[3] am I to still be hurt?"

After this I returned to Paris, and went on taking lessons both in singing and acting, but in a rather dilatory way. I had seen by that time a good deal of back-stage politics and meanness, and my ambition to go on the French stage, or any other stage, was not so ardent as it had been.

In Neuilly I had, as my near neighbor, Natalie Clifford Barney, who also had a small *pavilion* surrounded by fine old trees. She and I had known each other from childhood, especially during American summers in Bar Harbour where we used to go horse-back riding all over the island of Mount Desert. So, in reality, she was an Amazon long before Remy de Gourmont christened her so.

In her house, these old days in Neuilly were a foreshadowing of the kind of center

---

[2][Ed. Text elliptical. The word 'be' has been added. -J.P.A.]

[3][Ed. *Sic.* -J.P.A.]

which she afterwards created in the rue Jacob. One sees in the diagram of her salon, which forms the frontis-piece to her *Aventures de l'Esprit*, a tangle of names somewhat difficult to decipher; but, when the eye lingers a while, these names, taken anywhere, seem to reveal a truly magnetic attraction which must have been, and which was present at the start: Pierre Louÿs, Philippe Berthelot, Paul Claudel, Maurice Maeterlinck, Emma Calvé, Aman Jean, Lucie Delarue Mardrus, J. C. Mardrus, Rodin, Milosz, Berenson, de Max, Lugné Poe, James Joyce, Isadora Duncan, Montesquiou, Colette, Gertrude Stein, Richard le Gallienne, Salomon and Théodore Reinach, Paul Valéry, Sir James and Lady Frazer, and a few princesses and duchesses here and there. Some of these were already her friends in Neuilly, enough of them to show the trend, and to make my mother's fear for my future isolation appear in an unexpected light. I had left a two-sided atmosphere in New York: of social service on the one hand, and of hospital service on the other, both of which commanded my sincere respect, but could not reach beyond; and I found myself near such people as these, incomparably more interesting and entertaining.

Natalie moved in the midst of this going and coming with a certain laziness which was perhaps an indispensable component among her many keen and acute characteristics, (her eyes as Madame Mardrus said, were created to see and not be seen, as are those of most women), and this may have been the quality which served to harmonize the unusual combination of elements which were welded together in her nature. For to minds that are keen, laziness, or what seems to the outsiders to be laziness, may be the initial virtue without which all the others are destroyed or distorted: the "solid basis", the necessary condition for the "probing of conscience" which she herself has described.[4] It may be even a well of life for those who know the technique of drawing the inner mind into the outer consciousness, or vice versa. I should say that the stages of this technique are probably unfamiliar to Natalie, that this quieter side of her nature is not very different from ordinary, everyday laziness, and that she has no technique at all in what is usually called "meditation." Nevertheless, the combination of this ordinary laziness, and a mind as high-strung and hard to fool as hers, produces a result which is unique. She does not seem to venture far on the less known side of consciousness (she may be prevented both by her sense of humor and her extreme dislike of shams), but the mere fact that she is lazy, that she sometimes leaves her mind alone, lends a certain glow

---

[4] Natalie Clifford Barney, *Aventures de l'Esprit*. [Ed. Only the author and the title of the book are given in the MS. Barney's book was published in Paris (Editions Emile-Paul Freres, 1929), and was reprinted in the United States by Arno Press, A New York Times Company, New York, 1975; all pages references to this edition. The frontis-piece mentioned in the MS was not reproduced in this edition. -J.P.A.]

(which does not spring from her mental brilliance) to her poetical work, and to her prose, and still more to her conversation.

Natalie had been called everything, everything but one thing. She perhaps likes best being described as cruel, heartless, and indifferent to the feelings of others; but this may be because these beliefs concerning her give her free play to do as she pleases, as it were, behind the scenes. It is true that she is pitiless to attitudes of life which are not united in root and branches. How she chooses, for instance, to recall only one impression of Maeterlinck in his country home, which is sufficient to make his whole structure topple:

> This mystic on a motorcycle, seeking a renewal of life, amused himself by bracing his gun on the edge of a balcony, from where, in a reclining posture, he shot fan-wise at the whole plain; while a girl at his side changed his cartridges.[5]

Or this about André Gide:

> One should not play with the forces of nature when one has practiced only her weaknesses.[6]

And she says about herself:

> To cut open another's brain to remove all the sicknesses of habit, to scalp it if necessary in order to see what is inside, to touch its content, to feed on its authentic substance! What am I? A vulture? A woman? No, an amazon. And one is not an amazon without a semblance of cruelty. As a matter of fact, it is not displeasing to be thought evil, if this interpretation can spare us from becoming so.[7]

This is Natalie all over. Rather boastful about her inhuman attitude toward others, but giving herself away in the end by a confession which slips in because it is also a witticism, and she secretly thinks that people do not look beyond the surface of a jest. "It is not displeasing" she says, "to be thought evil if this interpretation can spare us from becoming so." It is as if she were using her evil reputation, and reinforcing it of her own accord, as a shield to protect her against the superficial kindness of those who profess much; as if she were hiding her own secret flights of sympathy from the approval of the charitably-minded as from a pollution; as if she would be in danger of really becoming cruel by associating,

---

[5] Natalie Clifford Barney, *Aventures de l'Esprit*. [Ed. No page reference; the passage in pp. 53-4: "Maeterlinck, ce mystique à motocyclette, à la recherche d'une vie à renouveler, s'amusait chez lui a braquer son fusil sur le rebord d'un balcon d'où, au repos, il tirait en éventail sur toute la plaine, une fille à ses cotes pour changer ses cartouches." -J.P.A.]

[6] *Ibid.*

[7] *Aventures de l'Esprit*. [Ed. This passage in p. 274: "Mettre le cerveau à vif, l'operer de toutes les maladies de l'habitude, le scalper au besoin pour voir ce qu'il y a dedans, palper son contenu, me repaître de sa substance authentique. Serai-je donc vautour? femme? Non, amazone.
Et l'on n'est pas amazone sans un semblant de cruauté. Même il ne nous déplait pas d'être crue mechante, si cette interprétation peut nous épargner de le devenir." -J.P.A.]

on a level of equality, with those who appear to be kind.

But listen to Pierre Loüys who was then threatened with total blindness:

> Forty-five days ago [I received] a most precious letter from you. You wrote it hurriedly on
> the 20th of May; I have not been able to answer; it made me timid. If I have ever in my life
> received two pages of such simple friendship as this letter brought I do not remember it.[8]

And another time in comparing her to Renée Vivien he writes:

> Under Pauline's violets I feel in her a sort of instinctive self defense against an imaginary
> malevolence prowling about, or lying in wait...But you were born with everything in your heart
> which she lacked. You write open-heartedly as naturally as she with her heart closed. And
> your word is generous, with a charming carelessness of future ingratitude...Her verses (which
> are very beautiful) are not confessions but illusions about herself. She is consumed by
> devouring passivity; whereas you are affectionate in the most active and beautiful way.[9]

Natalie's immortality rests largely, no doubt, in Rémy de Gourmont's "Lettres à
L'Amazone." When, ill and disfigured, he first knew her, his life had been bounded for years
by the walls of one room.

> Having persuaded him to venture as far as the Bois de Boulogne, I used to row for him on the
> artificial lake. He became so used to going out that I succeeded in making him mount my
> river-boat, and we went to Normandie, stopping at Rouen. He pitched about in the narrow
> streets, then climbed back with stumbling feet over the little gang-plank...[10]

And these were not passing fancies, not crazes of the moment. For five years this
man "devastated in the flesh, in revolt against God, having resisted all belief, found at last
a compromise between love and religion: this religion of friendship."[11]

After his death she wrote:

---

[8] [Ed. No reference in the text. The letter in *Aventures de l'Esprit*, pp. 33-4: "4 juillet. Dear Miss, Depuis
quarante-cinq jours, une lettre de vous m'est chère entre toute. Vous me l'avez écrite au courant de la plume,
le 20 mai; et je n'ai pas pu lui répondre; elle m'intimidait. S'il m'est arrivé de recevoir deux pages aussi
simplement *amicales* que cette lettre, je ne m'en souviens pas...Pierre Loüys." -J.P.A.].

[9] [Ed. No reference in the text. *Op. cit.*, p.35: "Sous les violettes de Pauline je vois une sorte de défense
instinctive contre une malveillance imaginaire qui rôde alentour et la guette Cela se manifeste par une étonnante
parcimonie de l'expression... Vous, au contraire, vous êtes née ayant au coeur tout ce qu'elle n' avait pas. Vous
écrivez à coeur ouvert autant qu' elle à coeur fermé. Et vous avez la génerosité du mot avec une charmante
insouciance de l'ingratitude future...Ses vers (qui sont fort beaux) ne sont pas des confessions mais des illusions
sur elle-même. Autant elle avait de passivité dévorante, autant vous êtes affectueuse dans le sans le plus actif
et le plus beau... Pierre Loüys." -J.P.A.]

[10] [Ed. No reference in the text. The passage in p. 53: "L' ayant décidé à s'aventurer jusqu'au Bois de
Boulogne, je ramais pour lui sur le lac artificiel. Il s'habitua si bien à sortir que j'arrivai à le faire monter sur
mon bateau de rivière, et nous allâmes jusqu'en Normandie, faisant escale à Rouen. Il tanguait avec difficulté
à travers les ruelles, puis remontait d'un pied trébuchant la passerelle. -J.P.A.]

[11] [Ed. No reference in the text. The passage in p. 55: "Dévasté dans sa chair, en révolte contre Dieu, ayant
résisté a toute croyance, il trouva enfin un compromis entre l'amour et la religion dans l'amitié--cette religion
de l'intimité." -J.P.A.]

I have not seen Rémy mortally sick, or dying, or on his death-bed. I did not assist at his burial. I hardly know his grave.

To each of us his own kind of piety, his own way of living with his dead, of continuing them in himself.

To contemplate an end forever is to create it.[12]

Natalie's kind of piety has kept her dead alive for her, and also for the rest of us.

And who knows? Perhaps the one word about her which has not been said, and which will go along with her, and after her, is that she is amazingly kind, and that her kindness carries.

---

[12] Natalie Clifford Barney, *Aventures de L'Esprit*. [Ed. The passage in p. 50: "Je n'ai pas vu Rémy mortellement malade, ni mourant, ni sur son lit de mort. Je n'ai pas assisté a son enterrement, je connais à peine sa tombe. A chacun sa pitié, sa façon de vivre ses morts, de les continuer en soi. Contempler sans cesse une fin, c'est la créer." -J.P.A.]

CHAPTER 6

Penelope

During this period in Neuilly the idea of going on the stage no longer urged me to any outward effort. On one occasion Natalie wanted to get up some theatricals in her garden, and this gave me a momentary spurt of energy. Collette and I were slated to act the "Dialogue au Soleil Couchant" by Pierre Louÿs, as she has charmingly recorded in her autobiography "Mes Apprentissages." I was rather frightened. I had been studying for a number of years and had never done anything, and there were so many people there that, as Collette says, we thought that all Paris was thinking of nothing but us. We imagined afterwards that we had been very successful. But presently Pierre Louÿs deflated our sails. He came up and told us that he had the greatest emotion of his life.

"Oh dear Louÿs!" said Collette.

"I have had the unforgettable impression of hearing myself interpreted by Mark Twain and by Tolstoi."

I was terribly hurt, and only some time afterwards I reflected that if I was as much like Mark Twain as Collette was like Tolstoi, I need not mourn over the resemblance.

After that, my dreams of great tragedy having culminated and probably terminated in a pretty garden party, I went for a while across the Channel. In traveling about, I happened to see, in Glasgow, an announcement that the Beerbohm Trees were acting that night in *Hamlet.* I went back of the scenes to see them before the play, and Mrs. Tree, who was in a rather gay mood, asked me to come on the stage with them. She dressed me up in one of her Ophelia dresses, took down my hair, and told me to do anything I liked, as lady-in-waiting to anybody. With this blank cheque in my hand, I stayed on the stage whenever there was the ghost of an excuse for a lady-in-waiting to be there; and, as I had no lines to say, I acted whatever pantomime occurred to me. Mr. Tree was amused and played up to me, and afterwards offered to take me on tour. But we were all in a laughing mood, and I do not know whether he meant it or not. During one of the *entr'actes* a married couple came backstage: Could they ask a question? They had made a bet: the husband thought my hair was real, the wife was sure it was a wig; could they feel it?

I returned to London after this and found an invitation from Mrs. Patrick Campbell to come and see her. She would like, she said, to act Pélléas and Mélisande with me. Would I come and join her company?

I was tremendously pleased.

The dying embers of my childish ambition flared up again, and all my theatrical visions of myself were suddenly as glowing as when I first decided to go on the stage. Presently, however, it appeared that there was a condition attached to Mrs. Campbell's proposal. She made it clear that, in order to act with her, I should have to give up a friend of mine in Paris of whom she disapproved. What she objected to was an occasional theatre or dinner engagement, or a ride or drive in the Bois de Boulogne. I was not living with this person, and Mrs. Campbell knew it. She was quite explicit about the fact that she considered my personal behavior exemplary, but that I was careless about the people with whom I was seen, and that this carelessness was bad for my reputation. I suggested that when she and I would be acting together we would undoubtedly be either in England or in America, that therefore these dinners and the tea parties in Paris which she objected to would automatically cease, so what difference did it make to her if I continued to maintain a friendly feeling toward this person whose name she had brought up?

"No," she said. "There must be no friendly feeling, and there must be no correspondence; there must be an open and permanent break if you are to act with me."

Seeing me hesitate, she said that the offer she was making me would put me within[1] one leap on the top notch of a professional career, that I was not likely to get another such chance; and that, if I refused, I would be forever just a rich dilettante, an amateur smatterer on the outside fringe of the theater; whereas, with her, I could start at once with a role that suited me, and after that it would be up to me to move on to any other plays that I might be dreaming about.

I knew that what she said was true. Everything I had been working for years was right there waiting for me to pick it up; and, if I did not stoop to take it, I knew that the road I had been following would be definitely closed. On the other hand, the thing which Mrs. Campbell was asking me to give up was not any matter of life and death to me, the atmosphere around it was not one where I felt at home, and in accepting her offer, along with her condition, I should not have suffered any overwhelming distress. It was merely an old friendship to which I preferred to be loyal. This was proved shortly afterwards when I left Paris forever.

Whereas my heart leapt at everything Mrs. Campbell was saying, I imagined her as Péléas and felt she would perhaps be better than in anything she had ever done on the stage;

---

[1][Ed. 'With' appears in the MS. -J.P.A.]

and the role of Mélisande was one which I could have acted in my sleep; and it would have been pure fun to pull up such a beautiful lover to my balcony with my braids. Everything about the outlook she had opened to me was delightful. I loved her little house in Chelsea, and I love[d] the thought of working and traveling with her. In fact it was all an ideal climax to my hopes and efforts up to that time.

What then was the adamantine thing in me that stopped me? What was the obstacle in me, below reason and below impulse, which made me refuse Mrs. Campbell's offer? No doubt it went against me to give up in such an uncalled-for manner, a friend who had done me no wrong, and I hated this smug case in judging a person dear to me whom she did not know. But what rankled most was her phrase: "It is bad for your reputation." This criterion she was setting up I considered not only mean-spirited for a great actress, it was positively unethical. I knew that my own life could not be regulated by "what might be said of me by others," that my actions would be judged by a more uncompromising critic than idle gossipers, and I felt that if Mrs. Campbell had nothing against me personally, and if she felt that together we could produce a fine play, it was up to her to go ahead without bothering me with such fantastical nonsense.

But added to all this, was there in me a sub-consciousness that I was not really on my own right path? Faced with a rare-opportunity which was closing in on me, did the theatre, as I knew it then, suddenly seem very small; and was I merely clearing the way for the growth in me of another theater-consciousness of which then I had no knowledge? Was it this that somehow made Mrs. Campbell's foibles loom large at a moment when I might so easily have fallen for her generosity? Anyway, I refused her offer, and I did this in full knowledge that life and effort and ambition, as I had known them up to that time, were at an end.

After this, in pure idleness, I went to Spain. But when I had seen the Prado and some of the northern towns, I returned to Paris, expecting to stay there forever, because no other place seemed any better. My future was blank.

In this frame of mind, which threatened to become permanent, I went one day to lunch with Paul Hyacinth, son of a former priest, whose eloquence had long resounded in the aisles and chapels of Notre Dame. Hyacinth had said:

"I am having Raymond Duncan, brother of Isadora, and his Greek wife. She will interest you. There will be no one else."

So again I heard Isadora's name, which had been spoken to me for the first time by Mrs. Campbell:

"Oh! There is a new dancer," she had said, "absolutely wonderful. But I am not going to tell you her name. You would go off your head about her."

And of course I did. We all did at that time. When Hyacinth said this to me I had seen Isadora dance quite often, and had met her once or twice, but I did not know her well; her brother and his Greek wife were a blank to me.

When I entered there seemed to be only one person in the room, or, if your like, two. A woman, simply dressed in white, who had not only the grandeur, but the very features of Michelangelo's Delphic Sibyl. The second person in the room was the child at her breast. After a while, during the conversation of the others, the child went to sleep. She then rose with no effort, carried her baby to a neighboring room, and left it there alone. She came back, and we all went to lunch. I suppose that the rest of us talked during the meal, but all I am conscious of is that she said absolutely nothing. After lunch Hyacinth asked her to sing. She did not wish to; but finally she rose from her chair and sang two Greek Ecclesiastical melodies, the first quite slow, the second rather rapid.

On me the effect was catastrophic. It was as if a wet sponge had been passed over a closely written black-board. I felt that I had heard music for the first time; heard a human voice for the first time.

After singing, Penelope lapsed again into complete silence; except that before leaving she asked me to come and see her.

This episode occurred in the spring, *toward the end of April, 1905*.[2] That year, the communists had announced a general strike for the first of May. There was an uneasy feeling abroad that street-fighting might occur; and the Government had ordered whole regiments of infantry and cavalry into the city. As these paraded about, my anxiety grew; not so much for Paris in general, or for many old friends in particular, but for this woman whom I had seen exactly once. I went to their studio in the rue Bonaparte, and offered to take them out to stay with me: bag, baggage, baby and all. I explained that my house was outside the walls, therefore they probably would be out of danger, and that after the first of May, they could return to their studio if they wanted to. So, presently, we were all driving up the Champs Elysées, Penelope and the baby, Raymond and I, with all their belongings and ourselves, in two little one-horse cabs. We dismounted at my tiny house, which was just large enough to give us each a room with one extra one for a living room.

The first of May passed off quietly; but the few intervening days had been sufficient

---

[2] [Ed. Italics in text. -J.P.A.]

to make Penelope and me feel at home together. My house, small as it was, seemed to be all we needed.

Meantime my older friends, dropping in as usual, were rather taken aback, on seeing a baby carriage in my garden, an infant four months old installed on a rug on my lawn, and two entirely strange people at home in my house.

In a few days, as we quieted down, after this first rather sudden upheaval, I became gradually conscious of Raymond. I had met him once before with Isadora, during the period she speaks of,[3] "when she wore Directoire dresses, and he knickerbockers, open collars, and flowing ties."

When he came to my house with Penelope they both wore white cloth dresses, somewhat Chinese in cut, with rather large sleeves; each had an Indian camel's hair shawl, hers dark green, and his dark red and they both wore sandals. To me this attire seemed natural enough, because, for many years, I had made ever renewed efforts to imitate the Greek clothes we see on statues, bas-reliefs and vases. When in New York, I would buy many yards of very expensive crèpe at Vantine's fine old down-town shop, stuff that really came from China, but not at all like what is now called crèpe de Chine. It was heavy and supple, and therefore rather good for draping in Greek folds. When in London, I would be tempted in Liberty's shop by the soft camel's hair materials and slinky silks. None of these stuffs were what I wanted, but they were the best I could find for the purpose, and out of these I had made a number of dresses which at least were cut in straight lines. I had also worked in leather, and had copied some of the complicated sandals on Greek statues. Penelope and Raymond had made attempts to solve this same problem. They had found a way of pleating dresses by wetting them, twisting them tight while wet, undoing them after a day, and twisting them again, and this several times over; the result looked more or less like certain types of archaic Greek costume, but the process required three or four days in drying, and would spoil very quickly when worn because the pleats loosened and widened in the middle as soon as one sat down.

Owing to these somewhat parallel attempts, our conversation centered largely on the difficulty we had all found in making any modern stuff look Greek in the wearing. One day Raymond said:

"If we had a loom perhaps we could do it."

I looked at him, my attention immediately arrested. I had never seen a loom in my

---

[3] Isadora Duncan, *My Life.*

life, and had no idea what one looked like; but the idea seemed promising. During all these first days in my house, Raymond had been very busy. From about the first moment, he had started to paint a little frieze in one of the rooms just under a low ceiling. He put in a terra cotta background, and silhouettes of athletes, in various postures, running all round, and looking somewhat like a black-figured vase. He had also acquired a sheet of copper, out of which he produced clasps for our chlamyses, with archaic animals chasing each other round the edge. He was evidently an excellent craftsman. So when he said: "If only we had a loom perhaps we could do it", I thought that perhaps we could.

I asked him if he could make a loom. He said he had seen them in Greek villages, and he thought he could. Penelope said she had woven a little in a peasant's house when she was a child and that she knew how it was done. I proposed immediate trial and took Raymond to a carpenter's shop to buy the wood. From that moment our days were very busy. Raymond proved to be a good carpenter, sawing, planning, and hammering, almost without rest, until our toy was ready. We had bought quantities of thread; but not one of us had any idea how to set it up. We spread it out on my lawn in hundreds of lengths of about twenty yards each. But it took a long time. Rains came; cats and dogs also; it got tangled; and finally, with much patience, we salvaged about seven yards, and wound it on one of the beams. Penelope spent days making heddles, whose function I knew nothing about. Then came the threading through the heddles and the reed, which took forever, because we did not know the right way. Raymond had said:

"With quite a heavy warp, and a very thin weft, we might obtain the effect we are seeking."

So the thread we got was heavy white wool; and when at last the warp was stretched and ready to weave, we threw across a fine silk weft, each one of us working in turn. This first effort made enough stuff for a dress for Penelope. After that we made a silk dress for me, with somewhat less trouble, though we were still all greenhorns. Then Raymond made a linen dress for himself; but we did not again attack the problem of a long warp. From this first loom in my house, each of us obtained a hand-woven dress.

While writing this chapter, I received a letter from Mrs. Eugene Vanderpool, of the American School of Classical Studies in Athens, which says:

> We have just been to a lecture by the director of the American School, who said: "While excavating a Geometric tomb we came upon evidence bearing out the theory of Eva Sikelianou." It seems that they found an iron object which had lain against the shroud of the body buried in the tomb; and which, during the process of rusting, had picked up the imprint of the cloth. It clearly showed the pattern of the weave: a heavy warp, and an almost

imperceptible weft. Mr. Morgan said that it not only proved your theory, as shown in the weaving of the Delphic Festival, but it showed that ten centuries earlier in Geometric times, this method was used for the same reason: to produce the richness of folds seen through Greek and pre-Greek vase painting.

The last thing one would have hoped for is this astonishing ratification by archaeologists that these first efforts of ours in Neuilly were on the right track, and that we really did discover the ancient Greek method of weaving. At that time not one of us knew how to set up a warp, or how to throw a shuttle.

Since then, living in many different Greek villages, gleaning here and there tricks in weaving that the peasant women know, and still more through an effort to discover the least fatiguing and at the same time the most rapid way of weaving by hand, I probably have acquired a manner of my own in using a hand loom. Nevertheless, it will be evident from what I have said that the original idea of copying ancient Greek stuffs, by using a heavy warp and a thin weft, which the Director of the American Excavations in Athens ascribes to me, is really attributed to Raymond Duncan.

Occasionally, during intermissions in our weaving, Penelope would sing to me. It seemed another world: one that took me back to that summer in Bar Harbour when I first looked into Jowett's Plato. I was about eighteen. It was an incredible experience which had no breaks, no contrast. From the first Dialogue to the last my feet did not seem to touch the ground, and wherever I went I had the sensation of flying.

> "Then felt I like some watcher of the skies,
> When a new planet swims into his ken."

I was absorbed in the many problems which Plato always evokes, and all but one of these problems was an added intoxication: How much of it all is Plato, and how much Socrates? Have the ideas an actual reality? and so forth; for each question believing that I could find the answer; at least the one that would be satisfactory to me. But one problem evoked no response from me. It left me dull and sad, so that only through the will to forget it could I regain the strange equilibrium which the rest of the work gave me. What did music mean to Plato? What was he talking about when he exiled one mode from his *Republic*, and preserved another? What was the Dorian mode which he retained, and what was the Lydian mode which he rejected? Whatever is a musical mode, anyway? Of course I had learned the school-boy stuff about the Dorian mode beginning on D, and going straight up the white keys of the piano; and the Phrygian mode beginning on E, and so forth; and I had heard some rather silly compositions which were supposed to represent these modes. I had also heard in Paris a whole opera which claimed to be written in a purely Greek manner, which was nevertheless insufferably dull.

But how could such possibly be the kind of music which Diotima told Socrates to write?   How could the Greeks, whose whole curriculum in education was based on mathematics, athletics, and music, be satisfied with such trash as this which any child of ten could produce today? And always the knell sounded from the lips of modern musicians. The Greeks knew nothing about what is now called harmony; *ergo,* although they were fine architects, fine sculptors, probably fine painters, and certainly great philosophers, great poets and the rest of it, in music they were morons. This conclusion seemed final. There was no getting around it; no fooling oneself into believing that they did know anything about harmony; no escaping the fact that, today, music without harmony is pure nonsense, a contradiction in terms. I could do nothing but accept the fact: that in spite of all they wrote about it, in spite of all their apparent adoration for it, and deep and devoted study of it, the Greeks were childish and silly in regard to music. With this, my state of levitation was in decided danger. But I succeeded in steering my mind away from it; in pretending that I did not care. There were so many other things in which they excelled. What matter if the Greeks were not musicians?

This distress which I had shrouded in Bar Harbour, because the Platonic wind was then carrying me above the earth, was not securely buried. It remained a blind and dark alley in my inner being; and every once in a while I would wrestle with it in this darkness, as a ghost might wrestle to recover the consciousness of a beating heart, and warm blood flowing.

But here was Penelope talking about music.

"A mode" she said, "is not a scale; it has nothing to do with the piano. Each mode has special intervals of its own, which do not exist on the piano. A mode is a mood; and a Greek song uses the mode which suits its content: one mode if the words are gay, another if they are melancholy, another if they are martial, and so forth. We have many musical modes. We therefore have infinite melodic variety."

I understood only very vaguely what she was talking about. But when she sang, I was in ecstasy.

One day we went to hear Raymond lecture in Paris. He spoke in vile French. This was not a crime in itself, but afterwards, in talking about it, he seemed to be proud of it. He had said a number of things in his talk which were shocking to his audience, so several people got up and went out. He seemed also to be proud of this afterwards. And so I heard him propound for the first time his doctrine: That it makes no difference whether audiences are for one or against one; the important thing, he said, is that they should swing violently in one direction or the other; that often it is better to have them disgusted rather than pleased, because this excites curiosity in others; and that in any case their mentality is too low to be worth considering.

At that time I did not take these harangues of Raymond's seriously. I thought in fact that he was propounding these theories rather as a joke. I liked him as a craftsman, and I did not imagine that a really good craftsman would believe and act on these things he was saying. So this blew over; and our quiet life of weaving, metal-work, book-binding, leather-work, went on as before.

Another day, walking in my garden with Penelope, she said a short poem to me in Greek, which she afterwards translated. She said it was by her brother, who often stayed on a small island by himself, near the large island of Lefkas, where her father and mother lived. The sound and the meaning of that poem affected me somewhat as her first song had. I was like a princess in a tower who had never heard a poem before; never heard a poet spoken of before. I told Penelope that I wanted to know her brother, and that I wanted nothing else.

"Let us go then," she said, "to my country."

Then among my friends, the unexpected happened. Every one who knew me, those who cared and those who did not; those who liked, and those who disliked each other; from near and far, rich and poor, wise and foolish, all were for once unanimous. To use every means in their power to prevent my going to Greece. It was strange, because I had crossed the ocean a number of times alone, and nobody cared. I had gone to Spain alone, and nobody cared. But when I said I was going to Greece, they all took on as if I had been headed for an African jungle. Was it, I wonder, because they all realized subconsciously that I would never come back?

To please them, or did that make matters worse, I left everything behind. All my belongings, especially all my clothes. My closets remained full of dresses from Doucet, Paquin and so forth; and hats from I don't remember where. With me I took a few straight dresses made with stuff from Liberty's or Vantine's, one or two from Natalie's garden-party, my one handwoven dress, a few wraps, and off we started.

CHAPTER 7

Kopanas

Arriving in Greece, we went straight to Kopanas, that is, to the foundations for a house which had been started a few years before this by Isadora and the whole Duncan family. They called it the Palace of Agamemnon, but it looked more like the remains of a medieval fortress, standing as it does, about five miles from Athens, on the summit of one of the foothills of Hymettos. I found myself within a large rectangular space, bounded by a well-built stone wall about ten feet high, with sky overhead, and nothing inside but a few lean-tos. These, on investigation, proved to be one good-sized room with a nice fire-place, and a number of small cell-like rooms, each with a door on the court. And that was all. There was no well, and no house or store anywhere near. It was evening when we arrived, and they installed me in the large room which they considered the best. I spread a few blankets and lay down, but it was not pleasant because the last use of the room had evidently been as a sheep-fold. So I took my blankets into the open court and had my first experience of sleeping under Greek stars. That alone was worth the journey.

The next morning I saw Penelope talking with a shepherd. She asked him something, and suddenly, at his answer, her face turned sad.

"What's the matter, Penelope?" I said.

"Oh," she answered, "he says that summer is over."

I could not imagine what she meant. The morning sun was blazing overhead, and a fearfully hot day was evidently ahead of us. So she explained:

"It has already rained once; and, after that, even though the hot weather may last for some time, we call it the end of summer."

It was then about the middle of August.

With the help of the shepherd we bought a few jugs of water and a few provisions; then I started off with Raymond to draw a deposit which I expected to find at a certain bank. We found the bank but not the money, which, through an error I could not have known of, had been forwarded to another bank. And so it happened that for about two weeks we lived on the top of a barren mill, with no money and no friends. The shepherd was kind and brought us water every day; and, in the evening, we would walk some distance with Penelope, who, fortunately, was a connoisseur in wild herbs, which were just sprouting under the dried grass and thistles because of the recent rain. She would pick herbs, and Raymond and I would gather sticks to cook them, and this was about all our food. Every morning we trudged into Athens to the bank; and then, when our energy held out, to the National Museum. And in the evening again we gathered herbs. They tasted good, and none of us minded the diet. The weather was perfect, the place a dream of incredible lines and ever-changing colors: the bay of Phaleron on our left, the tiled roofs of Athens on our right, the Parthenon directly ahead. I would have eaten the dried grass and thistles rather than miss it.

But one thing fell athwart my pleasure. Before starting off from Paris, as I did, with only a few straight dresses in my trunk, I had imagined that the tacit right of every individual in the public streets to the consideration of the others, depends not so much upon all of them being dressed in a given fashion, as on their own outer bearing, and their inner attitude of respect toward each other. I had never before worn Greek clothes outside my own house, though for many years I had worn them within these limits; but I really had no misgivings in leaving my French dresses behind, because I believed that if one's garments be an outward and visible sign of a simple and unaffected attitude toward life, and if one's appearance harmonize as far as may be with one's own spirit, the effect of that appearance on others will also be simple and free from strain.

But the first day that I walked into Athens with Raymond, we no sooner reached the village of Pangrati than we were joined by a mob. Children, men, women, everyone seemed to have abandoned work and play to come and look at us. They were not disagreeable, but terribly talkative; and it was a relief when the limits of the village were passed.

In Athens the same thing occurred, and continued to occur every day because the necessity of following up my expected bank order made it impossible to avoid these journeys. The little money that was left on our arrival had gone for small portions of rice, coffee, bread, sugar. I could not go out and send a telegram for the clothes I had left behind; I could not buy new ones; I could not stay home and hide. I was completely discouraged. I felt that all my notions about clothes were childish and silly, and I cursed my own impulsiveness which had prompted me to abandon everything I then needed.

But one day, Penelope decided to leave the baby with Raymond, and go with me into the city. That day we might just as well have been walking in our private garden. Nobody followed us, nobody spoke to us or about us, except for an occasional friendly greeting as we passed. I then told Penelope of my distress on other days, and asked for an explanation. But all the answer I got was: "Oh, my child!"

The next day I steeled myself for another ordeal, and sure enough the same hubbub resulted. I had begun to realize, however, that Raymond himself was not as troubled by it as I was; that in fact he seemed to like it; and I remembered his harangues in Paris when he maintained that the important thing with audiences is to swing them violently in one direction or another, regardless of whether they hate or like what you say. At present it was not what he said, but what he did. And yet it was not that either; because he did not in any way provoke the bystanders or passers-by with words or gestures; and, except for a few derogatory remarks, under his breath, about modern Greeks, he walked right ahead quietly enough. It was rather an indefinable attitude within himself, which did not resist, and did not protect him against this kind of disturbance. There was something in his aura which seemed to evoke the sarcastic, idle, or voluble curiosity of unknown people in the street. They would crowd around him through no apparent summons on his part, so that it was like going out to walk with a bitch in heat when no dog appears to be near, but presently a whole pack gathers from nowhere; or like accompanying a corpse, when out of a spotless sky, vultures signal to each other from afar.

Years after that, I was walking one day in Athens with Penelope. Some street urchins referred to me as "Miss Duncan." Then unexpectedly, Penelope's long restrained fury broke out, and her extraordinary Greek curses followed each other like flashing swords, but I remember only the end of her outburst:

"That is not her name, and if you ever call her that again, I will hang you on the highest tree by your own entrails."

Then she said my name, her brother's name, and the age-old pride in her voice has been a beacon in my life ever since.

Penelope loathed publicity; she hated acting. So, when, a few years later, in Paris, we gave the *Electra* of Sophocles, in ancient Greek, at the Chatelet, and afterwards at the Trocadero, her heart was not in it. She acted Electra, her gifted and beautiful sister Eleni acted Clytemnestra, I was Chrysothemis, Raymond was Aigisthos, and Denis Devaris, who afterwards became a distinguished newspaper correspondent in Athens, was Orestes. Our performance went well in Paris, but Penelope took no interest in her own success; and when this same performance, without me, had traveled all over the United States, she returned to Greece, worn and tired and terribly thin.

Some people are natural vegetarians. I myself am one; so that as long as we were staying on Kopanas with Raymond, his strict vegetarian diet suited me very well. But Penelope was naturally a meat-eater. Her mother told me that she alone, of all the children, had wanted an almost exclusively meat diet as a child. So, whenever they were in my house, in order to avoid reproachful looks toward her at table, I used to have food, saved, or specially cooked for her, which she ate in the kitchen; and so all went well, but when she came back from her long theatrical tour, she looked only half herself. Later, she caught malarial fever at Santi Quaranta; and after that her powerful lungs were consumed by galloping consumption at Davos.

But her lungs were an athlete's, a flutist's, a singer's. How could they have diminished and perished if her purely musical spirit had not first succumbed?

CHAPTER 8

Anghelos Sikelianos

During the long days of isolation on Kopanas, broken only by the journeys to the bank of which I have spoken, there was nothing within the bare enclosure of "Agamemnon's Palace" which provided any sort of occupation. Raymond had borrowed a few tools, and had found a little wood, and was often engaged in knocking together some pieces of rough furniture. Penelope and I usually sat quietly and talked.

My reason for coming to Greece had met with an unexpected setback, but it had not receded at all from my mind. On the contrary, Penelope's brother became more vivid to me through hearing more about him. Often I questioned myself, lying under the Greek stars at night, or watching the sun sink behind the Parthenon, which seemed to glow as if by its own inner light, what it was that had brought me so far. Why was the reaction in me so immediate when I first heard his name? Why had that first impression increased rather than diminished? I had lived with writers and painters and artists all my life. What was there in the few short poems which he wrote as a child, and which Penelope happened to remember, that had seemed to me so tremendously important? I did not know; and though I kept Penelope talking about him whenever I could, and though I learned something about his personal appearance, and though I heard her recite more of his poems, the "Why" remained unanswered in my consciousness.

The day came when the bank-clerk whom we visited so often asked if I had tried at any other bank to trace my lost money order and my mail. On that day, Raymond and I drove back with two cabs filled with furniture and provisions. By that time I had appropriated a small cell-like room near the entrance-door of the outer enclosure. This room had nothing but a door and two iron-barred windows just below the roof, about half a yard wide and six inches high. These windows did not open and were almost useless for giving light, because the outer walls of Agamemnon's Palace were thick enough to withstand the onslaught of a primitive siege-tower. The sunlight, however, streamed in through my open door, and when the great outer door was also open I could see the whole range of Hymettos.

So the next day, having made our cells somewhat more habitable, Penelope and I felt free to recall what we had said in the garden in Neuilly. We went again to Athens together, and sent a telegram to her home in Lefkas, in the Ionian Islands, to her brother, Anghelos Sikelianos.

I first saw him standing in the blazing sunshine outside my door; but the darting reflections from parched earth and stone walls, usually hard and glittering, had suddenly concentrated in light which was not glittering at all. He seemed at home and at ease in the intense brightness; and even after he had walked through the strip of sunlight in the center of my room into the shadow of its edge, he seemed to retain the glow which at first had appeared to be merely the reflection of the sun in his hair. He was quite pale and apparently cool, in spite of the intense heat in the courtyard and on the road outside.

Before he came, I had thought that I knew his appearance well, but it was something like imagining the lines of Greek mountains before one has seen them, or the colors of a Greek sea. Later I knew that these things not only cannot be imagined: they cannot be remembered, even after one has lived with them for many years. The mind can only retain special moments of Greek lands and seas, or else a composite impression of many moments. It cannot remember the light, the incredible lines and ever-changing colors because Greek earth is alive; and compared to it the mind is always static. In the same way, the mind cannot visualize a poet.

But what I had not imagined at all was his voice. It affected me very much as Penelope's singing had when I first heard her. All former impressions were wiped out, and I wanted only to hear him talk, at first not hearing what he said, as long as I could hear the quality of his voice. At that time he spoke little English and I little Greek, so our conversation was in French; even years after, when I spoke Greek with everybody else, I did not yet dare to say a word to him.

I do not remember how we started speaking about the advantages and disadvantages of discussion, but I remember his answer.

"Discussion," he said, "is good, but it is good in its place. It never produces agreement. It is an athletic contest on a mental plane, in which the wrestler uses all his strength to overthrow his opponent. Human pride and prowess have a share in it, and the personal victory of an individual or a nation is the reward. All nations are at war, or carry within them the germs of war toward each other. But understanding between them hangs on one question which has never been elucidated: are there in all of them, beneath their uneasy struggles, their paltry friendships, their latent or open antagonisms, any principles which are common to all?[1] Is there in all of them any germ of wisdom, which, however hidden, is

---

[1] The term "universal principles" sounds very like what Mr. Stuart Chase would call "bad language." In fact his book *The Tyranny of Words*, and another recent work by Professor P. W. Bridgman called *The Logic of Modern Physics*, [N.Y. 1927] have made one self-conscious in using words of such import. Nevertheless,

more vital than opinion? If there is, then the clarification of those principles which embody
the true wisdom of each, is the only path to the mountain peak where peace reigns. If there
are no such principles, then all effort toward human solidarity is nonsense."

"I believe," he said, "not only that there are such principles in the inner essence of
man, but there are, today, individuals in all nations who have a clear vision of what these
principles are. Those who do see clearly, beyond all dogma, the inner truth and unity which
is partially expressed in all dogmas, should have a home in the world where they could meet.
They should form a council, a nucleus for the protection of all human beings from fanaticism
and selfishness; and this nucleus should gradually grow into a University which would
further the study of Universal Truths, and teach their application through Science, and, as far
as possible, through the already existing Religion and Art of each and all nations."

"No doubt," he went on, "when this vanguard of the thinkers, the seers, the scientists,
the 'non-attached' will once have met, when they will have a home, however small, which
represents them in the world, when they will have spoken once above the clamor of dissent,
and voiced the clarion-call of agreement, when they will have looked into each other's eyes,
and each seen himself in the eyes of the others; then they will find how many are those who
vibrate to their call, who are now silent through discouragement or fear. But how bring
together those who really know? How give their voice a hearing?"

In listening to him I became tremendously excited. At last, here was a foundation for
what my father had called "Courtesy," which, by itself, had grown to seem a flimsy thing
indeed as a means of overcoming violent passions, exorbitant ambitions, bigotry and hatred
among mankind. Courtesy superimposed on all these was, after all, nothing but a polite
varnish, a gentleman's pastime, a parlor trick, if the basis of it all was the seething cauldron
of a man's worst passions and nothing else.[2] But here was something underneath these
passions and more real than they; something which could be gotten at, and clarified, and
developed, which would be a bond mightier than all discordant contentions. Anghelo called
the awareness of Universal Principles a tiny compass in a raging tempest. I felt that his

---

the Delphic Concept of reducing warring dogmas to their lowest terms, and so discovering where they can "agree
to agree" is just another way of getting rid of meaningless absolutes, and may come out on the side of "good
semantics" in the end.

[2] [Ed. There is a discrepancy betweeen the two manuscripts I have collated. In the copy, which I take
to be the final and more complete version, the text of the next sentence reads as printed here. In the copy I titled
MS2, which I believe is flawed, the following words are missing: "and nothing else. But here was something
underneath these passions"; I have opted for the fuller version of MS1 and the insertion of the missing words
since they help make the meaning clear. -J.P.A.]

compass was pointing safely to the Polar star.

As we talked, Penelope came in and said that she had prepared supper; and we went in with her to the large room. Raymond, with his carpentering, had arranged the place very nicely. He had four long, narrow couches against the walls, and tables of similar shape in front of each, but somewhat lower, so that they could be pushed under the couches when not in use; and each couch was covered with bright-colored Greek blankets, and had hard round pillows at each end, so that in eating one rested comfortably on one elbow. The stone wall behind each couch was also hung with warm, gay blankets; and, to make it all look homelike in the growing chill of evening, Penelope had lit a great fire. She had also prepared delicious food, but Angelo said he wanted to eat nothing but Hymettos honey. And sure enough, during the days he was there, he ate nothing else. As we lay there, archaic fashion, each on his own couch, with our long narrow tables nicely spread before us, I watched Angelo who was lying opposite me. He looked very fine in the candle and fire light, and I wondered if the extraordinary color of his skin came from eating honey. But that could not be so because it seemed to be a recent craze which set Penelope laughing; and besides, she herself had the same quality of skin, healthy, but rather pale, what the French call *mate*, and which is apparently immune, in all changes of temperature, from going red or blue, or any other unbecoming color, from heat or cold.

At that supper I heard Anghelos and Penelope talking [in][3] Greek together for the first time, and I was both delighted and exasperated. The sound of it was amazing; but I felt somehow cheated, as if they had filched from me something that belonged to me. I had no curiosity about what they were saying, but considerable jealousy, because they knew Greek and I did not. Presently my aggravation got the best of me, and I brought them back to a language which they both spoke easily by asking a question.

"Your thesis concerning Universal Principles," I said to Anghelos, "seems to presuppose the equality of the races. But do you believe that all races are equal?"

"No," he said, "I do not. But those who are superior are only a short way ahead on the road as long as they imitate the savage in their means of attack. Education through violence may and sometimes has inculcated higher principles in backward individuals and races, but it is terribly slow. It creates resentment which may endure for centuries; whereas science and art both possess means which are rapid, sometimes immediate, and they leave no residue of bitterness or thirst for revenge; both can cause the hidden germ of innate nobility

---

[3][Ed. 'In' added. -J.P.A.]

to blossom like the almond tree in winter in one sunny day."

He went on talking about this innate germ in races and individuals, and said that local characteristics should not be levelled down, but consciously developed, and that, through an appreciation and understanding of the finer qualities of each, the greater races could show their true superiority.

But in listening I grew to long for the sound of Greek again, even though I did not understand it. His answer to my question had been what I had wanted and expected to hear. Then, as when he first spoke in my room, the sense of what he was saying became lost in the sound of it. But I knew then that, however fine in French, the sound of his own language was incomparably better. So I asked them to go on talking in Greek. This time I gave myself up to the pleasure of it. They seemed happy together, and often their talk was broken by the laughter of either, or both. I was watching them, and the fire, and the candles, and thinking how my eagerness to meet him had been met by what seemed an immediate expression of my own thoughts. Had he divined them and used his voice to express them, or was it my inertia which waked into awareness in meeting his thought? No doubt the latter; and yet it is now over thirty years since that evening, and I have never once felt unexpressed when he was speaking. Even then, through an unknown language, which was simply music to the Schopenhauerian sense: a thing-in-itself, unattached and free, I felt at home.

As they talked, and laughed, I watched the candles grow shorter, and the fire grow dim, until we all separated for the night.

CHAPTER 9

The Delphic Idea

The next morning we had breakfast together, which consisted, for Angelos, of a small cup of black coffee and a crust of bread. I asked him if that was what he always ate for breakfast or whether it was part of his momentary fondness for honey. He said no, that that was all he ever ate in the morning. The rest of us had warm milk and cream in our coffee and nice toast and butter, but he did not seem to envy us at all.

I told him that I was anxious to hear more about his vanguard of human solidarity. Had he thought of how it could be started? Did he have any special place in mind where he thought it should be founded? In Athens, or where?

"Pascal is right," he answered, "in saying that God is a circle, the center of which is everywhere, and the circumference nowhere; and eventually it will be true that the center for human understanding will be everywhere, and the circumference nowhere. There will be centers founded in all parts of the world, each manifesting the Oneness of Man and of all Creation, through the outwardly diversified means and inclinations, due to the climate, the race, the traditions, and the language of each. Each nation will find that in lifting up its own sacred hope, and in expressing it in its own greatest artistic form, it will become itself and embodiment of the Spirit of God in Man. Rooted in its own Earth, and clarifying its own Divinity, each will become a Witness, to itself and to others, of the oneness of man."

"Nevertheless, at present, when not one spiritual, or scientific, or artistic center is fully aware of its great mission, the establishment of the first Nucleus cannot be a matter of chance, or of personal preference. It should be identified with one of these sites which history has chosen to further the spiritual advance of the human race. The reason for this is that each one of these spiritual centers had reached out in the past beyond its own national or racial boundaries, has enlightened other races to some extent with knowledge beyond themselves, which has remained a part of their spiritual heritage, and therefore connects them still, consciously or unconsciously, with itself and with each other. Thus each of these ancient centers is potentially a home for all those whose constant residue of spiritual attributes has once drawn from its source."

"Each great civilization possesses such a site or sites. Brindaban in India is one; Jerusalem is another; Glastonbury is another. In Greece we possess many such sites, Eleusis, Dodona, and Delphi being best known. The last especially seems to have been the basis of all Greek Culture. But also, to the extent to which Greece has influenced all European countries, all of America, North and South, and even to a certain degree Asia and Africa, to all these, whether consciously or unconsciously on their part, this site is a mother country."

"All the ramifications of Greek thought and activity are not known. Nevertheless, in all nations, enough has been written and spoken by students of Art, of Science, of Religion, of Philosophy, of Politics and Economics, to make it evident that our foundation is also, to some degree, theirs. Moreover, the ancient site of Delphi has been for centuries, and is today, a strategic center between north and south, connecting Central Europe with the Mediterranean. It was not in vain that Zeus let fly his eagles from the extremities of the earth to find its center, and that these eagles nested together in Delphi."

This remark was afterwards verified during the war of 1914-1918, when the Allied fleet cast anchor in the harbour of Itea, which is Delphic harbour. The Allied armies were stationed at Bralos, which is just back of Delphi in the Theban plane; and the road built by the Allies over the flank of Parnassos, to connect Bralos with Itea, passes through ancient Delphi on its way. Thus the very cross-roads where Oedipus killed his father are as important now strategically, as they were then; but spiritually[1] they are more so, for, as Angelos reminded me, the ancient sanctuary of Delphi had made the only serious effort in history to unite the East and the West.

"Delphi therefore is the chosen center where a new Temple must be built; not one of marble columns, but a temple whose pediment shall be Education, Economy and Justice for the whole earth."

"But how," I cried, "can this thing be done? How can we sink this anchor, and get it deep enough, and heavy enough, for all the storm-tossed peoples of the world to moor their battered ships? How can it be done, not ever so many years later, but right now, before you and I grow old, and before Europe and perhaps the whole world is wrecked by other wars?"

"I do not know," he said, "but I have thought of nothing but that question all my life. That is to say that whatever I have done or written, as far as I can remember, even though to others it might seem irrelevant, has always, for me, radiated from or worked toward this secret pivot. I do not know how this anchor can be laid; but I do know that if a group of

---

[1]   One of the short-comings of the English language is that this word happened to be derived from Latin instead of Greek. Both words 'spiritus' and 'pneuma' originally meant "breath"; but in English the word 'spiritual' always connotes something vague and mysterious, and suggests disembodied spirits floating about; so that one misses the straight hit of the Greek "pneumatikes" which, beside implying immaterial values, also evokes "genius," "intelligence," "penetrating insight." It is a pity for such a word to have fallen to such base uses as to be now only the compressed air in the tire of an automobile.

men, men of large vision and competent mind, who certainly exist in many countries, could be brought together, and allowed to work in the way I am suggesting, it would be a true starting-point for the conquest of savagery, for which so many people everywhere are longing and praying."

One day I said to him:

"If you were able to draw from all parts of the world men of the type you speak of, who undoubtedly exist today, are you not at all afraid that, however perfect their vision and their language, they would soon sink into discussion and sophistry, if they were isolated for long in the manner you describe, and what good would this center then be to the world?"

"Most certainly," he said, "they would so degenerate and fall into the mazes of discussion if they were isolated. But the very essence of the Delphic Idea is that they would not be isolated. There must be a medium, a means of communication between them and the rest of the world. Their spiritual intuition must be constantly reinforced by the power, and joy, and suffering of all humanity; and humanity must be constantly renewed by their vision of the potential understanding and joy of all men in the world. There must be a bridge, a causeway, between those who see and those who only feel. There must be an interchange between the lungs and the heart, or both will perish."

"This," he went on, "is possible only in one way. There is only one causeway which can unite in absolute equality those whose thoughts are of great expanse, and those whose thoughts are narrow. There is only one bridge which can span the chasm: and that bridge is Art: though not the little sentimental effulgences which are sometimes called so. And in the realm of great Art, there is one whose power is supreme: and that is DRAMA: though again, not the trifling exertions which often gather little crowds to little theaters: but the great Drama which held masses, fifteen, twenty, thirty thousand people in the grip of great poetry, great music, great dancing."

"To a certain extent this is done today," he said, "in the religious services of those churches which still use art as a medium of communication and unification of masses of people. But the ultimate possibilities of this method are lessened in churches by their only partial use of all the faculties of man; and also by the limitations of their dogma, whose appeal, however nobly represented, cannot reach beyond the confines of its own flock."

"But tragedy has no such limitations. It uses and harmonizes all the faculties of man, Poetry, Music, Dancing, Acting, Architecture, Painting, Sculpture, have once been united in the Drama. A whole people has been quickened into life; overpowering emotion has made them one: spiritual understanding has become pure beauty. This is what Aristotle means by purification through tragedy.[2] It has been done once. It must be done again."

"Then, when such Art as this has performed the miracle, when the spirit has led masses of people to the mountain top through representation: when they know through their own spontaneous emotion that they are indissolubly one: then is the time for reasoning, for pedagogy, for discussion. Then all superficial differences will have become insignificant; and those differences which are real will be approached in a spirit of temperance. Then discussion will no longer be a battle of wits: but a meditation: a prayer to reach the light.

"And tragedy has the inestimable advantage of being entirely non-political, entirely non-dogmatic, with no alloy of party or sectarian prejudice. It is so large that warring states and warring religions can sit together in the same great theater, and quietly suck the warm milk of love and pity from its great breast. Tragedy alone can declare the truce of God. It is for this reason that the Sanctuary of Eleusis ordered Aeschylus to "Write Tragedies."

So we talked: he speaking, I ecstatically listening, feeling that all my dreams and hopes and efforts, and my father's and my mother's hopes and dreams would somehow not be lost.

But one night, very late, after he had left me, I heard a cry from without the outer wall. My name repeated three times:

"Eva! Eva! Eva!"

It was Angelos' voice, and I ran quickly to find him. But the night was dark. There was no trace, no sound. I went and called Penelope. She also had heard the cry, and she came out with me to call him and search for him. But we both knew it was hopeless. He was a swift runner, and he already had a long start.

"We will go," said Penelope, "to my country."

---

[2][Ed. The Aristotelian term in the *Poetics* is 'katharsis'. -J.P.A.]

CHAPTER 10

Lefkas

Sacred lion-sleep
Of the return, in the great
Stretch of the beach:
In my heart
My eyelids closed:
And shining, deep within me, the sun.[1]

The return. For him to his home: which was at once the outward aspect of this shining Ionian mountain rising out of the sea, and the vision, the feeling, the knowledge (they are one) of this sun within, which made his flesh transparent. For me also it was a return home, but from what, and to what? From things familiar which had always seemed strange, to things unknown which were the blood in my arteries. And the great stretch of the beach, the unimaginable cleanness of the sea, breathed in me and round me as my own infinity. Inward and outward seemed to meet in this island which was Spirit, in these white egg-shaped pebbles which were our bed, reaching beyond the visible horizon, and down to the bottom of the sea. I even knew that this Oneness was not for a moment in time, but had always been, and would be forever.

Was this, I wondered, what Greece had always been saying? Was this why the world may struggle to be rid of her, but can never escape? Is this why Greece, however many times destroyed and abandoned, is nevertheless clean and new? Because Greece has once made the Spirit transparent Flesh, and the Flesh evident Spirit. And is not this the inner goal of all our earthly striving: that the outward and the inward be one?

In Lefkas, the Ionian Island, in Anghelo, its son, this outward and inward breathing, this heart giving out life-blood and taking in Spirit, were real. It was not in him an attitude toward life, or merely an incredible spontaneity in language; he actually was the golden eagle "nourished by facing the sun," and he was the dead in the graveyard; he was the swift boat, and the shadow of clouds; the leaping dolphins, and the beggar in the ditch. Then he saw the peasant's spade cleave the earth apart, he was the worm speeding back into its hole; and he was the tormented bull, racing from the gadfly, and brought to a halt on the cliff's edge by the sound of his own ringing cry. The serpent bending the grasses it moved; the oxen

---

[1] [Ed. A. Sikelianos, *The Seer*, opening lines of the poem. As far as I know the translation is her own. -J.P.A.].

under the yoke, the swift stallions in the threshing-floor bounding through the hay. Everything around him seemed to be not separate entities but part of his inner consciousness, as we went from village to village, from mountain to mountain, from harbor to harbor. All that we saw in his island or on his sea became, in a way, ourselves.

I asked him how he first became conscious of the Greek race, how it affected him as a child. It was, he said, in some National Celebration where he heard speeches about their long slavery under the Turks, and of the Revolution which freed them. After that he was afire with excitement about the heroes of 1820.[2]

"But my father," he said, "who is a saintly and scholarly man, quietly dissipated my childish enthusiasm. He used to take me on long walks through these great olive groves, or through the salt-marshes, or up the mountain to the old monastery overlooking the Ionian Sea, and he would talk with me. Little by little he made me aware of how, through our Revolution, which was won partly through the bravery of our heroes, and partly through the intervention of modern diplomacy, Greece had exchanged Turkish dominion for Western "protection;" and how this diplomatic process was, in a way, more dangerous than slavery for a newly liberated people: because, after winning our confidence, this "protection" was extended to us more through self-interest than through sympathy, and in total ignorance of our deeper roots and capacities."

He spoke of the Greek people as in a lethargy, unaware that without spiritual independence true freedom is impossible.

One day Anghelos and I were passing some Cyclopean ruins, and he told me how he became conscious of the immense age of the monuments around him, of his vain search in archaeological books to find a key to their meaning; of how passionately he had longed for a teacher; one who really understood the whole of Greek history, and who, in the widely-branching tree of Greek genius, could show him the trunk. But he found no one anywhere who knew or cared for what he was seeking; only worthy and honest people who were dazzled by their imagined freedom; or, occasionally, the bitter sarcasm of the few who, themselves, had made similar attempts and found it hopeless.

As I grew to know the peasants better, he also told me how he had turned to them, and often found among them, in their language, their customs, and their life-movement, the glow of a true and autonomous tradition: but only as a brightness, and only within the limits

---

[2] [Ed. The year should be 1821, when the Greek War of Independence broke out. Probably the author meant to refer to the 1820's. -J.P.A.]

of the village and its surroundings.

So nothing remained for him in his search but to go on alone; and nothing to help him but books. Gradually I became aware of his truly vast reading: in Greek, in French, and in Italian, and many translations from German and English. He seemed to have left nothing unread that I had ever heard of. He described his meeting with Plato, and especially with the Presocratics, and with all the remnants of Greek writings which have come to be known to us. And he told me how, little by little, all these widely differing personalities seemed to lead him to a single goal: the Delphic Sanctuary. He was struck at first by the serious relationship of all the great men in Greece to it, over centuries of time, and by the fact that so many of them were seconded and sustained in their work by the Sanctuary: law-givers, reformers, wise men were anointed: poets, historians, philosophers were recognized and sustained; slaves were systematically liberated, the equality of the sexes was recognized. At no period, for more than a thousand years, was there any effort to obtain control of the conscience and actions of the people, or to form a theocracy with a powerful priesthood as in Asia and Egypt. There is no parallel in the history of any other country of a religious center which instituted Courts of Justice: Congresses of Arbitration for the spiritual encounter of all peoples of the earth; Festivals of lyric, dramatic, historic, and athletic contests, which embraced in a spirit of one-godliness the whole terrestrial Myth, and hospitably received all the currents of the earth in order to unite them. The Sanctuary also indicated new sites for colonizing cities, which in itself implies a startling knowledge of geography, considering the number of Greek colonies which were founded in the whole Mediterranean and beyond, and also the beauty of the sites which they chose; and these expeditions were always accompanied by two Delphic priests.

And over and above all the branches of this amazing organization, which itself was the principle source of Greek education, were the highest initiates who were called the *Epoptai*, which literally means "overseers," but in a sense which is unfortunately lost in the English word, together with its true function. These priests were obliged vigilantly to follow, and overlook all the comtemporary historical currents of all peoples then known in the world, and to attract them, above obscure fanatacisms toward a hearth of knowledge of the Universe, and knowledge of one's self, without the slightest trace of dogmatic slavery; and these priests were also called Guardians of the Sacred Archives.

"And today," he said, "there are such men in the world, whose vision is clear, and whose heart is strong. There are enough of them to do a great work if they were together, but they are weak and helpless because they are scattered and unknown to each other."

So Anghelos brooded on his Delphic Idea as we rode together over the island.

One time we took a week's trip to Sappho's promontory, a very high ledge of rock at the other extremity of the island. From passing steamboats I had seen it looking shiningly white in the sun, and hence the name *Lefkas*, but from above it looked brilliant pink; we leaned over, or rather Anghelos did, and I crawled to the edge to look down from a really immense height over a wall that one could not see, for it was so steep it jutted inwards. There was nothing but the water below, a quiet little bay with bright red fishes swimming about. It was from here that Sappho is said to have leaped to her death; and she certainly chose a sure place to die.

During this trip, Anghelos was overjoyed with a book he had with him by the great Polish hellenist, Thaddaeus Zielinski. It was a series of lectures about the importance of classical studies, delivered to his students in St. Petersburg, and for which Zielinski was afterwards exiled from the Soviet Republic. Here is one of the pages that warmed Anghelo's heart. He read:

> All states of antiquity," he read, "were based either on a military or an economic idea. In Greece alone dawned the thought that the state should be a means for the ethical perfection and conduct of men, and that politics should be a fulfillment of ethics all along the line. The realization of this thought was undertaken by Delphi, the greatest spiritual and ethical organization in Greece, down to the fifth century: and also the education of the whole of Greece, according to the spirit of Apollonian Ethics. Thus Greece, from the most ancient times, by means of Delphi, places over all one-sided problems the most central of all human problems, that is to say: how should a state be organized educationally in order to ensure not only the harmonious solidarity of peoples among themselves, but also the possibility of the greatest physical, spiritual and ethical perfection of each individual separately.[3]

Shortly after this Anghelos went to Egypt to see his brother Menelaos who lived near the Libyan desert. While there, in about two weeks, he wrote his first great poem,

---

[3]   [Ed. The title of Zielinski's work from which the passage is taken does not appear in the text of either manuscript. The author gives here the impression that at the time she met A. Sikelianos in 1907, he was already familiar with Zielinski's ideas. The lectures Zielinski gave on the suject of classical Greece before his student audience in Petersburg took place in 1903. It is possible that A. Sikelianos (1884-1951), who was then twenty-three years old, had read the lectures in a French translation. Since it is unlikely that Eva P-S had committed to memory the text she cites, she must have been transcribing from notes she probably kept or from her own copy of the Zielinski's book, available in a French as well as a Greek translation. A. Sikelianos quotes extensively from Zielinski's lectures, delivered in 1903, in his 1931 essay "The Delphic Union," in *Prose Works* (Πεζὸς Λόγος), ed. G. Savides, Vol. II, (Athens: Ikaros 1980), pp. 325-83. The passages Eva P-S cites in this chapter correspond to "Delphic Union," p. 356. Zielinski's collection of essays "We and the Ancients" was translated into Greek by I. Sykoutris and printed in 1928. See Th. Zielinski, ʹΗμεῖς καὶ οἱ ʹΑρχαῖοι. Μετάφρασις καὶ ʹΕπιλεγόμενα ʹΙ. Συκουτρῆ. (ʹΑθῆναι, Δ. καὶ Π. Δημητράκος, 1928), σελ. η+268. -J.P.A.]

Alaphroiskiotos,[4] which might be called *The Seer*. It is his island and his people, his mother, Penelope and myself, projected through his consciousness, and more than ever ourselves.

When he returned with this manuscript, and read it to me, I felt for the first time the sort of ecstatic torment which I have known ever since, with each new poem that he writes: how could I project this thing, which his voice was giving to me through the medium of the Greek language, beyond that language?

I did not know.

Often I have thought that all the hours of my life would be a small stake to put up for such a large result. But can anyone but a poet translate a poet? Could even a poet give however partial a rendering, in any other language, of the richness and beauty of Modern Greek: These questions have grown more insistent as time went on, and as Anghelo's poems followed one another with ever-increasing mastery of his medium:

> **The Dedication**
> **The Prologue to Life (including)**
> > **Consciousness of my Earth.**
> > **Consciousness of my Race.**
> > **Consciousness of Woman.**
> > **Consciousness of Faith.**
> > **Consciousness of Personal Creation.**
> **The Mother of God.**
> **The Easter of the Greeks.**
> **The Dithyramb of the Rose.**

These and many other works, published and unpublished, have constantly intensified my first delight and anxiety. Who could interpret them in English, or French, or any other language? Once I took heart when George Cram Cook came to Greece. He became ecstatic when Anghelos recited, and then translated for him some of his shorter poems. He vowed that his life work, from then on, would be to leave everything Anghelos had written adequately translated into English. He actually began enthusiastically to study modern Greek; he really seemed to love and understand what he had heard, and I felt then my hope would be realized. But "Gig" died within the year; and so far, no one has taken his place.

In Greece, however, beside many shorter appreciations in magazines and newspapers, three books [in Greek] have been published which give the measure of understanding meted

---

[4] This word is difficult to render in English because of the ambiguity of our adjective "light," which may mean either the opposite of dark, or the opposite of heavy. In this word, "alaphrós," or "elaphrós," means light in the latter sense; and "iskios" means "shadow." So, literally, the whole word means: he-whose-shadow-does-not-weigh-heavily. Among the peasants it also means: one who sees visions and dreams dreams, and it was they who called him by this name. The opposite of this word also exists in Greek: "variskiotos," which means dull, glum, stupid; literally heavy-shadowed.

out to him at home:

> Takis Dimopoulos. *The Delphic Idea* (1933).
>
> Theodore Xydes. *The Religious Will of Sikelianos* (1932).
>
> Takis Dimopoulos. *The Dithyramb of the Rose*. Text, Notes, Epilegomena (1934).

This last book is a most scholarly and truly beautiful study of this poem and its writer. He calls him "our poet in God," and says:

> Whatever to our eyes may seem soulless and gloomy, under his glance and his word takes on a distinctive life, and appears *sub specie aeterna*, flashing out the radiance of eternity...
>
> With him it could not be otherwise, because he actually realizes in his own being the first Orphic demand: Unity. You feel that his thought is poured into his body, and his strong soul gleams through his flesh. And you feel the coexistence and mutual justification of austerity and swee_ness; of modesty and authority; of the deepest concentration of thought, and, along with it, the gayest childlike joy.[5]

The book by Theodore Xydes considers one by one the characteristic qualities of Sikelianos to show that they all constitute what he calls "the coefficients of a complete religious will." I will quote from this book a few passages:[6]

> [V] Let us follow him. His presence always holds us under pressure. And that pressure is all the magnificence of his enchantment. But how shall we get near him? His poetry, Titanic in magnitude, and absolute in worth is a mere dripping as manifestation of himself. It is certainly a manifestation. [VI] Yet Sikelianos himself becomes the object of broader research, so broad that even his poetry, which for others is everything, becomes a detail, an impressive one most certainly, but always somehow incapable of interpreting his life. Because, for the Delphic poet, inspiration does not exist as an element of his poetry. In vain we shall seek for it. His inspiration is his life itself. In all his moments he is the inspired one. For him, and perhaps this is true only of him, every moment is poetry itself. That which we call important or unimportant does not possess the same substance for Sikelianos. This is simply because for him every instant is important. The voice of a child, the scent of a rose, the murmur of the sea, the beauty of a mountain slope, the transparency of the sky, do not constitute motives for writing verses. They are his very life. His life which becomes alive in the universe...
>
> [IX] The equilibrium between the worship of Apollo and Dionysos which was consummated at Delphi, is the same in the poetry of Sikelianos. It seems as if the Apollonian paeans and the Dionysian dithyrambs determine the most ravishing symphony. Spirit and nature cannot live together in greater accord. It is as if the spirit impregnated nature and as if nature surrendered herself to the control of the spirit. It is as if the spirit were incarnated and as if the flesh became spirit...
>
> [XIII] Sikelianos possesses an incomparable grandeur which cannot be turned, to use the common phrase, into small change. The assemblage of his spiritual creations is completed and perfected by its universal beauty. Thus the study of special aspects of his work is a descent.

---

[5] [Ed. Text in T. Dimopoulos, *The Delphic Idea*, p. 98; the translation is by Eva Palmer-Sikelianos. - J.P.A.]

[6] [Ed. The text in Th. Xydes, *The Religious Will of Sikelianos*, (Athens, 1932), passim. The translation is by Eva Palmer-Sikelianos; page numbers in brackets are to this edition. -J.P.A.]

As many as grasp it complete, these have grasped its complete beauty. As many as search for his details and ignore the work as a whole, these are as if they broke up a statue to examine it anatomically...His poetry is one and indivisible. As a poet he was born; as a poet he was shaped; as a poet he exists.

Proof of the gravity of the Sikelianic work is the inner certainty, the steady and persistent line which the poet follows with faith...He knows his work...And this inner certainty, most lyrically established within himself, far from egopathetic boundaries, proclaims him prophet, herald, apostle, master-craftsman.

[XIV] His knowledge of himself is again the essential cause of the courage which is enclosed in his verse...The most natural expression for him appears to us most daring. Its context, precisely because it is supreme leaves us at a distance, so that we follow it from afar, as a meteor on the horizon. In this way every great action holds those who perceive it in astonishment, and neutralizes their reality by its authority; and then, as a conqueror, transports them. We experience the same sort of conquering siege in the essays of Sikelianos. Here the poet does not retreat in the least. As in a musical composition, the modes leap from the words of his rhythmic prose, because each one of the essays of the poet is rhythm. The impetus of the prose and poetic work is the same, and with the same athletic presence the runner runs his course...

[XIV] The religiousness of Sikelianos is in most symmetrical accord with the ethnic mission of his work which certainly embraces the world, but its core is profoundly Greek. Whatever its cosmic extent, its nature is Greek: and although the poet has entered the international order, he remains on a Greek foundation. [XV] He is a Greek of all centuries. In his soul lives the history of a race. We cannot refer his work, to any one historical period. It encloses what is deepest in all epochs, and also in all places where the essential distinctions of our race have been developed in detail. Only a religious interiority such as that of our poet would have been able, in these numberless elements, to find the accord which is outside of the boundaries of time and space. That is why he has sung the life and teachings of the Nazarene with the same warmth which we find in his ancient hymns. The most Greek of all poets sings to us with most Christian seemliness the whole Christian legend.

[XVI] The ethical significance of the Sikelianic work is of extraordinary importance. His educational power is most unusual. On every page he brings us back to our unknown self, and to our conscious relations to the universe. Thus only can the people obtain their spiritual well-being. And in this his word comes straight, calling the peoples of the earth to brotherhood on a spiritual basis.

[XVI] What is the deeper relation of Sikelianos with our people, with the peoples of the earth? He has lived near the people as if he belonged to them. He has rejoiced in their joy, grieved with their grief, celebrated their holidays, learned their customs; he has felt them. His immediate relation to the people brought him nearer to the earth. And that which exists in the people as fragments of original human virtues, as qualities and tendencies, in our poet is the fullness of life. [XVII] How deeply I was moved when I saw men of our people come near him whole-heartedly, giving him whatever they had in their heart, and how he, with his piercing glance and his Olympian laugh, met them with real accord. How often the shepherds of Parnassos, or the country people of Korinthia, or the villagers of any other part of Greece have surrendered to him with their purest devotion.

[XVII] With the spiritual elevation which Sikelianos teaches comes the true promise of deliverance. Every other promise can cause only a surface healing. The proclamation includes in itself complete recovery. It is not right to awaken the instinct of the people toward revolution only for physical subsistence and for material revenge, thus enslaving them in a way which is antispiritual; but he leads the people directly into spiritual joy, and makes them commune with the deepest causes of life; and he levels with condescension his own complex inner impetuosity with the demands of the people, and so establishes them in their true place. In the village, in the warmth of the house, the poet finds complete repose, blessedness.

[XVIII] Sikelianos teaches that for the restoration of our people it is not enough to provide them only with material benefits. Because these alone, unless accompanied with the indispensable development of ethical benefits, can only brutalize and degrade them. The poet of course does not deny the power of material well-being; but he does not feel that this includes all their rightful demands. To believe this would be a blasphemy against all peoples. Because, in taking a broader outlook, it is clear that the germ of every phenomenon of our life exist in the people. They give them to us with generosity, and we repay it only with system-atized organizations which are usually dangerous, unnatural, and useless. How many errors and how many illusions have been caused by our remoteness from the people, and also by our ignorance concerning their longings and their interests. Incapable of seeing them, we have not enjoyed the fruit of their realization. Even as we have become estranged from our deeper self, so we have wished to lead the people into the error of our own crooked ways. And just as we have degraded whatever was gentle and transparent in our soul, so, sadistically, we have wished to deform their uncorrupted disposition. Sikelianos rejoices in this disposition and strengthens it.

[XIX] The poetry of Sikelianos is a phenomenon of poetical health. And his health is due to his direct inspiration, and to his physical life. There is not a sickly breath in any one of his poems. His vibration is like Adonis, sun-born; it gushed forth like music; it burst into effulgence like the garden of paradise. [XX] And this is because the poet did not sing separate conditions of the soul. Even his grief is expressed with the resignation of Olympian consent. And his joy blossoms without the slightest egotistical arrogance and becomes the joy of all. The song of Sikelianos is truly the song of life.

CHAPTER 11

Weaving

In ancient Greece, Zeus, the greatest of the gods, was the Protector of strangers. Whether with the irresistible power of his thunderbolts, or through the majesty of his word, we do not know; but, whatever his method, he must have performed this function with amazing thoroughness. Today, very few country-people in Greece know the name of Zeus: and perhaps not one of them has ever heard that he considered strangers sacred. Yet however unknown he may be to them, it is still as if a great god were secretly watching over the stranger on anyone's threshold.

On these walks or rides, when Anghelos and I were exploring the whole island of Lefkas, I came in touch for the first time with the Greek spirit of hospitality. At first it seemed as if Anghelos' name must have been the reason for the beautiful friendliness of the peasants wherever we went; and no doubt, in a way, this was so, because his family had been loved and honored for centuries on the island. But later on, in places where his name was not a local talisman, with him or without him, with other strangers or alone, I met with the same glowing reception from the peasants.

How have they preserved this trait for so many centuries in the face of the ever-growing danger of being imposed on by unscrupulous passers-by, and when the religious belief connected with this courtesy has been extinct for about two thousand years? One does not know. But their dignity and kindness to people unknown to them was a constantly recurring pleasantness.

In almost all the houses at which we stopped there was a loom, and usually the eldest daughter was weaving her dowry. This seemed often to consist of bright colored woolen blankets, very soft and fluffy. They were woven with heavy thread, spun usually by the mother, and sent when finished to the water-mill to be thrown into a pool under a cataract where the action of the water produced the fluffy effect. The mountain villages often have these water-mills, and when they have not, several houses club together to send their stuffs to a neighboring village. The best of these blankets are lighter in weight and warmer than anything which money could buy in New York.

In these villages, some of them on high plateaux, others on cliffs overhanging the sea, I had opportunities to see weaving at all its stages. I saw the women spinning with their distaffs as they walked through the streets, or calling on their neighbors, or even while walking in the mountains, and often with loads on their backs; or coming from the well, with a large jug of water on their heads. I have even seen one woman walking along with a magnificent swing, through the olive grove, carrying on her head a cradle with her baby in it, and spinning. Spinning with a distaff is a most sociable occupation, especially when old women gather round their neighbor's fire-place to sit spinning and gossiping at the same time; which always seemed a pleasanter way of paying a visit than our stand-up-and-do-nothing tea parties. There is also the setting up of the warp which requires neighborly good will, for this is usually done in the village street, several women working together, and helping each other by turns: mine today, for instance, and some other day Maria's or Ioanna's, when each one happens to have finished her spinning.

Then comes the weaving itself, which is endless in its varieties and possibilities. There is nothing one cannot make on a loom. Clothes of all kinds for men, women and children. Rugs, curtains, sheets and so forth, besides all the finer kinds of cobweb weaving in silk, linen, or cotton.

During the intervals between our trips, I became absorbed in this art. I had ordered a loom made of walnut, and I soon set about systematically to make my own clothes; for I was still getting along with the few things which I had brought from Paris. I needed clothes of some sort, and I was definitely weaned from letting anything touch my skin which had been made in a factory. At first this was chiefly a matter of personal taste. But when I got the thing really working, and felt the fun involved in all the different stages and processes of weaving: from shearing the sheep, through washing the wool at the spring, then carding, warping, weaving, with the satisfaction of unrolling the finished stuff from the loom, and finally of sewing one's own dress, it gradually came to mean more than just an indulgence in the sort of clothes I happened to prefer. It took on, for me at least, the proportions of a solution for certain social evils, such for instance as the problem of unemployment, where hand work, all along the lines, seemed so much pleasanter than either starving or being fed on a pittance by public charity.

But another problem was evoked by the sight of these busy women, occupied with any one of the various processes connected with weaving; and this became more insistent as I became more familiar with this craft myself. What are we in the world for at all, unless it be for each human being to enlarge his consciousness through the development of his own creative capacity: and how can this be done when in the bare process of living man himself is turned into a machine?

To me this mechanization of human beings seemed even more disastrous to those who buy the goods than it is to those who produce them. For the workers at least are working, however monotonously; but the consumers are being vulgarized and hardened by the acquisition of things ugly and cheap, and are even growing proud of their own helplessness.

Then the whole question of cheapness seemed to be involved and there too I began to wonder. I had been to a factory near Athens, and had seen little human automatons making everlastingly similar gestures around enormous steel monsters, which were grinding out thousands of yards of cheap material in the midst of a distracting and ceaseless din. The director of this factory who was showing me round them took me beyond a partition into another section of the building where I saw other steel monsters, as large as the first but lying idle, and apparently rusting. Here he explained to me that, in order to meet the present competition in commerce, one has to keep abreast of new inventions: and that these great machine looms, however expensive, have to be replaced every five or six years, even though they may still be in good working order. This shocking waste of great machines, not to speak of the comparative uselessness of modern stuffs, which are usually worn a very short time, and then thrown in the garbage can, seemed to suggest a fallacy somewhere in the common reasoning concerning the comparative cheapness of machine-made stuffs.

I wondered if this fallacy could be traced. With the American interest in statistics, I wondered if anyone would take the trouble to calculate the cost of the mining of metal, the melting and tempering of steel, the manufacture of looms, the repairs and replacing of parts, the payment of expert draughtsmen for detailed designs and for new inventions, the waste of material which machines cannot handle (which, in the case of silk, and perhaps of other raw materials, is enormous) the short wear of these cheap stuffs; and then compare these items to the cost of a good hand-loom which lasts for generations, the complete economy of material when manipulated by human hands, and the durability and also the cleanliness of stuffs which wash in soap and water and last for many years.[1]

And how about the comparative slavery connected with all the processes on the one hand, and the pleasant, free activity of all the processes on the other? Is this whole rigmarole, from miner's hovel to ready-made-dresses-bought-over-a-counter based, perhaps, on the

---

[1] When the great Exhibition of Decorative arts was preparing in Paris, I was asked by some friends in Athens to send an exhibit of my weaving for the Greek Pavilion. I refused on the ground that I had nothing new to send. "Oh, send something old," they said, "no one will know the difference." So I sent a dress that I had worn for at least ten years, and I won a gold medal. At present I have dresses over thirty years old which are still good.

strange passion of women for changing the shape of their clothes? And is this again due to the strange shapes in which their clothes are cut and sewed, which they would naturally get tired of very quickly[?][2]

But when dresses are perfectly straight, and worn with a shawl also straight which can be put on in many different ways, so that the dress is never twice alike in wearing it, why should one ever be tired of things which become better, softer and pleasanter, and one dreads the day when they may eventually wear out? So that one's new dresses are put to hard use, and the old ones become very precious.

Since that time when I visited the villages, I have woven at least a hundred kinds of stuff. I have taught many people to weave, and no one of them has done anything that resembled any of the things I have done; each one, on becoming efficient in this craft, does something which fulfils her own needs or desires, or expresses her own character or taste; and, these desires once fulfilled, other vistas are opened which otherwise would have remained closed. There is something alive about the loom, something eminently sociable on the one hand, because of the different stages in setting up a warp where several usually work together, and something restful and rhythmical in loneliness when the swift shuttle seems to clarify one's thoughts, much better than merely lying down or sitting idle in a chair.

For long I was so entranced with this fascinating craft that I believed that with this, or with other kindred crafts, men all over the world would again acquire a pride in the skill of their hands, and also a sensitiveness to individual talent in the objects around them. I thought of the great army of artists in Europe and America, and especially of the painters, whose works, or some of them, are exhibited every spring in the great cities. I remembered years when I had been traveling and had seen the Salon in Paris, and the Salon des Independants, and the Royal Academy and other exhibitions in London and similar ones in Munich, and Rome, and Berlin, and New York; and how each one of these exhibitions in which one had seen literally miles of pictures, had left me completely exhausted, and wondering what in the world it was all about. Almost all of these pictures were trash: but all the same, the urge to paint them argued that all these artists were making brave personal efforts to escape from the dreadful routine of the growing monster of the mechanical world. Could they not, I thought, as my shuttle flew, make the world really more beautiful and more free (and thereby also, incidentally, earn a livelihood) by using their artistic instinct to make

---

[2][Ed. Question mark not in the original. -J.P.A.]

a chair or a table which would be unique in line, in polish, and in comfort and so be a permanent delight to the person who used them: or in making a very fine saucepan, or a beautiful spoon?

With the years that have passed, I have entirely recovered from this prepossession. I see the whole new world of the Soviet Union absorbed in perfecting machinery, and believing in it as the ultimate solution of all human ills. I see the whole of America given over with no misgivings to mass production of one kind or another, and completely satisfied with the results they have obtained. In these results one sees a great people who built towns from one end of a continent to another which conform to a plan as fixed as the architecture of a bee-hive; and the men and women living in these towns, surrounded by a maze of mechanical gadgets, are sinking into an easy conformity where no individual initiative is required, and where personal responsibility has nothing to undertake.

America is in the lead in these innovations, but other countries are following hard upon. Human beings seem to have grown envious of the carefree mentality of a kind of living organism that has attained everlasting survival at the price of everlasting sameness. In all ways men are learning to act and look like insects. Their airplanes are like dragon-flies, their automobiles are like beetles or like cockroaches, their stream-lined trains are like processional caterpillars, their gas-masks are probably like themselves when the ultimate metamorphosis will have been perfected; the whole reminding one of Rudolf Steiner's horrible prophecy that in one cycle of existence the mechanical inventions of a former cycle become the surviving living organisms: therefore that mankind will pass away, but that their motorboats and airplanes will become living beings. Without going so far as to believe in this grotesque nightmare, it is nevertheless evident that men do, already, advance in swarms: they stop all together and move on again all together, having no personal volition. Their military discipline, their industrial standardization, their political organizations, their labor syndicates, are centralizations of various kinds of power which all require masses to feed on, but they do not require men.

One country alone forms an exception to this general trend toward the perfection of insect routine, and that country is Greece. In living there so long I probably came to project their characteristics on countries which are fundamentally different. The central revelation which the ancient Greeks bequeathed to the world was the importance and the dignity of human individuality, and the immense variety of their contributions to civilization stems entirely from their courage in training men to think and act as individuals.

Through the vicissitudes of over two thousand years, this characteristic has not changed. Perhaps the topography of the country, with its mountains and valleys, islands and inlets, where no two villages are alike, has helped to preserve this special sense of individual human worth which was so deeply rooted in their nature from the start. However that may be, the fact points to a special mission for Greece in this age of the world. There are still people in all nations who prefer quality to quantity, and who know well the limitations of machines wherever quality is asked for: and they also know the diminishing capacity of workers to produce quality in anything. The Greeks are natural craftsmen. They do not like to limit their work to certain mechanized gestures: this we can see by the large number of Greeks in America who have chosen any trade that preserves their freedom in working (they often keep restaurants or small grocery stores: or they raise and sell flowers or fruit) and the insignificant numbers who have ever worked in factories. (They are still the nation which slavery and misery and poverty cannot tame.)

Let the Greeks then use their special talents, and thus provide for themselves, and for those in all countries who still care for such things, objects useful to life and unique in beauty, with the inimitable quality that only human hands can produce. In this way they will secure an enviable living for themselves, and at the same time eliminate one nation from mechanical competition.

CHAPTER 12

America

My mother was anxious to see Anghelos, I was anxious to have her know him, and also to see her again; and he liked the idea of going to America. And so, in the early summer of 1907, we decided to take this journey. We went first to Paris, and out to my little house in Neuilly, which was just as I had left it. There I found, to my unexpressed anxiety, that Anghelos was very much entertained by the closets and drawers full of my French clothes which, also, were still as I had left them. He said he would like to see me in them. So, sharing his amusement, outwardly at least, I put on one of them; and in the evening I changed to another. The next day there were other dresses that he wanted to see worn, and the next others; and there seemed to be no limit to the fun he got out of going around Paris with me in all my discarded clothes. Day after day I kept up the game, but inwardly I was becoming more and more anxious; for I began to fear that what was to me a carnival amusement, a mere masquerade, gave him genuine and perhaps permanent pleasure. For about two weeks this game continued, and I had almost given up hope that our intuitive and unspoken agreements were as complete as I had supposed, when one day he said to me:

"Aren't you ever going to throw away those clothes?"

Well, it did not take me long. I felt as if a life sentence in prison had suddenly been annulled.

Arriving in America was not so easy as traveling abroad had been. The rumour that I was differently dressed had gone ahead of us, and I found on the pier in New York a jam of reporters who were waiting for pictures and interviews. I had no notion of what American journalism was like at that time, and I thought the simplest way out of the difficulty would be to tell them that I had nothing to say and no pictures to give, and also to cover up my head if they pointed cameras at me. Alas for my supposed dignity and cleverness.

The next day the New York papers had pictures of various young women, none of them in the least like me, wearing draped sheets or whatnot, and with the captions: "Eva Palmer arrives from abroad," "Eva Palmer in Greek toga," and other such.

One of these pictures represented a young lady with a French dress in the latest fashion, a French toque on her head, stepping down the gang-plank of a ship, her skirt airily held up with one hand to show, underneath, her bare feet and sandals. I was terribly chagrined but my chagrin was nothing compared to the utter disgust of my family. I tried to sue the papers for libel on the grounds that I had said none of the speeches they had quoted, and that the pictures were not of me. But I was told that nothing libellous had been said, and that there was no law against using anyone's picture and calling it any name they pleased.

The result of all this was that instead of going to my mother's house in New York we went to a hotel; and there I had constant delegations of my relatives and friends, who tried to impress on me the evil and selfishness of my ways. It was pointed out to me that my mother was not well, that she was no longer young, that what I was doing might have a fatal effect on her health, and that, as long as I was living abroad anyway, why for goodness sake couldn't I be considerate to her for the short time that I expected to stay in America, and do as I pleased after I left?

The situation was difficult. I cared very much for my mother; I thought of her extraordinary kindness to me during my whole life; how in fact she had consistently spoiled me ever since I could remember with unnumbered cares and considerations. I remembered her delightful habit of getting Christmas or birthday presents for me at any time of the year if she happened to see anything that she thought I would like. Each time she would imagine that she would put it away and have it ready for the holiday. But she was never capable of hiding a present for more than a few days, and so one was apt to receive several presents before Christmas actually arrived. This sort of thing she did for all of us, but there were certain things she did only for me. Whenever I was in America she would have a single gardenia in a little glass of water at my place at table, every night, whatever the season. I remembered her anxiety, whenever fish was served at dinner: "Be careful, Wink, not to swallow a bone." It was as if she had never quite got used to the fact that I had really grown up and was alive, and though that at any moment she might lose me, through any simple occurrence such as possibly choking on a fish bone. And I remembered how she and I had gone off together on a sort of a lark, to see the first Chicago Exhibition, and what a nice lazy time we had, being wheeled around in chairs through the endless grounds and buildings.

As these discussions were going on, some one of us, I do not now remember who, subscribed to a press-cutting bureau. Then, every day, teeming envelopes would arrive with copies or embellishments of the New York notices, from papers all over the United States; and most of these cuttings had pictures of the same young women who were still flaunting my name. It was painful enough; but thinking back on it now I am struck by the fact that I never considered the simple solution of changing my clothes temporarily to please my mother. Everyone was urging me to do this; yet the only choice I saw ahead was either to carry on as I was doing, or else to burn up all the dresses I have woven, and wear French clothes for the rest of my life. Anything else seemed to me to put the clothes one wears on the level of a masquerade, the expression of a passing fancy, a means of fooling one's self and others. With me it was a matter of dressing as others do forever, in order to please a few people I was fond of, or else of following my own convictions and preferences, and doing this also forever. The middle course did not exist.

I may say now that I really leaned heavily to the easier course of pleasing my mother and ordering a few new dresses, to have done with it; but what settled it was something I did not speak of then, and probably have not since. It was a conversation of my father's which had impressed me tremendously when I was quite little. He had been reading Swedenborg, and he quoted one day, rather jokingly, a passage in which there is a description of angels, who are wearing swallowtail coats and high hats. I suffered a shock at that moment from which I have never recovered; especially when my father went on to comment on this quite academically, remarking that, as a matter of fact, all ghosts actually do appear to wear the clothes they were used to wearing while on earth; and that if ghosts and angels exist at all, it is extremely likely that they continue to dress in precisely the way they did when alive.[1]

As the years went on this suggestion became a sort of obsession. I thought over the fashion plates one knows of different periods of human vanity, and imagined living spirits still dressed up with hoop skirts, or bustles, Turkish trousers, Spanish mantillas, or Elizabethan ruffs; or men everlastingly dressed in heavy coats of armour, or with long pointed shoes tied to their knees, or tight black Toreador Breeches, or with long streaming feathers of the Three Musketeers. I imagined living souls doomed to go on using such outworn, tiresome fashions that they were sick of, with no way of escape, until they had the luck to squeeze into a new incarnation, and so take a bath, as it were, and change. My father disbelieved all this, and I did not know what I believed; but it seemed a risk; and I felt somehow on the safe side in choosing clothes that I did not get tired of in this world, so why should I in the next? But also, I felt that this sob-sister method of inducement was worthy neither of my mother nor of me. So I crossed that particular Rubicon, and announced that I would not wear machine-made stuffs any more, or dresses cut into arbitrary fashions.

In spite of the uncompromising attitude which I then assumed, there came a time, a

---

[1] I found, later, that Goethe evidently believed what my father had laughingly suggested. After the death of Winckelmann he said to Eckermann, "He had the advantage of figuring in the memory of posterity as one eternally able and strong; for the image in which one leaves the world is that in which one moves among the shades."

few years later, when I made a concession. Mother had gone to Aix-les-bains for her health. I was in Greece and she wanted to see me, and begged me to bring along some ordinary clothes. This time she really was not well, and I, feeling that I had gained what I had fought for in America, decided to do as she asked. So I went first to Paris and bought a whole wardrobe (I had given away all my old clothes on the day when Anghelo asked me to get rid of them); gowns for morning, afternoon and evening; hats, gloves, stockings, shoes and slippers in the latest fashion, coats, negligees, everything. Mother was delighted. But the funny thing was that she missed my own clothes and felt unhappy not to see them. My sensations during these two weeks were horrible. After several years of walking easily I went mincing around on shoes like stilts, and with dresses that were like a plaster-cast. I wondered how so many women stand such senseless, hideous and unhealthy discomfort; and also how I myself, in former years, had stood it.

On leaving Aix, I got into my railway compartment and undressed quickly as I could. I slipped on one of my straight dresses and my sandals, and then I started feverishly making a bundle. Everything I had bought in Paris - dresses, shoes, coats, hats, stockings, slippers, gloves - everything was piled into a railroad sheet, which afterward I paid for. Then up went the window, and out went the bundle as the train thundered through the night. My relief was intense. That sort of thing was definitely over for me. I would never again wear clothes cut and sewed in silly shapes, and I would never again be touched by stuffs turned out by machines: machines of metal, and machines of flesh and blood.

As the train rolled on farther and farther from my bundle, I felt translated into heaven.

While the controversies I have spoken of continued in New York, Mother had meantime gone up to Bar Harbour. From there she wrote me that she would be glad if we would come up and stay with her. She said she did not mind how I dressed in the country, and that I could do as I pleased. She also added that she loved my clothes in the house, and found them very beautiful; that, in fact, she felt there was nothing wrong in what I was doing if I would only stop wearing sandals in New York. And this was the crux of the whole difficulty. No one would have thought twice about the matter if only I had not worn sandals in the street. And how right they were.

Years after this my dear Hindu friend, Kourshed Naoriji, told me that in India, the English had never attempted to make any change in ancient Hindu costumes except one. Everyone is allowed to dress as he pleases; but at all state functions presided over by the

English, the Hindus, Maharajahs included, are not admitted unless they wear English shoes.[2]
This is a master-stroke on the part of English diplomacy. For, with the amazing grandeur of
Hindu clothes and Hindu jewels, this one little change is enough to make their whole outfit
look ridiculous. Anybody with the slightest sensitivity, and the Hindus have plenty, would
prefer to change off to clothes bought in Piccadilly rather than wear their own fine costumes
with stuffy shoes in which they cannot walk. At a stroke they are changed from people of
power and dignity to comic opera magnates with mincing steps and silly gestures. They are
no longer solid on their feet; and this is reflected in their minds and in their general attitude
toward life. In fact an effective method of breaking the spirit of a man, or of a woman, who
really knows how to walk, is to confine the feet in modern shoes. And this is especially so
if all the other parts of their habitual costume remain untouched. It is not half so serious for
a man's character to change altogether to English clothes, because, in doing this, he can preserve inviolate an inner image of himself, and can, on occasion, change back again, and with
no harm done; but this subtle change from true gravity and beauty to burlesque is enough
to warp a man's inner image of himself forever.

Curiously enough, this premise also holds the other way round. There is nothing
ridiculous, either in outward appearance, or inner personal impression, in wearing modern
clothes with sandals. I have often seen men wearing sandals with long or short summer
trousers, or women with duck skirts, or slacks, and they all looked very well and were
perfectly contented.

There is probably no change which could be so easy and so practical as this of
wearing sandals in summer; but even today, when so many conventions have gone by the
wall, most people still shy off from it and consider it shocking. Who can tell what would
happen to men and women if their feet were strong and free? Would they not find their way
out of the tangle of modern industrialism if they could move their toes, and feel the supple-
ness of their own insteps? And what would become of the robots? Is it perhaps a true
instinct, an obscure sense of self-preservation which has made sandals taboo?

Up in Bar Harbour Anghelos was happy. The beautiful island was in its glory, and
I took him to all the places I cared for most. First up Duck Brook, just back of our house,
where I had the fun of seeing him play our old game of jumping from rock to rock up the
center of the stream without falling in. And we climbed Newport, and Sargent, and Green

---

[2] I have learned more recently from an English friend that this was an old law which has now been
abrogated.

Mountain, (these names have been changed now to I do not know what), and we saw Eagle Lake, and the Bubbles, and Jordan Pond, going over the fascinating foot-paths which were blazed in the old days by George Dorr and others, while we younger ones used to play "Indians" on the almost perpendicular side of Dry Mountain. Anghelos loved it, and I was happy because Mother loved him. In fact, during this ideal month in Bar Harbor, toward the end of which we were quietly married in Mother's house, only one thing went wrong. Courtlandt had to go abroad shortly after we arrived, so that Anghelos hardly saw him, and hardly heard him play. This disappointment was one of those things in life that start wrong with no reason, and keep on going wrong, still with no reason. Nobody has wanted it. But here we are, after thirty years and more, and Anghelos and Courtlandt have been together only two days.

CHAPTER 13

My Son

We called [our son][1] Glaukos, or Glafkos, as it is pronounced in Greek, after the fisherman who longed so for immortality that he leapt into the sea in order to reach the gods, and who was received by them on Olympus. And he was also named, in a way, for me; because the first of Anghelos' names for me was Glauke, or Glaukomata, which has been variously translated as blue, grey or green eyes: or eyes-like-the-sea.

When he was very little I took him from Athens to Lefkas; and from there to the tiny island of Saint Nicholas: a flat, narrow strip of land, about a quarter of a mile long, with a two-roomed house at one end, and a shrine to Saint Nicholas, protector of sailors. This island near the main-land of Acarnania is the only one in a large quiet bay reaching from Lefkas to Preveza, and protected from the open sea by an extraordinary formation of adamantine rock called the Plaka, which is an almost perfectly flat causeway, barely above the level of the sea, and with only a few rocks jutting out here and there. One can walk along the top of this natural wall, which is sometimes a few yards wide, and sometimes broadens out into what might be an excellent dancing floor. There are only two breaks in this wall, both extremely narrow, about five and eight yards wide, and it is a quite exciting trick to maneuver a sail boat through these passages; but it is the only way to get to Saint Nicholas from Lefkas, unless one goes by the long coast-road of Acarnania, which we never did.

There is no fresh water on Saint Nicholas; and twice every day our fisherman, Spyros, would fill large earthen jugs at a spring on the mainland; this was all the water we needed for drinking and cooking and washing the baby's rather scanty clothes; and for everything else the sea was a perfectly good substitute. In fact, the sea was so extraordinarily clear, and the sunshine so brilliant, and the Ionian winds so clean, that soap and fresh water grew to seem a poor makeshift resorted to by those dingy mortals who live in the darkness of houses.

Every day Glafkos and I went into the sea, in our large, quiet, and perfectly isolated swimming-pool; and we could see the high waves of the open sea breaking against the Plaka a little distance off; we could even see the wind-mills on the coast of the main island, and a little church in a grove of sea-blown scrub pines, where Anghelos' ancestors have been buried for hundreds of years. Glafkos would swim a little with me holding him up, and then play with the sand, and shell, and the quietly lapping waves; and it was fun to see him trying

---

[1][Ed. 'Him' appears in the MS. -J.P.A.]

buried for hundreds of years. Glafkos would swim a little with me holding him up, and then play with the sand, and shell, and the quietly lapping waves; and it was fun to see him trying to rise to his feet on the shore, for he never seemed to want to crawl on all fours. He learned quickly to walk holding one of my fingers, and this habit he kept up long after he could have walked alone. Probably both of us found this a pleasant way of getting around, and saw no reason for dropping it. And I was amazed to see that his feet, pink on the bottom, and apparently tender, were not bothered at all by sharp pebbles and stones, which I could not walk on without sandals.

The island of Saint Nicholas was nothing but a stretch of pebbles, with two scraggy trees on the other end from the house. One would hardly think that a spear of grass could grow there; yet, within a single month, I picked and pressed a collection of over fifty varieties of wild flowers.

Fishing was our great amusement, we had a boat of our own, a *monóxylo*, a peculiar kind of craft, used, I think, only in Lefkas, flat-bottomed, yet quite swift for either sailing or rowing. In rowing, the man stands in the stern, facing forwards, and at each stroke, after dipping the long oars, he takes two steps forwards on a slightly slanting floor, so that the weight of his body propels the boat with very little effort; then, as the boat goes forward, he takes his two steps back.

We had our own fishing-nets, and would throw them out in the evening, and gather them in again before sunrise, full of brilliant colored fish. But the most exciting kind of fishing was at night. We would have a rower behind, and Spyros, the champion fisherman, standing in the prow with a harpoon like the trident of Poseidon. Right under him, in front of the bow, was a flaming torch of pine-wood, heavy with rosin which threw light into the water from a reflector which protected Spyro's eyes so that he could see the fish in the sea as we rowed quietly on. With unerring aim, and with movement older than Greek art, but very like it, he would throw his trident whenever a big one came in sight. Then we would row back to the island, and Spyros would light a fire by the shore and cook any fish; we preferred cleaning it first in the sea. Then he would sail back to Lefkas with the rest of his catch, which he would sell in the morning for himself and his family.

These feasts at night on the shore of Saint Nicholas, with black bread and good Greek wine, inviting any fisherman who happened to be passing, have spoiled the taste of fish for me forever. How can anything ever again be so fresh?

One day Spyros came from Lefkas with brand new fish-nets which weighed down the prow of the monóxylo. They were his own, and he said it was the proper time to dye them because the following day the moon would be full. He had also brought with him a large sack full of the bark of pine-trees broken up into very small pieces, and also an enormous copper cauldron. The next morning, very early, he had started his task. The cauldron, full of fresh water and the pine bark, was mounted on an iron tripod, and already had a bright fire burning under it when I arrived on the spot, long before sunrise. All day Spyros was fetching jugs of fresh water from the mainland, and kept the cauldron full, and the fire burning brightly. Near the cauldron the nets were rolled up waiting; and on the other side of it, a small empty skiff was also ready. About an hour before sunset he let the fire die down. Toward sundown he dipped out the pine bark with a sieve and threw it away. Then, as the sun set and the moon arose, he started dipping the long net into the dark, reddish-brown liquid, and from the cauldron dropped it into the skiff. The nets were very long, and it took some time for the whole length to pass through, letting each bit drink its fill. During the process I ran to the house, and snatched a very nice white silk dress, which I had taken some trouble to weave and embroider on my loom, and I threw that also into the cauldron, and thence with the nets into the skiff. Finally the end came, the skiff was full, and Spyros covered the whole thing for the night with a large woolen blanket. By that time the great round moon was well above our heads.

The next morning, before sunrise, he pushed the skiff into the sea, and turned it upside down, leaving all the contents floating about, and turning the whole sea terra-cotta. This color gradually cleared away, and the nets and my dress were gathered in and spread on the shore to dry. My dress was a success.

We had one other member of our little island colony, beside Anghelos who came and went, myself, Glafkos, Spyros, and any stray fisherman who happened to pass. This was a peasant woman named Patra. A two-room house may seem small for so many, but it was not. We had two small tents on the shady side of the house, but these were only a midday protection for the others against the sun. In Greece it does not rain in July; in fact, it usually does not rain from May to September; and the sky is one's best roof at night.

Patra did the cooking and took care of me and the house. For Glafkos she did nothing, because I never let anyone touch him until he was able to take care of himself. Yet one thing she did do. She played ball with him: that is, using him as the ball. She would throw him way up, and catch him again, any number of times running. He loved it, and so did I, because he laughed adorably when he was high in the air. And we had a very large sheep-dog, who took him riding on his back; and Spyros took him riding on his head. When he was carried by any of these strong creatures his arms never dropped to his side, but he held them always straight out, as if he were embracing the world.

When we got back to Lefkas in the autumn, I used to let Patra carry him beside me to the olive grove. He did not like being wheeled, though we had a very nice-looking carriage which Raymond had made for me, something like an ancient chariot, with a carved frieze of deer all around it copied from an ancient vase.

As Patra carried Glafko with her swinging walk, I would hear her, in spite of my remonstrances, muttering curses under her breath at passers-by who spoke of the baby. These blasphemies would always end with the unpleasant wish: "garlic in your eyes," which she said quite loud; and then, with the semblance only, very gently, of spitting three times at the baby, in order to aver the evil eye.

The Greek peasants are definitely afraid of admiration. They explain this by saying that in admiration there is apt to be an alloy of envy, and that envy can do harm. I do not know the origin of this rather general attitude on their part, and I simply accepted it as a harmless superstition until the following incident occurred. Glafkos was about two. We were living in a large house which I owned at that time in Athens, and one day a lady came to see me. I knew her very slightly; but she was pleasant and generally complimentary about what she saw. She admired my loom, my room, the bright fire burning in the grate, and so forth. Suddenly Glafkos burst into the room. She had not seen him before; and she exclaimed not about his hair, or his eyes, which I was more or less used to, but about his legs. How strong his legs were, and how beautifully shaped! That night I put him to bed as usual, and he went to sleep quietly, with me sitting beside him, as we always did. But at about one o'clock he woke up howling with pain in both of his legs. He was evidently in torture, and it took me a long time to smooth away the pain, and get him to sleep again.

This phenomenon is inexplicable to me, and probably to everyone. It cannot be accounted for on the theory of fear of harm projected into him by a third person because I was the only one present, and I did not believe in any such danger, and in fact never even thought of it. I was simply surprised, and rather pleased, because no one had ever paid him that particular compliment before; and I had never attached the slightest seriousness to Patra's curses. However, after this incident, I allowed her, or anyone else, to curse Glafko's admirers to their heart's content, and without any further remonstrances.

Around this house in Athens we had a garden, with lemon, orange, and mandarin trees, some large pines and cypresses, and peacocks decorating the lawn. Glafkos had many other animals, especially a baby fox, which he used to hang around his neck, as a boa. Peasants from the villages often came to see us, and with these, and also with workmen he was always happy; in fact he was with everyone, except the well-dressed-young-gentleman type which he never could abide.

From the beginning, he had a poise of his own which I have always envied. When he was very small this was occasionally interrupted by moments of real gaiety. As he became older this poise made him almost silent for long intervals; but then it was broken by moments of spontaneous speech, or of conversation, when he was interested, which sometimes betrayed the import of his silences. Now and then, people have said that he looks like me, or that I look like him, or that our characters are alike. No other personal remark ever make me so happy.

Years have passed; and the direction of our lives are, and probably will be, different. His mind is turned toward Science, and is therefore moving in realms which are beyond my apprehension. But however different the direction of our lives may be, or however far removed in space, we possess between us a golden hoard which is ours; an unimpaired capital which cannot be lessened. It is our knowledge of each other, built up by both of us, during the first years of his life.

CHAPTER 14

Greek Music

From the time, at the house of Paul Hyacinth in Paris, when I first heard Penelope sing, the lightening-flash impressions which had seared my brain then had not been armed. Often I heard her sing again; often I heard peasants singing in remote parts of Greece which were still uninfluenced by recent Athenian fashions, and before American phonographs, radio and jazz had been generally introduced in the little cafes of Greek villages.

So another impression different only in its increasing expectedness, came to support the first, and to lighten the darkness which had closed in after Penelope had first opened her lips. For that day I had been carried away, but I did not know why. I longed to hear more and more of her singing merely as an aesthetic delight; and I listened to her theoretic explanations in my garden in Neuilly with vivid interest, feeling vaguely in what she was saying the possible solution of the old platonic problem, but not really understanding what she meant. There were too many years of opposite notions in my brain. There was too old a habit of thinking of music in a totally different way.

In Greece, however, I had time to analyze this new, but ever more insistent impression. Penelope was often with me; and besides that there were the songs of the peasants which were sometimes quite as remarkable as hers, and it was from the peasants that she herself had learned what she knew.

I was not enough of a musician to write down the songs I heard on paper; and, at first, I could not even hum them to myself. But I soon found that I was not the only one in such a predicament. A number of musicians who were my friends could do no better; and I would hear them trying to play on the piano a peasant song which they had just been listening to, only to get up in despair at the complete lack of resemblance to the original in what they were playing.

I realized then, what I have occasionally been able to verify since; that musicians cannot hear intervals which they are not used to; and that this is not so much the fault of their ears as of their minds. They have a fixed notion that intervals not included in the tempered scale must be out of tune. But modal music does not <u>sound</u> "out-of-tune," and this probably causes a mental syllogism to form itself unconsciously in the mind of the musician; as for instance:

A. The only intervals which sound in tune are those of the tempered scale.
B. Modal songs sound in tune.

C. Modal songs must fall in the tempered scale.

So they go to the piano humming a song (which incidentally proves that their ears are all right) but they cannot play it; and usually they get up cursing Greek music, as being impossible for educated people.

It was evident, as Penelope had told me in the beginning, that Greek modes have nothing to do with the piano. But how was one to learn them? And how get one's ear and one's voice trained to receive and to transmit what they were singing? I no longer doubted the existence of musical modes. Here they were alive and healthy, and perhaps even similar to those which Plato had accepted and rejected in his *Republic*. What I doubted then was my own capacity ever to understand or reproduce them.

One winter, after my return from America, Penelope told me she had decided to study the theory of Greek music with Professor Psachos, who taught Byzantine music at the National Conservatory in Athens. She said that he was an authority on Greek Ecclesiastical music and that he had been named by the Patriarch of Constantinople "Master Teacher of Music of the Great Church of Christ."

I used to go with her and listen-in to these lessons; but my dilemma constantly increased. I was more than ever fascinated by Greek music; but also more and more sure that it was beyond both my ear and my voice to get into any closer connexion with it.

This sort of inferiority-complex lasted for several years. But after we had lost Penelope, and I could no longer obtain my vicarious delight in music through her, I went one day to Professor Psachos and asked him to teach me the theory of Ecclesiastical Music. I told him that probably I was incapable, owing to my long familiarity with European music, of either hearing or singing correctly what he would teach me; but that I should like to try; and that, in any case, I could learn the notation. Professor Psachos said there was no reason why familiarity with European music should be a hindrance in learning Greek music, and he accepted me as a pupil. I studied with him for over five years.

I expected to find a maze of difficulties ahead of me. But I was carried along rather easily by the logic of the method and by the beauty of the church songs, and these two things more than counterbalanced the effort involved in learning the signs of Byzantine notation. Here at last was a kind of music which seemed to lead one on from step to step by persuasion instead of by grinding work. There were no scales, no arpeggios, no exercises of any kind; for a mode is not a scale, and cannot be taught in a mechanical way; its very essence is melodic, so the teaching is all through melody. And as soon as one can decipher it at all, the whole thing becomes a simple progression from one melody to another. Then, when one advances a little further, and becomes familiar with the sound and character of each mode, the lessons become more complicated, with songs which skip from one mode to another with perfect freedom, in order to express a change in meaning of the words.

I was more and more struck by the perfect oneness of word and music. After a few years of work I realized that not one of all the church songs I had been learning had ever failed in this inter-penetration. Moreover, as I went on advancing from mere reading, or learning by heart and singing, and reached the point of starting to compose, I saw also why the ancient Greeks attached so much importance to accent and quantity, and also why, to modern grammarians, and to students of Greek in general, these are considered mutually exclusive. When approached from a musical angle the answer is simple; accent and quantity both existed, and actually do not interfere with each other at all.

One day Professor Psachos said to me:

"Greek music is subordinate to language. It has always been considered, both by the ancients and by the Church as having properly no independent existence. Its function is to enlarge and enhance the word, to make the greater meaning and emotion of the word distinctly comprehensible in very large churches or in the open air."

This startling statement left me speechless. I wondered if my Professor knew what heresy he was talking from the point of view of any modern musician. But at that time I was not equipped to discuss the point with him, or even with myself. I merely stored it silently in my memory.

He also spoke to me very often of his idea of building an organ which would have all the intervals required by all the Greek modes.*[1]

[A. No one mode has any greater number of intervals than the European major or minor scale. Sometimes in fact they have fewer: being usually tetrachords repeated, with or without a tone between. But these tetrachords have intervals which differ one from the other according to the mode. For this reason, when all are put down together to form a keyboard, the result seems incredible to those who are accustomed only to the tempered scale. In building our organ, Professor Psachos wanted fifty-six intervals in the octave, but owing to the technical difficulties of building such a keyboard he compromised, and made forty-two.]

He felt that this was becoming more and more necessary in order to preserve the fast disappearing tradition which he believed to be very ancient.

In listening to him I gradually formed the idea of founding a school of music which would possess an instrument, by the help of which the musical tradition actually existing in

---

[1] [Ed. At this point and further down the author had inserted two long footnotes to provide pertinent technical information. In editing the text I decided that the logical place for this material would be in the text itself. The asterisks mark the original place of the footnotes; the transferred text is now enclosed within brackets. -J.P.A.]

Greece could be taught, regardless of whether this tradition is ancient or not. I also believed that it is ancient, and that was my principle reason for hoping to stem the tide of destruction which is quickly overtaking it.*

[B. When I first went to Greece, over thirty years ago, one could hear very remarkable singing in almost any little cafe in Athens. But now, to hear the same sort of thing, one has to journey to almost inaccessible villages. This, I believe, is due to the following facts:

When a Greek peasant is in mourning, one of his outward indications of grief is that he stops singing and dancing. In the Balkan War, which immediately preceded the European War of 1914-18, Greece was victorious, but at a heavy cost in men. This was followed by a long mobilization during the European War, and then by destructive fighting in Turkey. The result of all this was that for a long time there was hardly a family in Greece which had not recently lost a husband, a father, a brother, or a son. The whole nation, therefore, had ceased to sing just at the time when American phonographs and radios were introduced, and the younger generation heard these almost exclusively.

The other fact I had in mind is that in Athens, where there are two very good conservatories of music, the tide had turned altogether toward the West. All the talented people of Greece were learning the music of Bach, Haydn, Mozart, Beethoven, Chopin, Schumann, Wagner, Brahms, etc., and all fashionable society had grown to know and care for this only, and not one of them could read a line of their own notation. Musicians were bored by music which they called old-fashioned; or, whenever this appeared with any pretention of excellence, they were simply exasperated.

This attitude on the part of the Court (which was foreign), of society, of all educated musicians, of course reflected back in the villages also in an attitude of disdain for old music and dancing, and in the desire to be up to date. And so an art at least as old as Christianity, and probably much older, was destroyed under one's very eyes, in the course of about ten years.]

But there were other reasons for my desire to build the organ and to found a school. For me, Greek Ecclesiastical music, and Greek peasant music, along with their peculiar omission of voice, and their manner of dancing, are in themselves beautiful, and should not be lost to the world even if they were invented last year or yesterday. However, as this is a matter of taste, and as I had the current of taste going against me, I did not mention this as one of my reasons for building the organ, but only the following three:

1) The historic interest of preserving the religious and secular songs of Greece as they have come down to us.

2) The probability that nations which possess a musical tradition older than Bach, could, through Byzantine notation, find a way of preserving their own traditions which, also, are now being quickly destroyed.

3) The probability that, once we had a school of modal music, and an instrument with which these modes could still be taught (in case the few remaining Greek musicians were to leave no successors) there would be a new development of music on Greek basis, not to replace, but to supplement the education of today.

The time came when I decided to take what seemed the first step toward the founding of my school; namely, to start building the organ. As Professor Psachos had had this dream for many years and as he was undoubtedly an authority on the question of intervals in Greek music, and as he had also invented a keyboard for such an organ, I asked him to go to Germany and start the work in the factory of Steinmeyer, near Munich. I also sent with him Dr. Vrachamis, who was a mathematician, and who was interested in the technical problems involved. These two, and afterwards, on a later trip, Mr. Psachos alone, completed this work; and when it was drawing to an end, Anghelos and I went to Germany to see it. But on arriving there we found that there were still delays ahead before its final completion. So, after a while, Anghelos returned to Greece, and I went to Paris.

There I met my lovely Hindu friend, Kourshed Naoroji; and I became so much interested in her that I felt the delay of the organ had been providential. All her brothers and sisters had been educated at Oxford and Cambridge (her father, or grandfather perhaps, had been the first Hindu member of Parliament in England); she, however had chosen rather to go to Paris to study music. She told me that her reason for this had been that Hindu music was being quickly destroyed by European influences; that there is no Hindu notation, and therefore it is extremely difficult to do anything to counteract the inroad of phonographs, radio and jazz. She had come to Paris to learn the piano and composition, in the hope of alleviating this national need by writing the Hindu songs. But she was fearfully discouraged. She had been there years. She could play Beethoven quite well, and Chopin really charmingly; she had learned a good deal about composition.

"But," she said sadly, "I must be very stupid. For still I cannot play the simplest Hindu melody on the piano, nor can I write any song of my own country."

Of course I jumped a foot. Here was the chance I had been longing for. I told her that her failure was not her fault, but was due to the inherent difference of two systems of music which cannot represent each other.

I told her about my organ which soon would be finished; and that the reason for building it was what she had come to Europe for: to save the ancient oral tradition of music all over the world, but especially in Greece, because there we have a notation which can write it. I told her of my belief, that this notation can write not only Greek music, but the music of any ancient nation. And I told her about my Greek Professor, who could write the most difficult songs from dictation; that I was very anxious to see if he could do this with ancient songs which are not Greek; as, for instance, with Hindu songs, Chinese, American Indian, and so forth. I explained how, if she wished to help in this experiment, she could sing her Indian songs to him, he would write them if he could, and then turn his manuscript over to me to read; and if she found that I was singing her songs correctly, we would have the proof that in Byzantine notation we have a precious means of helping not only Greece, but perhaps all ancient nations to preserve their oral traditions. And would she come to Munich to try?

So we made this journey together. Kourshed was happy, because with me she felt free to wear her Indian clothes, which she had given up when she came to Europe. On arriving in Munich we immediately tried our experiment, and she said to me,

"You are singing my songs."

We took her to Steinmeyer's factory where the organ was then finished.[2] She went to try it; and in about half an hour she was playing her Hindu melodies with perfect ease. She was delighted and so were we; and we decided to have a celebration in the factory. We invited Professors from the University, and everyone else we knew in Munich; and the whole village of Oetingen turned out for the occasion. Psachos played, Kourshed played, and I played on the organ; and they also heard a phonograph attachment which Psachos had insisted on, but which I afterwards felt was a mistake.

It had been very complicated to make so many intervals (forty-two in the octave, four octaves, and four registers: 1672 intervals in all) and I would rather have had another octave on the keyboard. Also, the central reason for taking all this trouble seemed to me turned aside from its objective by making the organ primarily a thing to listen to; whereas I had thought of it as an instrument with which to study, to teach, and also as a help in composition. Perhaps this is because I do not really like the sound of an organ. However, at our celebration, the phonograph arrangement worked very well. Everybody made speeches and the party was a great success.

After that Kourshed came to Greece with me to study Byzantine notation. On her first railroad trip in Greece, from Patras to Sykià, on the south side of the Corinthian Gulf, she made the statement that she felt as if she were seeing India, but India "all joined together," as if she were seeing North, South, East and West, all in one.

"A sort of essence," she said, "of India."

We had the joy of seeing her, and hearing her sing, seated on a pillow, with her little Indian drums, one between her knees, and one on the ground beside her; and her tiny hands and delicate wrists would bring out extraordinary resonance from these fascinating

---

[2]   The arrangement of the keyboard invented by Professor Psachos is very satifactory, because it resembles a piano sufficiently to make it easy for any pianist to play on it. The white notes make an octave as they do on the piano. The black notes, instead of being five in the octave, are subdivided with very small keys which the fingers can reach easily. The total number of intervals in the octave is forty-two.

instruments. Or she would dance for us on our little terrace overlooking the Corinthian Gulf, singing her own music, and keeping time with her bare feet, and with jingling bracelets of little bells on her ankles. Or sometimes she would sing Ravel's songs with Mitropoulos at the piano. He also was staying with us that summer, after his fatiguing work as assistant director of the Opera House in Berlin. The following winter he became director of the Symphony Orchestra in Athens. Since then, to our joy, he has gone from one triumph to another; first in various cities abroad, and afterward in America as director of the the Minneapolis Orchestra, and as guest conductor of the Philharmonic in New York.

Kourshed stayed with us for several months; but that was not enough for her to acquire the technique of writing Byzantine notation which was what she needed for her musical mission in India. Circumstances prevented us then from going on with this work; and since then, another mission for India has absorbed her. She is a devoted follower of Ghandiji, as she calls him, and she has spent much time in prison.

We called her Boul-Boul, the Nightingale.

On leaving Germany, I took with me two other instruments we had made in the factory; one small one with two octaves which had served as a model for the organ, and which I gave to Professor Psachos; and one larger harmonium of four octaves on which I then hoped to study myself. The big organ was carefully boxed for shipment, and stored in Steinmeyer's cellar, until such time as I could found my school.

In writing about Greek music, it is a constant temptation to enlarge just a little, on the technical aspects of this study. But this "just a little" is a snare. Each by-path, and there are many, leads on into mazes: sometimes mazes of difficulties, but more often mazes of delight; and one no sooner retraces one's steps from one of these lures, than another appears close at hand. Yet, always, a technical dissertation or discussion concerning unfamiliar music is as meaningless as a description of color to the blind. Music must be heard and felt. It cannot be explained.

The most tempting, perhaps, of these possible digressions is the stenographic notation of the Greek church, invented, they say, by St. John of Damascus, superceding the ancient Greek alphabetical notation, and also an intermediary system called the *Ekphonitikón*, which was used only for singing the Gospels and the Epistles of Saint Paul. The Stenographic System obtained for about a thousand years, with occasional changes and enlargements by different Greek masters, and culminated in the final notation of the three musicians, Gregory, Chrysanthos, and Hourmouzios, which was authorized by the church in 1818, and which writes in detail what had formally been written stenographically. A number of Scholars have patently examined these older musical records, but those in Europe have been hampered in their studies by a scarcity of manuscripts, and also by an hereditary attitude toward music which is different from that of the Greeks. Their conclusions, in fact, are apt to be diametrically opposed to the Greek interpretations,[3] because they generally ignore the value of the stenographic signs to which the Greeks lend a musical meaning. Indeed certain European scholars believe that the elaborate system in use today is not a mere long-hand writing of what everyone already knew (as if one were to write "Company" instead of "Co", or "Street" instead of "St.", or "Massachusetts" instead of "Mass.") but that it was a pure invention on the part of the three named above. Theodore Reinach (author of *La Musique Grecque*, Paris, 1926) told me himself that Byzantine music was all Turkish.

If these opinions concerning this vast musical treasure-house be correct, if these three men devised this wonderful method, and composed these divine melodies with no background to support them; or if the Turks[4] invented this great musical literature out of whole cloth, what can one say except "Hurrah for Three", or "Hurrah for the Turks?" Whichever did it, they were the greatest, the most prolific, the most melodious geniuses the world has ever seen.

In all these discussions, there is one generalization which may be useful to the beginner in Byzantine music: European Scholars, without exception, are equipped with considerable knowledge of European music, but with no practical understanding of the meaning of a musical mode. Reinach says, in his preface,[5] that he had studied Greek music for forty years, but that he does not know what a Greek mode is. At least he is frank. But the consequence with him, and with all European writers on this subject, is that they are always talking about one thing in terms of another; and these two things do not and cannot represent each other. It is impossible to take the first step toward comprehension of what the ancients were talking about as one remains barricaded within European conceptions of inter-vals (which have existed, even there, only since the time of Bach) of what, in Europe they

---

[3] See K. A. Psachos, *Parasemantiké tes Byzantinés Mousikés* (The Notation of Byzantine Music), pp. 51-54, 78-79.

[4] There exist musical manuscripts which are several centuries older that the occupation of Constantinople by the Turks. These may be seen in the Patriarchate of Constantinople, in the monasteries of Mount Athos, in the private collection of Mr. Psachos, etc.

[5] *La Musique Grecque*, p. 5.

call "harmony".[6]

But there is a first step which can be taken, and which may lead to incalculable results: Go toward it as a little child. Learn the songs. Practice the modes by singing tunes. Get a monochord so that you can be sure of your intervals. Learn what the great Greek masters have said; what the Greeks are saying today. And above all do not approach it as an intellectual stunt. Use it. Sing it. Dance to it. And see what happens.

For this sort of approach, it is necessary, in the beginning, to forget everything one knows: to let it go altogether, until these queer Byzantine signs become alive, until musical modes are no longer a perplexity and a bewilderment, but something more like an emotion, with one's heart going faster or slower, according to the heroic content, or the soothing lilt of the melody. These emotions, these modes, these moods, may or may not be the same as those which the Greeks called Dorian, Phrygian, Lydian, and so forth; (and here is another tempting digression) but they are MODES, MOODS, EMOTIONS; and at least, with these in one's experience and one's consciousness, one will no longer be perplexed at Plato's distinctions. One knows then what a musical mode is, as well as one knows what a piano is, or a violin.

Then all that the European scholars have amassed will become valuable. They cannot help us at the start; but they are excellent aids when one sees the way. And then, also, one can open again the great gates of European music, and let it take its course in one's heart and in one's mind. For these two are: TWO GREAT MUSICAL SYSTEMS WHICH HAVE DIFFERENT FUNCTIONS. THEY ARE NOT HOSTILE TO EACH OTHER.

Only today, one of these has the world in its hand, and the other is impoverished and abandoned. Greek music is the lost sheep; which may sometimes seem more precious than the ninety and nine.

---

[6] Harmony is a Greek word. But to them [the Greeks] it meant an aesthetic agreement of notes which were sounded consecutively, not simultaneously. Often it meant a musical mode. Plato and Aristotle both use the word in this sense: "-And which are the harmonies expressive of sorrow?/-You are musical, you can tell me./ The harmonies which you mean are the mixed or Lydian tenor; and the full toned, or base Lydian." Plato, *The Republic*. [Ed. The passage occurs in Book III, 398d-e. -J.P.A.]

CHAPTER 15

The First Delphic Festival

When Kourshed and I arrived from Germany in the harbour of Patras, Anghelos came to the boat to meet us, and almost the first words he said to me were these:

"I think I have solved my problem."

I knew well what his "problem" was: how to bring together those initiates of today, those seers and scientists, those *Epoptai*, "Overseers," whose function is no longer clear, and whose very name, in English, is degraded. How give them a chance to vigilantly follow and oversee the contemporary historical currents of all peoples now known in the world, in order to draw them, above obscure fanaticisms, and above political intrigues, toward a hearth of knowledge of the Universe, and knowledge of one's self, without the slightest trace of dogmatic slavery?

"I think I have solved my problem."

As we journeyed along the Southern coast of the Corinthian Gulf, with Kourshed absorbed in what she was seeing from the car-window, and occasionally turning to tell us what I have already recorded about the similarity of India and Greece, Anghelos explained to me what he meant.

"I have never believed," he said, "that anything vital can be accomplished by merely talking. An infinite deal of wisdom is expounded every day in public and in private; but it does not pierce even the crust of human inertia. It would not be very difficult for us," he went on, "to bring together from many places men whose actions show that they would understand and encourage the thing we are dreaming of. We could institute a round-table conference in Delphi or in Athens. But this is what I have tried to avoid for so many years. It would have no more effect than the rest of the conferences, whether official or unofficial, which are held now in many places. Fine speeches would be made, and applauded, and quoted in the newspapers, and then all the delegates would separate and forget. But to reach below the surface where speeches cannot penetrate, our action must be organically connected with the very roots of the Greek people. We must use the great medium which alone can unite opposites: ART, and especially DRAMA."

And he went on to tell how with a festival we could bring home the Delphic idea to the whole people at once. Only so can one begin. Would I help?

He had the program all arranged: a performance of the *Prometheus Bound* of

Aeschylus in the ancient theatre of Delphi; an Athletic contest in the ancient stadium; an exhibition of peasant handicraft in the village which is now called Kastri. Would I undertake the Athenian side, while he himself would work in the village?

He knew that I had come back to found a school of music. But we had both visualized this school as a part of his University. We saw the festival only as a starting point, but a true one, for our ultimate goal; as a beginning for the kind of activity and the kind of University which he hoped to found, as a positively efficient means of pricking the inflated Hobgoblins which now stalk the frontiers of all nations, terrifying the human beings on both sides of the lines. To make the peoples understand each other. To make them conscious of their sameness, tolerant of their differences, loving instead of hating the infinite variations of the world, and all of them competing nobly for ultimate excellence in God's own Athletic contest for the manifestation of his image on Earth. Here was the way open. By all means let us do everything in our power, and not wait for others any more. The School of Music could wait.

Years had passed since I had first heard Anghelos speak of his Delphic Plan. I had always imagined in the meantime that his friends of the Greek Government, or some unknown miraculous individual would take definite steps to start, in a practical way, the work which he was describing. It was a commonplace, in the old days, to see people carried away by his voice and his earnestness and his spontaneity, and to believe each time one saw them hanging on his words that now, at last, we were on the threshold of definite action. He never expressed any disillusion at these repetitions of ineffectual zeal around him; but, as the years went on, he talked less, saw people less, lived more alone in the mountains; was in fact in danger of losing contact altogether with those he had known, or might know, in Athens.

And now he was saying:

"Let us do what we can alone."

To direct an ancient play, in an ancient theatre, was what he was asking of me. Could I, would I do it?

I was well aware that this was a thing that neither I nor anyone else knew how to do. But my attempting it seemed to be the only stepping-stone toward realization of the dream: "Tragedy is so large that warring States and warring religions can sit together in the same great Theatre, and quietly suck the warm milk of love and pity from its great breast. Tragedy alone can declare the Truce of God."

I remember what he had said years before.

I told him I would try.

I had dreamed about Greek Tragedy from years earlier than my summer with Plato. I owed this dream originally to Swinburne. I knew all the choruses of *Atalanta in Calydon* and of *Erechtheus* by heart when I was about fifteen, and was fascinated by the sound of them which seemed unlike anything in English. This was at the time I was at school in Farmington, Connecticut. Miss Porter, who founded it, was still alive but very old, and the direction had fallen to Mrs. Dowe. A few of the older girls had got into the habit of having me recite for them. Gradually a few more, and a few more came, so that my room became crowded on all free evenings for a sort of continuous performance of recitation. One day Mrs. Dowe called me to her office, and said that she did not approve of what I was doing.

"There is nothing," she said, "positively wrong about it, but I consider these evenings too exciting both for you and for the other girls, and I shall have to ask you not to recite any more."

So after that "Hounds of Spring", and "Who hath given man speech", and "Who shall put a bridle on the mourner's lips to chasten them", and "Thou art goodly, oh Love, thou art fair", and

> "Ah, broken is the golden bowl: the spirit flown forever!"
> Let the bell toll!--a saintly soul floats on the Stygian river,"

and "I dwelt alone
in a world of moan,
And my soul was a stagnant tide,"

and "Here once through an alley Titanic
of Cypress, I roamed with my soul--
Oh, Cypress, with Psyche, my soul.
These were days when my heart was volcanic
As the scoriac rivers that roll
As the lavas that restlessly roll
Their sulphurous currents down Yarnak
In the ultimate climes of the pole--
That groan as they roll down Mount Yarnak
In the realms of the boreal pole."[1]

Swinburne and Poe! How the English language was feeling out at that time for its complement in music! I too was trying to push language further into the realm of melody, and to discover the technique for doing this. But I did not even imagine that there *is* a technique beyond, and altogether different from the sort of impassioned recitation with which I held a few school-girls spellbound. It must have been painfully Victorian, and Mrs. Dowe probably did well to stop it. But this interruption was for me in a way, an end. My passion

---

[1] [Ed. The verses from the choral dramas of Algernon Charles Swinburne (1837-1909). -J.P.A]

for Swinburnean choruses, for melody in words, from that time struck inward instead of outwards. As far as personal performance was concerned it never came to the surface again, not even in the few amateur plays which I directed, or in all the work I did in Paris for the stage. Perhaps Moréno sensed it when she said:

"You can destroy what you've got if you want to, but you cannot acquire a French intonation."

I was never again carried away and sure of myself as I had been in my little room in Farmington. I became suspicious, perhaps even ashamed, of my love for melody in language, and all my French training was of course against it. For this sort of singing speech is contrary to the genius of the French language, whereas, and in spite of the present trend against it, English has in its bones the lyric lilt of bards and minstrels. So this impetus toward the singing of words was for long obscured; and Mrs. Dowe's negative imperative was perhaps still working, while entirely new conceptions of Greek Choruses were building in my consciousness. But then I no longer was interested in either reciting or acting myself. I had come to long for many voices, for many women, or preferably many men, expressing in perfect individual freedom, and in perfect composite unity, the complete inner meaning of the word.

After my set-back at Farmington, I turned to reading translations of Greek plays, Gilbert Murray's and others, and finally to the critical studies of scholars concerning the Greek Theatre. These last seemed rarely to be in agreement with each other, and never with the impression I got from the actual plays themselves. I did not feel that I knew anything about producing Greek plays, but I did believe, later on, from reading, and from many performances which I had seen in various places, that no one else did either. The written work which interested me most in this regard was Nietzsche's *Birth of Tragedy*, but even with this I agreed only on part. As a guide on my way, or rather at first as a torment, I held for years to two short sentences: one from *The Republic* of Plato, and one from Aristotle's *Poetics*: "The tragic chorus is the union of poetry, music and gymnastics," and "the tragic chorus expresses in movement the character, the sufferings and the actions of the actors."[2] I think that now I am just beginning to see what they meant; but all I got out of it then was that outside help from scholars and archaeologists seemed to bring one no nearer to the goal, and that the true way of presenting a Greek Tragedy would have to come somehow from within,

---

[2] [Ed. The reference can only be to *Poetics* 1456a25-26. The author is paraphrasing a passage where Aristotle states that the chorus must be an integral part of the whole enterprise, since it must be regarded as one of the actors. -J.P.A.]

rather as an enlightenment than as knowledge acquired from books. As years passed I had formed certain notions about it which were still too immature for me to refer to them even in conversation. So, when I told Anghelo that I would try to direct the play, I was inwardly, thinking:

"I will follow what I myself feel."

On arriving in Sykiá, I encountered my first difficulty. Anghelos and I were sitting in the pine forest, near our house, and near the sea. He told me that for the music of *Prometheus Bound* he felt that only two musicians in Greece were great enough to attempt it. One was Demetrios Mitropoulos, who was then staying with us, and the other was Manolis Kalomoiris, Director of the National Conservatory in Athens. He said that he had already spoken about it to both of them and that Mr. Kalomoiris had accepted. My heart sank. How was I to explain to Anghelo, after so many years, that the inner impetus of all my work in Byzantine music was my belief that the method brought down by the Greek Church was definitely connected with Greek Drama; that this, in fact, was the very pivot around which any true interpretation would swing: and that it was inconceivable to me to produce a Greek play with a musician, Greek or foreign, who knew only European music.

Anghelos said he understood what I meant, but that there were no composers who knew anything about the Greek theory, and what could we do? I suggested Professor Psachos, but he answered very truly that, outside of ecclesiastical compositions, he had never done anything: and how could I be sure that he would be able to apply his knowledge of modal music in the way I imagined? I said I was not sure; but that knowledge of the method, of the applicability of musical modes to words, and to the accents and rhythms of words, was a basis which could not lead one absolutely astray, and might lead to great results; that, in short, with him I felt that I could do something, and that with anyone else I knew that I could do nothing. Anghelos said that the play was in my hands, and to do as I thought best.

I went immediately to Athens to see Mr. Kalomoiris, and I told him all that Anghelos and I had said, only at somewhat greater length. I explained how, for so many years, my interest in Greek Ecclesiastical music had been neither archaeological nor religious; that I had built the organ, and hoped to found a school in order, eventually, to bring out its relationship to and perhaps even show the direct descent of ecclesiastical music from ancient drama, that in no case would it be a matter of applying existing church songs to words of Aeschylus, but using the method brought down by the Church in free and original composition. I spoke of how the architecture of a Greek theatre provides no place for hiding the musicians or any extraneous accompaniment, whereas the text of the choruses demands a musical variety expressive of all human emotions. In short that Greek Drama demands, as Aristotle says, "melody and rhythm" and nothing else, and that modern harmony has nothing to do with it. Could he write melody which would stand up without harmony, melody which would render the power and the variety of an ancient Greek play?

Mr. Kalamoiris was wonderful. He said that he agreed with Anghelo that a purely ecclesiastical training was not sufficient to produce a dramatic composition.

"But," he went on, "try Mr. Psachos, and if you are not satisfied, come back to me, and I will write it for you in the kind of music which I know."

I then went to Professor Psachos, only to encounter a new difficulty. He said that he had already decided to go to Mount Athos and become a Monk; and anyway that he knew nothing about writing music for plays, and that knowledge of ecclesiastical music had nothing to do with it. Then I had to begin all over again, to explain to him what he ought to have known, and what Anghelos and Mr. Kalomoiris had understood. It was a long uphill undertaking to persuade him; but finally he accepted and said he would do it. Shortly after this he went back to Germany, this time for his health, and said he would send me the music for the play from there.

The rest of my summer was spent in listening to Kourshed, or Mitropoulos (who besides being a very gifted orchestral leader, is a remarkable pianist), or to both together studying Ravel; and by myself, I studied the fine translation of *Prometheus Bound* by the poet Jean Gryparis, which Anghelo has chosen as the best in modern Greek. We discussed the possibility of giving the play in ancient Greek, but against this he had three sufficient reasons. First the pronunciation; for if we chose the Erasmian method, the Greeks would be dreadfully shocked: but if we pronounced it as the Greeks do their ancient language, European or American scholars would think it quite horrible. Second, he wanted the peasants to understand it easily. And third, we wanted to establish the fact that Greek is not a dead, but a living language.

On arriving in Athens, I started my task in two ways. First I set up my loom to weave the dresses for the play myself. These were to be made of silk (contrary probably to archaeological propriety, though at present this is debated), because I thought that for the Chorus of Oceanides the sheen of silk would be appropriate. I knew that the ancient Greeks were supposed not to have silk, but I did not really care. I was not trying to be strictly correct, and I felt that if Aeschylus did not have silk he would have liked to have it for this particular play. My idea was to make very elaborate dresses for all the minor characters: Force, Violence, Hephaistos, the Ocean, Hermes, and the Chorus of Oceanides, because all these are supernatural beings far removed from human suffering;   and to dress the two principal characters, Prometheus and Io, very simply because they are in torment and mortal distress.   This involved a great deal of embroidery in my loom: sea-forms copied from Mycenean vases, fish, coral, sea-flowers, sea-birds, which were amusing to do, but took considerable time.   Yet I was chiefly interested, of course, in making stuffs, especially for my Oceanides, which when they would be dancing, would look like the folds on a Greek bas-relief.

Having the costumes under way, I called a meeting of the older members of the Lyceum Club, the only woman's club in Athens, and told them what we were planning. Could I have their daughters for my Chorus, and could I have the ball-room of the club for rehearsals?   My idea then was as follows: I would give lessons on the theory of Byzantine music, alternating with gymnastic exercises which I considered a basis for the sort of dancing that I would teach them later;   and we would go all together quite often to the National Museum to study, and especially to make copies of the infinitely varied poses of figures on the ancient vases.   I felt that these three things would be a foundation for the Chorus I was imagining.   The truth was that I was feeling my way, and I told them so quite frankly.   The girls came for three or four lessons and we went twice to the Museum but after that they all came to me together and said that they did not want to learn the theory of Byzantine music, that they were bored by the Museum and did not see the use of it, that they were not interested in gymnastic exercises, and wouldn't I teach a dance?   I realized that the work I had hoped to do with them had to be done alone, and I sent them all home.

Shortly after that I received the manuscript of the first chorus from Germany, written in Byzantine notation, and I started to work on that.   I made a great quantity of sketches in the Museum with a friend who was a sculptor and then, phrase by phrase, I tried to fit the highlights, as it were, or the principle accents in meaning and music, with what seemed to me appropriate gestures from the vases.   But what with all the other things I was doing at that time, (obtaining permissions from different ministries to hold the festival, and this was not always easy) it took me months to work out one Chorus.   So the following spring I called the girls together again, and said I was ready to do what they had asked, and I started teaching them the music, entirely orally, because they had not wanted to learn to decipher it, and then definite gestures for every word or phrase of the text.   I had not wanted the things to be fixed in this way, and had hoped that each one of the girls would do what I had done, and work out her own interpretation.   In this way it would have been more interesting, and more like what a Greek Chorus should be, developing harmony out of variation, allowing each one to keep her own individuality, and making the whole thing more vivid and expressive, but the girls were not capable of doing that at the start.

So the work for the Festival went on. Summer came, and I took a house near the Bay of Phaleron. It had a large courtyard in which I marked off in bricks the size and shape of the Delphic orchestra, a circle about fifteen meters in diameter; and the girls came every day toward sundown to rehearse. New manuscripts arrived from Germany. But by that time I was in the swing of it, and the dances did not take me so long to compose. And the weaving always went on, for me mostly at night, for the daytime found me hurrying to various ministries: Education, Interior, Communications, Foreign Affairs, Tourism, War, for one reason or another they all came into it. And there turned out to be so much of that sort of thing to do, that I taught three girls to weave, realizing that with all these other activities which I had not foreseen I would never get through the weaving by myself. As it was, I wove about twenty heavily embroidered costumes.

Beside the play, there were the two other parts of the program to be arranged: the Athletic Games, and the Exhibition of Handicrafts. The preparation of the Games turned out to be quite difficult. At that time, in the Ministry of Education, the director of all the athletic activities in Greece was an ardent admirer of Swedish gymnastics. The first time I went to his office he showed me a picture of a public place in Sweden arranged for the kind of exercises he admired. It was all marked off in squares, like an enormous checker-board; and on each square was a man. In the centre was a scaffolding supporting a similar square on which there was also a man standing. This central man, visible from all the other squares, was the teacher, whose every movement was imitated with automatic regularity by the thousands of mechanical dolls below him. If his hand or his foot went up, then all other hands or feet, in all the other squares, went up like clock-work, at exactly the same angle. This picture represented the ideal which the Greek director of athletics was striving to impose on all the youth of Greece.

I told him of our plan for the ancient Stadium in Delphi. He listened courteously, and said that he would give orders to his assistants to help me. I went away elated; but a month passed, and nothing happened. I returned to his office to experience an exact repetition of my first visit. He received me courteously, but in apparent ignorance of any previous conversation. He showed me the Swedish photograph, and gave me new assurances of cooperation, but again I waited a month with no result. I tried once more, this time reminding him of my former visits and his promises; but there was no response in his eyes. I only received more promises, and finally understood that his plan was to keep me hoping

Eva Palmer as a young lady in the U.S.A. (Archives of the philologist Vivette Tsarlamba-Kaklamani.)

Second Delphic Festival, 1930. Standing, from left to right: Koula Pratsika, *Korypheus* in the chorus of Aeschylus' *Suppliant Maidens*. George Burlos, in the part of *Prometheus*, in Aeschylus' *Prometheus Bound*. Sitting: Eva Palmer-Sikelianos, in archaic dress, woven by herself. Katerina Marouli-Kakouri, in the part of *Io*, in *Prometheus Bound*. Several masks of the representations of the above pieces. (Archives of Thanos Burlos.)

Eva Palmer-Sikelianos at Delphi, during the First Delphic Festival (1927). (Archives of the philologist Vivette Tsarlamba-Kaklamani.)

Eva Palmer-Sikelianos in archaic dress at Delphi, attending events given in her honour. This is the last known photograph of her, taken at the end of May 1952, a few days before her death on June 4th. (Archives of the philologist Vivette Tsarlamba-Kaklamani.)

for his collaboration until it would be too late to organize the sort of athletic games which we were planning. So it came to putting others on his track, which was effective eventually, but a great waste of time.

With the help of friends the athletic program was finally set in motion, with only one exception: the Pyrrhic Dance. I had had thirty suits of armour hammered out by hand: breast-plates, helmets, short swords and spears, copied from ancient models in the National Museum. They were gorgeous, and I was looking forward to seeing men dance with heavy armour which would force them into movements; there could be no graceful leaps, or pirouettes. But the Greek director of athletics was adamant. He did not even make a promise about the Pyrrhic Dance. He simply refused to countenance it. Then a friend came to my rescue, a gifted architect named George Kontoleon. He undertook to get thirty men and to teach the dance. But he encountered other difficulties. The men got together but were not dependable. They found the work too hard, so that he had to keep replacing them, and he was constantly starting afresh. The Festival was drawing near and he was hopeless, and thought we would have to give it up. Finally someone suggested the army; to get boys whose military duty would force them to come to the lessons. I also felt hopeless, but I went to see the Commander of the First Army Corps which was then stationed in Athens. I did not know this General, and I felt rather frightened. I did not see why he should grant what I had gone to ask. He was charming and immediate in his response. No explanations, no persuasions. He told me to send Mr. Kontoleon to choose the men, and that I could have as many as I liked. This same general came to the Festival and saw the Pyrrhic Dance. He sent word to me afterwards that if we ever gave another Festival I could have his whole Army Corps.

This request for men for the Pyrrhic dance occasioned my first meeting with officers of the Greek Army. Not long after this my second occurred. A number of small matters had accumulated which depended on the Minister of War. I needed many tents, several trucks to carry all the paraphernalia of the Festival from the harbour of Itea up to Delphi, more men for the Stadium, old cannon balls to produce thunder at the end of the play, and probably other things which I have now forgotten. The Minister, Mr. Mazarakis, whom I had never seen before, sat in the centre of the room near a large desk which had a semicircle of electric bells just beyond his blotter. I was again discouraged and rather frightened. In other Ministries I had met what often seemed like evasion, never whole-hearted cooperation. This was natural enough, because I was trying to do a thing which they rightly considered, first from one point of view, and then from another, as very risky. They were merely doing their duty, and being careful. Nobody was to blame. But anyway I was tired. I told Mr. Mazarakis the things I needed. His answer was to ring all his electric bells one after another. Immediately a line of officers came into the room. They saluted him and then stood at attention. He then turned to me and said:

"Madam, these gentlemen are in command of the departments from which you require assistance. Will you please give your orders?"

This moment of extraordinary courtesy was to me one of the high spots of the first Festival. And it had its sequel in the second.

The Exhibition of handicraft was the only part of the Festival which, for me, was pure fun without any work. I called a meeting of ladies at the beautiful house of Mrs. Angeliki Hadzimichali. Many of my dear friends were connected, either through their ancestry, or through actual living relatives, with some definite part of Greece: Macedonia, Epirus, Euboea, some special sections of the mainland, or of the Peloponnesos, or with an Ionian Island, or any island of the Aegean Sea. There were Miss Helen Eukleides, Mrs. Paul Melas, Mrs. Kallergis, Mrs. Maria Theotokis, Mrs. Edla Nazou, Mrs. Hadzilazarou, Miss Helle Papadimitriou, and others. I told them our plan: to show the ever-creative ability of the Greek people, how even today, and in spite of heavy importation of industrial products, there is hardly a village which has not preserved some local tradition in handicraft. In weaving, embroidery, in furniture, leather-work, basket-work, silver-work, rug-making, pottery, the Greeks still know how to use their hands. We wanted to show, not so much the beautiful work of about a hundred years ago, but the living talent of today. Would each one of those present undertake to collect from her own country the best examples of contemporary local skill, and would Angeliki direct the whole Exhibition? I knew that not only was she an expert in all local varieties of costumes and handicrafts, but that she knew, either through correspondence or personal acquaintance, the names and talents of the especially gifted workmen both in and out of Athens.

Angeliki said there was not a craftsman in Greece who had ever heard of an Exhibition; that they would not understand the usual plan of sending, to a distant place, the things they had made, to sell them at a Festival of which they knew nothing, or have them returned afterwards unsold. It had never been done. The only way, she said, to do such a thing would be to buy beforehand all the objects we wished to exhibit and sell them afterwards if we could. Everyone present agreed with Angeliki. We could not, they said, persuade the peasants to send their work until they had seen a Festival, at least once, with their own eyes. I said we would buy the objects if they would collect them, each one taking over a special section of Greece. They all accepted. It was also decided that separate houses in the village street of Kastri should be given over to special sections of Greece, and that the ladies who had made themselves responsible for those sections should themselves superintend their own exhibits, each one dressed in the costume of her own country.

I knew that I had experts all along the line, who each knew about village workmanship, who were themselves well known in the different localities, who were absolutely dependable, and who were not afraid of work. And so, from then on, this very important part of the Festival seemed miraculously to take care of itself.

I had thought, as the work progressed, that it would be well for the Festival to obtain the approval, as it were the patronage, of the foreign Archaeological Schools. I went first to the French School in Athens, and spoke to Monsieur and Madame Roussel. They were most courteous, and said that they would think about it. Then I went to the American School of Classical Studies, where I received the same answer. Then to the English School, with the same result. Finally I went to see Mr. Buschor, Director of the German School. He was more frank. He considered it a sacrilege to defile any ancient monument with a miserable modern attempt to perform ancient dramas.

"Leave them in peace," he said. "You cannot possibly do them right, so why do them at all?"

I sympathized with the way he felt, and I liked his frankness; but my visits to the Italian and Swedish Schools never came off. Somehow, I do not know why, Mr. Buschor came to the Festival, and after the performance of the play, he came to our house.

"You have solved," he said, "archaeological problems which we have been working on fruitlessly for years. How have you done it?"

"No," said I, "my dear Mr. Buschor, I have done nothing of the kind. I have read archaeological books only to forget them, and I never thought of your problems. And besides," I went on, "the performance was bristling with archaeological mistakes; but even you did not detect them, and you are not conscious of them even now. And that is because the play was moving around its own pivot; it was emotionally true, or almost true--and that was sufficient to make even you feel that it was correct archaeologically. But there is no such thing as archaeological correctness. There is nothing in Greek drama except the emotional truth and consistency of the performers, and the immense responding emotion of those who are present. The faculties of the actors, the chorus and the audience in the great circular theatre become one, and form an overwhelming magnetic force. It is a tidal wave which nothing can resist; not even archaeological conscientiousness."

Beside Mr. Buschor, there was one other person in Athens who was perfectly frank with me before the First Festival. This was Mr. Petrakópoulos, Director of the Grande Bretagne, which is the largest and the best hotel in Athens. I went to ask him if he would announce the Festival to his various correspondents abroad. As an answer to my question he took out his files and handed to me a circular letter which had been sent out some time before. In this letter he had already announced the Festival, but with unequivocal disapproval. He had recommended, in fact, that any travelers wishing to come to it should be discouraged, and turned away from it if possible, because the accommodations would probably be entirely unsatisfactory. This was rather a blow. I had thought it likely that Mr. Petrakopoulos would not care to help us, but I had not foreseen that he would use his influence as a hindrance. I said nothing, except to thank him for his frankness which I honestly appreciated. He then explained that he had no doubt at all that, from an artistic point of view, our performance would justify our own hopes, or even surpass them.

"The program you have announced," he said, "is extremely attractive. It will interest exactly the type of people whom I have been striving for over thirty years to bring to Greece. But those people demand the kind of accommodation which I can give them here in Athens. They are not used to any sort of primitive hardships; and I consider it impossible that, even with the utmost care and forethought, you will be able to supply these needs, in a distant, and almost inaccessible village. And so, in a single day, you could destroy the effort of my whole life, which has been given over entirely to the advance of Tourism in Greece."

I saw his point. And three years after that, when the Second Festival was preparing, I felt as if I had conquered a kingdom when Mr. Petrakopoulos joined the Guarantee Committee which was forming and became an invaluable, I might almost say an ardent helper in the cause.

Nearly three years had elapsed since Anghelos has spoken of his plan on my arrival in Patras with Kourshed.

One summer in Sykiá studying the play, a false start in the autumn at the Lyceus Club, and a winter studying the first chorus alone. Two summers of work with my girls in Phaleron, and one winter in the Greek Archaeological Institute. During this time my chorus of Oceanides had become word-perfect, melody-perfect, move-perfect. They sounded well, and they looked well. The dresses were finished. But I was not pleased. Their singing and their dancing seemed to me stilted and mechanical, and I did not know what to do about it. We started rehearsing with the actors, and they also became word-perfect and the rest of it; but I liked nothing as I had hoped to.

At that juncture Mr. Psachos came home from Germany, and to my horror he announced that he had an orchestral accompaniment, and that we must have rehearsals with an orchestra. All my house of cards seemed falling around my head. His music sounded beautiful as it was. What was the point in adding the very thing which I had been striving to avoid; why must the greatest expert on the Greek musical tradition bow to the prevailing fashion? But at that time I had an old habit of looking on Mr. Psachos as my teacher, and on myself as somewhat of an outsider. I was timid and tired, and my remonstrances were probably feeble. I engaged the orchestra with Mr. Oikonomidis leading, and we had two rehearsals in Athens. It did not sound very badly. The girls had the habit of my interpretation, and Mr. Oikonomidis followed them with great musicality. I saw at least that they would not have to change anything that they were doing, so I was partly reconciled. After that I went up to Delphi with all my girls and the actors, and the orchestra was to follow in a few days.

The arrival in the village was for me a high spot in the Festival. There was not a house which had not been white-washed inside and out. There was not a family in the village of Kastri, and in all the neighboring villages, which was not in some way a part of it. Anghelos had found, in all the villages of Parnassos, and much farther afield, all the best singers, all the best dancers, the best clarinettists, flutists, pipers, and drummers; the best runners, jumpers, and wrestlers, for the Athletic Games. He had arranged with everybody that only those who were actually performing were to come to the Festival on the first day, but that on the second day a free performance of the whole Festival would be given for them, and that all were invited. He appealed to them on the basis of hospitality to leave the grounds in and around the Sacred Enclosure entirely free for strangers who might come. He knew that there is no other appeal so binding to a Greek. All the countryside was ready.

With the girls alone I had my first rehearsal in the ancient theatre. It was a revelation. The thing that none of us had been able to do in Athens happened by itself on the great mountain. Their voices were free and strong, their movements beautiful and powerful. They were inspired.

But in a few days the orchestra arrived, and then a strange thing happened. Mr.

Oikonomidis who had followed the Chorus so beautifully in Athens found, when he was hidden with his orchestra under the stage, that he could hear absolutely nothing. The girls sang as loud as they could, but no sound reached him. He could only see the movements of their lips. And so it was demonstrated that in spite of the miraculous acoustics of a Greek theatre, which makes the slightest sound audible, not only in the last row of seats of the Theatre, but also on the mountain-side above it, this transmission of sound evidently did not work other ways. From Orchestra[3] to audience, or actors to audience, it was perfect; but from Orchestra to cellar of the stage, there was no sound at all. Here was a proof, if I had known it beforehand, that the ancient Greeks did not have hidden instruments in their theatres. The upshot of all this was that Mr. Psachos, standing by Mr. Oikonomides, following the lips of the girls and beat time with his hand, and Mr. Oikonomides, following this hand, was able to lead his musicians. It was all very complicated, and rather dangerous; but the thing went on in this way, and left the girls free to follow their own inspiration, and that was all I cared about. From the auditorium the instruments were hardly heard, and there were forty men playing. The effect of it was a sort of harmonious rumble, which to me detracted from the clarity I had been dreaming of but it was not positively disagreeable. Only it retarded the proof of my theory, that in the Greek Theatre, or in fact in any theatre, harmony is a hindrance and not a help.

Before the arrival of the orchestra, Angeliki had come with all her committee of ladies, and all their exhibits, in huge cases, were lining the streets. Their activity in the village was very exciting, transforming the houses of the peasants into characteristic suggestions of far away villages and islands. And the athletes were already there practicing in the stadium, with their short bright-colored chitons which Gladys Stewart-Richardson had woven; and the soldiers were there with their glistening shields, breast-plates, and helmets, practicing the Pyrrhic Dance. Mr. Phoskolos, the sculptor, was busily erecting his paper-mache rocks on the stage. And the singers, the dancers, the clarinettists were going over their parts here and there, in little cafes, or in the streets. It was all very gay, and everyone seemed happy.

I had little anxiety about the Festival itself. Everyone in it by that time, was in it whole-heartedly, and I felt sure that the thing was good, but would anyone see it? This

---

[3] The word "Orchestra" has lost its proper meaning in English. It is a Greek word which means a dancing place, and especially the circular part of the Greek Theatre between the actors and the spectators, in which the chorus performed its revolutions. In this sentence the word is used in the Greek sense.

question, toward the end, became more and more insistent. There had been practically no announcements of it abroad, except those which had been unfavourable and except for the foreign correspondents who had been invited, there was not much chance that anyone would come from far. There were, however, many strangers traveling in Greece at that time, and we had counted on their coming to see it. But this hope was gradually receding. The travel bureaus were afraid to recommend it, for the same reason that Mr. Petrakopoulos had been afraid, and a growing tendency had been evident in Athens to consider the whole thing a joke. Meantime the boats that had been hired would be empty; the automobiles would await passengers in vain; the restaurant brought from Athens, and the huge shelter built for it, with fir boughs over the roof, would have only the participants to feed. The last minute was on us. We had asked the peasants to stay away. All our preparations would be for empty benches or, if we gave it up, the work of all my friends in Athens, and Anghelo's work, with the whole country-side of Parnassos, for three years, would have been for nothing.

Facing this impasse, I sent telegrams to Athens that everyone was to be invited, that the boats and cars should be filled. I knew that this act was rash in the extreme. Up to that time the whole Festival had been provided for. It had cost, as we had calculated, about one hundred thousand dollars. But we had no more money; a small income from a trust-fund after that, and that was all. I was assuming the traveling expenses, the food and lodging of about two thousand people for three days. That is an extra responsibility of about thirty thousand dollars, which we had never calculated, and which I knew we could not pay. Our credit was good. I made the plunge. And today, nearly fifteen years after,[4] having lived through the continual harassment of these same debts ever since, and with no freedom to go on with the work we had started, I can truly say that I have never regretted this plunge.

The boats full of people had come: the automobiles were streaming in from Athens and from Itea. The foreign correspondents had arrived, and Anghelos was with them. It was the ninth of May, 1927. The day before there had been a terrible thunder-storm which had destroyed our last rehearsal. Everyone but Anghelos had been downcast in the heavy rain, but he was unperturbed.

"The weather," he said, "will be perfect."

And it was.

I walked down to the Exhibition, and was delighted. Every house on each side of the

---

[4]   [Ed. The year, when these pages were written, must have been 1942. -J.P.A.]

village street was filled with varied and beautiful treasures, all made by the peasants; and in every house a great lady was presiding in the local dress of her own home. All Greece was represented in the crafts; and all by accomplished craftsmen. Here was a dream come true.

But returning home I could hardly climb the hill to our eagle's nest; and how would my feet ever drag me as far as the theatre? And how could I ever dress all the girls? When they were ready, it seemed incredibly difficult to get from under the stage to the auditorium. I was paralyzed with fatigue. As if in a dream I realized that Prometheus, Force and Violence, and Hephaistos looked very well; that they spoke well; and that the audience liked them. But presently my Oceanides appeared, and I was immediately and immensely alive. They were completely free, and completely beautiful. I was radiantly happy. The great audience and the chorus were one: and I knew that I was truly on the threshold of Greek Drama.

Afterwards the telegraph wires were buzzing; the first news was passing to Athens, to Paris, to London, to Berlin, to Rome, to Madrid, to Lisbon. All that night Athens was in a turmoil of excitement . The next day the shops were closed, and people were kissing each other in the streets, as they used to at Easter. All of Greece was awake. And the news from Delphi continued coming. After the first short notices, the long and detailed ones came. Especially from Gabriel Boissy, Editor-in-chief of *Comoedia*, and leader of the French group: Mario Meunier, Marcel Boulanger, Pierre Plessy, André Billy, and others:

"The drama has been reborn" they were saying, "in the original land of its birth."

And the Greek correspondents were wonderful:

"They had gone to mock, and had stayed to pray."

For months the Greek papers had pages full of nothing but the Festival. They told me long after that the public wanted no other news.

Next morning in the Stadium, disks and javelins were glinting in the sun. There was running, jumping and wrestling, and the flashing suits of armour; and the singing of men as they danced. At the end of *Prometheus Bound*, eagles had come down from the summit of Parnassos, and circled around the hero's head. And in the midst of the games in the stadium, they came again, flying low in the arena. All of nature seemed truly to be taking part.

But the best of all was the following day, when the peasants came to see the play. They had kept their promise, and no one had come from any village on the first two days. But on their own day, they trekked for many miles, with their children, and often with babies in their arms. In the morning the theatre was filled, though they knew that the play was to be late in the afternoon; and during the day, the mountain above the theatre became black with people. The first day the audience of intellectuals had been very grand, but the second was stupendous. The Greek people truly were awake.

That night, when they had all gone, I sat alone in the theatre, and the future was clear before me. I knew that the response had been real, and that the result had been far beyond my own expectations. I knew that if we could go on then, the reality of the great dream was in our hands. But I saw well ahead. I knew that night that much would be said, and much would be written, but that no one would free our hands.

CHAPTER 16

America

During the following summer, the thing I had foreseen took its course. The wave of awakening consciousness in Greece, the zeal of many abroad, seemed to increase rather than diminish. The Greek Government exhibited interest. One Minister stated that, for the first time since the Greek Revolution, Greece had held up her head abroad; and they said that the Delphic movement could balance the Greek budget; another that we had demonstrated the creative capacity of the Greek people today. All were agreed that the Delphic deficit should be a public charge. There seemed, however, to be no fund from which they could draw for this purpose, and finally someone suggested a lottery. In Greece there had never been more than one lottery allowed. This was started shortly after the Revolution, and its original purpose had been the preservation and further excavation of archaeological sites. A little later, the need of a Greek Navy seemed to be pressing. So the proceeds of the first lottery were divided, and have continued to divided ever since, between Archaeology and the Navy: the latter, of course, receiving the lion's share. No other lottery had ever been permitted.

There was a good deal of opposition on moral grounds:

"Why multiply," said the Minister of the Interior, "a method which we recognize as bad, why not pay right out?"

I did not see why myself, but the majority were in favour of the lottery. Having reached agreement among the Ministers, the proposal had to pass through the Boulé, or House of Representatives. A bill was drawn up providing for many useful measures for the village and the future activity of the Delphic movement, with a clause which stated that the Delphic deficit (this included the three unpaid items for which I had made myself responsible in the end, the boats, the automobiles, and the food for those I had invited, and also the whole Festival itself) should be paid out of the first gains from the lottery.

Again my time was spent, as it had been largely before the Festival, in speaking with many members of the Government, this time in order to hasten the passage of the Delphic Lottery bill through the House. If we could have in our hands the sum with which we had prepared the Festival (I learned afterwards that altogether this sum was less than one tenth of what Austria had spent that same year for Salzburg) we would be able to continue the work while it was on the peak of accomplishment. This was immensely important. In fact the very reason for the Festival itself was at stake. For the essence of the Delphic plan is that discussion, in order to have any beneficent outcome, must follow agreement, and not precede it.   That is to say that agreement is essentially a religious phenomenon, that it is not necessarily concerned with this or that material demand of nations or individuals hostile to each other: that there does exist a realm of Agreement which is independent of material demands; and that these can be discussed intelligently only when the fundamental recognition of human relationship has already become a fact, not of the mind, but of the heart. This recognition could be brought about today only in one way. I cannot depend on the sort of fervour which made Cromwell's army cry: "The Lord of Hosts, the Lord of Hosts," because such purely religious victories have too often become coercive and cruel.

But there exists a means of evoking this same generous impulse in men without linking it to the constricting influence of religious dogma: this means is the instantaneous liberation caused by great drama. Its effect is exactly expressed by the Greek word metanoia (μετάνοια), usually translated as "repentance"; but it is not repentance: it is not necessarily connected with "feeling sorry", which is what the Latin word means. It is a change, usually sudden, of direction of the mind; its first meaning in ancient Greek is a "change of sentiment". This change of sentiment may be, it actually was at the first Delphic Festival, a change from hostility to understanding. On a very small scale, between representatives of different nations who were present, between members of families estranged from each other by recent civic turmoils, there took place a "change of sentiment" (which was afterwards lasting) from resentment and suspicion to spontaneous and affectionate intercourse. This wave of spontaneity and joy had already spread through the whole of Greece, and even beyond its borders. The spirit of Upward Panic was abroad.

The original Delphic claim had been verified. That great Tragedy still has this power. The time had therefore come for the second Delphic step: to call together the Seers of different nations, however few: to lay the corner-stone for the Spiritual Centre, for the Delphic University of Human Understanding. With the passing of the bill for the Lottery the next step we had dreamed of seemed within reach. Such an incentive was sufficient to carry me through the effort involved in getting the bill passed. This was accomplished rather rapidly, with great courtesy on everybody's part; so that presently there seemed to be nothing more ahead than the fun of designing our Lottery tickets, giving them to the printer, and afterwards on to the accomplishment of our real Delphic dream. The cup seemed so near the lip that for a moment one took heart. But "there's many a slip".

Having the whole weight of authority on our side: The House of Representatives, and all the Ministers, it seemed a small matter to print a few tickets. But this matter of printing was mysteriously delayed. Time passed again until I discovered where the obstacle had occurred. I went to see the Minister of the Navy.

"You are destroying" I said, "the whole Delphic Effort, in which, until now, you have shown great interest."

His answer was unexpected:

"No," said he, "my dear Madame Sikelianou, it is you who are destroying the Navy."

Did this answer slip from him, or did he say it on purpose? I have never known. But he went on:

"We are in debt for submarines," (he told me how many, the name of the creditor, and other details which I have forgotten). "Our only hope for these debts is in our own Lottery. But if yours comes out, all of Greece will buy that, and we shall not sell a single ticket. How can I possibly allow yours to appear?" I suggested that ours had only two drawings, whereas his came out every year; and that for our two times he could have his appear first, and so gain considerable advantage.

"No," said he, "if the people know that yours is coming, they will all save their money for that. What you are saying will do no good."

I had never thought of this rivalry before. But perhaps he was right! Perhaps we would have destroyed his Navy, and all Navies, if we could have gone on then. Europe was still in a fleeting condition. A number of sharp differentiations which are true now, did not then exist. The peoples were still dreaming of Wilson's 14 Articles. Perhaps he was right.

I had never thought of this rivalry before. But it did not occur to me at that time that we had the law on our side; and that public opinion was evidently strong in our favour since the Minister of the Navy thought that the Greek people would buy all of our tickets, and none of his. Perhaps one more push at that time would have sent the rolling stone of Sisyphus tumbling down the other side of the hill. Who knows? Anyway I did not even think of it. I was desperately tired. America was all that loomed in my thoughts.

I had received a letter from Dr. Ralph van Deman McGoffin, the President of the American Archaeological Institute, asking me to come to speak to various archaeological groups in different American cities to tell them what we had done in Greece and what we hoped to do. He said that the Society could not give large fees, but that I would be sure of intelligent audiences. Dr. McGoffin had been at the Festival, and expressed a friendly interest in what we had done.

It was over twenty years since I had been to America, and then, only for a few months, the summer when we were married. Before that I had lived mostly in Paris; and before that there had been much going and coming across the ocean. Somehow, "America" as a fixed quantity, still meant to me Gramercy Park. I remembered how at my father's house foreigners who were interested in a cause had only to ask for a hearing from him. If he considered their cause a worthy one, he would call a few friends to listen. If they considered it worthy, a committee would be formed, and sometimes almost overnight such matters might be established, and definite help obtained. I felt, in going, that I had something worthwhile to say; that we had deeds to show, and not merely words. I vaguely imagined that this remembered atmosphere of Gramercy Park would somehow still be there, and that I would somehow find it, forgetting that my father had then been dead about forty years.

Dr. McGoffin had been right.

I found intelligent audiences and charming people. Often, in the cities where I went to speak to them, other Societies would ask me to lecture; and besides these, I went to a number of Universities, Museums, Schools, and so forth.

Before leaving Greece, I had written down four lectures: one called "The Delphic Idea", another "Greek Music and Drama", another "Handicrafts", and one on Athletics. At first I read one or another of these papers according to what had been asked of me beforehand. But gradually I became weary of what I had written, and also less afraid of facing audiences. Once in a while I would forget about my manuscripts, and go off on some relevant explanation; and finally I abandoned them altogether, and simply talked on whatever happened to come into my head. It was fun to see the people, which one cannot do in reading; and fun to work out a technique for being heard in large halls without any effort, either for the audience, or for me.

Everywhere I had crowded halls, but all the response I ever got was the invariable group which gathers around me afterwards and always with the same words:

"Won't you please give another lecture?"

And most of my lectures were free. From one place to another, and another, I went on and on, always imagining that at the next place some one person would understand, and would ask me to stay there, not to give another lecture, but to form a committee, as my father would have done, and put the Delphic Effort on its feet. I reached the Pacific Coast, and went back again by another route, still lecturing, and arrived in New York, after about a year, without having covered my traveling expenses. Until the end I hardly saw anyone I had ever known before; and of those few, no one took any real interest in what I was saying.

On this whole trip, only two events occurred which are worth recording. At Yale University, Mr. Baker, then head of the Drama Department, asked me to stay at Yale and teach. I could have, he said, the whole time of his fifteen best students until Commencement, if I would teach them the choruses of *Prometheus Bound*, exactly as I had taught them in Athens. He wanted, he said, a model for a real Greek Chorus, and that neither he nor his students had ever understood before what a Greek Chorus is. I said that what he was asking had no artistic foundation. I would be teaching in a language which no student would understand, and in a kind of music which, perhaps, no musician in Yale would understand. The best I could do would be to produce a good class of parrots; but if those parrots taught the incoming class the following year, they would have no theoretical knowledge on which to base their teaching. The second year of his model chorus would inevitably be worse than the first, and the third year worse than the second, until finally, in the end, they would have only a caricature of one part of one Greek play, with no chance of ever applying their learning to any other play. I explained that the principles of Greek music were applicable to the English language, and that I hoped sometime to prove it; but that so far, I had never composed choruses in either English or Greek and that I did not dare to launch out in teaching.

Mr. Baker was not satisfied. The next day he sent his assistant, Mr. Alexander Dean, to try to persuade me. Mr. Dean said, quite truly, that it would be better for my Delphic Cause to have it connected with a great American University than to go off on a wild-goose lecture tour all over the country. I fully recognized this truth, but I was too conscientious to accept what he was proposing. I felt that the thing which they were seeking was, as it were, a spiritual entity within me, but not of instruction.

"Why not make the leap," they said, "and do now what you expect to do later?"

At present I feel that Mr. Baker and Mr. Dean were right. I could certainly have done something which would have made it worthwhile for Yale, and, at the same time accomplish a better thing for the Delphic Cause than my absurd lecture tour. And yet, again, do I feel this now, perhaps, only because it would be so easy for me, at present, to do what Mr. Baker was asking me to do then? I do not know.

The other event which I shall record happened before I started for the West. My dear friend Dr. Simon Flexner, Director of the Rockefeller Institute, and his wife, Helen, sister of Martha Carey Thomas, whom I had known and loved ever since the old Bryn Mawr days, took my cause to heart, and tried to help. Dr. Flexner obtained a hearing for me before the Rockefeller Foundation, and he advised me not to go alone, but to ask the support of one or two distinguished American citizens. I asked Dr. McGoffin to go with me, and he accepted. I wrote to Cambridge, to a dear old friend, Dr. Herbert Weir Smyth, a noble Aeschylean scholar, former Eliot Professor at Harvard, then Emeritus. He also accepted, and came down from Boston in a driving snow-storm. At a meeting among ourselves beforehand, it was arranged that Dr. McGoffin, as an eye-witness, should speak of the material good to Greece resulting from the Festival; and that Dr. Smyth should speak of it more generally as a classical achievement.

We were received by Mr. Applegate, who evinced a friendly interest in our mission. Dr. McGoffin began by simply describing the Festival. He spoke of the effect of the play on the audience, which was something he had never seen before. Then he spoke of the Games in the Stadium: of how Athletics had been removed from the commercial and professional basis, which is now so common, in order to become a practical ideal for everyone, including the peasants; and how, instead of one-sided excellence which is fostered today, and which often produces enlargement of the heart through over-strain of certain muscles, the Delphic Stadium had held up the true aim of Athletics, which is a harmonious development of the whole body. But he spoke more particularly about the Exhibition of Handicrafts, of how, in Greece, taste and quality of workmanship is still wide-spread. He spoke of the topography of the country, and the character of the people, which both set up a natural resistance to industrial standardization, and of the success of the Exhibition from a financial stand-point, showing that this gift of workmanship, still possessed by the Greek people, could be developed into a national means of support without injuring their spontaneous creative ability.

Dr. Smyth spoke of the humanizing effect through the centuries of the Greek language, of the literature in general, the poetry, and especially the drama. Of how it has never been replaced by any other influence which could compare with it in its ennobling effects on the human mind.

"But," he said, "its influence is waning; our strength is weakening amid a general ignorance and indifference around us: and the Delphi Festival has done more for the cause of the Classics in a single day than all the Greek professors, in all American universities, could do in twenty years."

Mr. Applegate listened very attentively and had kept us there over an hour. His expression had been sympathetic, and his few words encouraging; so that we all three came out of his office in high feather, thinking that our cause had won the day. But there had been a reef, which we had passed over so quietly that not one of us had seen or felt it, nevertheless the hull of our ship was fatally damaged. Mr. Applegate had asked me a question:

"When you say 'we'," he said, "referring to those who founded and organized the Delphic Work, whom do you mean?"

"I mean," I answered, "my husband and myself."

That was all; and none of us knew the pitfall into which I had stumbled. It would have been so easy to have given him a list of gentlemen in Athens, and to form by cable in a few hours, a committee of people who had already worked with their whole hearts for the cause we were advocating, and who would work for the rest of their lives, if it could only be started again. Or I could so easily have given him the names of Angeliki's committee of Ladies, who represented all Athens, and who had worked so remarkably and with such splendid results, and who would all have given me their names till kingdom-come without the asking.

I answered as I did as a sort of short cut, instead of explaining a long story; but I did not know, none of us did, that individual initiative is under a ban in the Rockefeller Foundation.

I went West. Months after this interview, on my return to New York, I received a letter expressing regrets that for so excellent a cause the Foundation could do nothing; it was against their policy to recognize individuals. The only activities which they could aid were those which had been founded, organized, and operated by committees or institutions.

After this I bought my passage and sailed for Paris. I was still convinced on leaving, as I had been on coming (in fact more so, because I had sensed them all along my way) that there were many individuals in America who were near me in spirit, perhaps the whole nation was near me, but there was a chasm I could not cross. It was a constantly losing struggle: to feel with my instinct so strongly the points of contact, and not to be able to express them with my eyes, my voice, to touch their hands. But, at that time, it was the height of prosperity. The crash into depression had not come yet. Everyone was happy, hopeful, self-sufficient. They could not sense the distress which was hanging like a pall, ready to fall on Europe, and to fall, also, very soon, on them.

CHAPTER 17

The Second Delphic Festival

In Paris, I simply settled down to study. I saw no hope of going ahead in any direction, so for the moment I gave up trying. One day Mr. Andonis Benakis came to call on me.

"Why do you not come back to Athens," he said, "we are all waiting for you."

I told him I had no means of going on with the work, and that it would be difficult for me to go back and do nothing.

"Come back," he said, "and we will form a guarantee committee for the second Festival."

"No," said I, "I cannot. When people give money for an objective in which they are interested, it is fair that they should have a voice in deciding how the money is to be spent. The gentlemen of your committee might have opinions different from mine concerning a drama of Aeschylus; their opinions might be better than mine; but I might not accept them."

"Come all the same," he said, "We will raise funds for the Festival, and you will direct it, with no intervention whatever on our part."

"Then," I said, "I will come."

And it was arranged that I should start very soon. He was leaving the following day. It was the late autumn in 1929. The second festival, he said, would take place in 1930.

Going back to Athens was not as easy as it seemed. It required a kind of fortitude which I had never practiced before. How could I walk in the streets of Athens without having paid my debts? The Orient Express rushed along taking me nearer to what seemed like doom. The rattle of the car-wheels seemed like the wheels of all the automobiles which had filled the roads around Delphi, and like the rattle of the thousands of plates in the Restaurant of the Festival. The whistle of the train became the siren of the passenger boats which had brought so many people to Itea. These three demons choked me with anxiety. I imagined myself accosted in the streets by creditors; or seeing them lined up around my door. As I left the train, the first radiance of the Greek sun was a kind of torture.

But in the streets I was soon accosted in a way I had not foreseen.

"Won't you take our daughter,"--- or "Won't you take our niece in your chorus? She is beautiful -- she dances -- she has a fine voice."

The days were over when I had to struggle to get a chorus, when girls would come and girls would go, and I was constantly beginning over again. For the *Prometheus Bound* I had started with the plan of having a chorus of fifty, but finally, after three years, I gave the play with only thirty, though I must have taught about a hundred. This time again I wanted fifty; but they assembled in a few days, and no one ever dropped out.

Anghelos wanted to give *The Suppliants* of Aeschylus, and I was delighted. The oldest of all existing plays, the nearest, not doubt, to the condition I was dreaming about. If the archaeologists would only dig up a play of Pherekydes, or of Pratinas, or of Thespis, I might have been better pleased, but here at least was a play where the Chorus itself was the Protagonist. There was of course an outcry. Why choose the least dramatic of all the Greek Plays? Why not do something of Euripides: the *Medea*, or *Hecuba*, or *The Trojan Women*? Professor Gilbert Murray wrote a very courteous answer to a question I sent him about something else; but in the end of it he said that he did not understand why we had chosen *The Suppliants*. It could not possibly stand up theatrically.

These opinions were right from the point of view of modern drama. But I did not think twice about them. I was extremely excited about something else: can a chorus as protagonist be, not *as* dramatic, or *as* beautiful as actors on the stage, but much more dramatic, more harmonious, more beautiful? And in my mind, of course, this question changed its context: can groups of people, nations, races, be not *as* intelligent; *as* harmonious, as their leaders are at present, but much more so?

This last sentence sounds communistic. It is not. The Soviets are not concerned with these problems. The question might be more clearly expressed as follows: did the ancient Greeks, in creating the form of a Tragic Chorus, do it consciously or not? Were they presenting a working model of a perfect State, much better than Plato's, in which social harmony is in equilibrium with individual expression, or was the fact that they did this by pure chance?

I divided my fifty girls into five groups, and gradually chose a leader for each. In one of these groups my leader realized my original vision. When I first started teaching the *Prometheus*, I had hoped that all fifty of my girls would approach the work individually, and produce her own interpretation, so that each one of the Oceanides would be a living entity, conscious of the general harmony, but conscious also, and expressive of her own soul. In feeling my way for the second play, I quickly realized that, in the fourth group, one of my Suppliants was a born leader. She had been with me the first time, but either I had not recognized her then, or, in the meantime, she had changed. This was Annetoula Kolyva,

Angeliki's sister. We went over the music together, then started working on the movements for her group: and she was so alive, so full of suggestions, that I saw I was not needed at all, that she could compose her dances, and direct her group quite well without me. From then on, I did nothing for these ten girls except teach them music. The interpretation was entirely Annetoula's.

For all five leaders I had to have people who not only could sing and dance, but who also could recite poetry properly. For this reason, the other four were not chosen from my first chorus. I had three excellent amateur actresses and one professional. Their names were Koula Kalliga, Ismene Dimakopoulou, Lela Isaia, and Anna Gallanou. They all had beautiful voices, poise and grace on the stage; and Anna, who was leader of the first group, had the power of rocks and rivers when her voice rang out in her prayer to the Earth. But none of these four had worked with me before, and had no idea how to express meaning and rhythm in movement. So only Annetoula could train her own group; and hers had a life and a vim which made them better than the four groups I trained myself. But she had the advantage of me, because I used to compose dances while I drove around in a cab from one group to another, and then I would sit down in the evening with a pencil and paper to figure out the movements of all five groups as a geometrical problem. This was somewhat difficult, because, although we all met about twice a week in the large hall of the Greek Archaeological Society, this hall was not, in fact no hall in Athens was, the right size and shape. They were all long and narrow; and I desperately needed the sized and shape of the Delphic Orchestra to rehearse in. So that until we all went up there, to the real theatre, I had no idea what the Chorus was going to look like. The first rehearsal in Delphi was, just as it had been in 1927, a revelation.

We had again asked Mr. Psachos to write the music. But I begged him this time to have a mere simple accompaniment. I should like, I said, a single flute, or an oboe whose function it would be to play introductions, and short interludes between the phrases of the chorus, which would give time for one group to retire and another to advance, and would also give the mode or key, and the pitch for the entering voices. Mr. Psachos came occasionally to my small rehearsals, but not very often. I hardly saw him during these months of preparation. He gave me new manuscripts from time to time, and that was all.

I had no trouble with the weaving the second time. The Chorus was to be dressed all alike, without embroidery. The design of the dresses was to be Egyptian, because the Suppliants came from Egypt. The stuff should have been transparent, as many Egyptian monuments lead us to infer, but this was considered immodest, so I did what was desired by the mothers of my girls, bought the threads, hired a few weavers, and set them going. I did no weaving myself.

In fact for this second festival, almost everything was taken off my hands. No running about to different ministries to be allowed to go ahead, no anxiety about any practical arrangements at all. Mr. Benakis' committee did everything. We had occasional meetings of about twenty gentlemen whom he had got together, but these meetings were a relaxation rather than a strain. There was hardly ever any discussion, never any disagreement, never any loss of time. The Rockefeller Foundation should have seen us then: they would have had all the names they wanted. In the matter also of directing the play, the committee was perfect. Only once did they intervene. They used to come quite often to my general rehearsals. On one such occasion, one member remained afterwards, and told me that the whole committee felt that I was making a grave mistake; they all disapproved of one of the people I had chosen for a very important part; they suggested another whom they considered better; would I think of it? They felt that otherwise the play would be ruined.

"The most difficult thing," I answered, "of the whole Festival, is to know, in Athens, what will stand up in Delphi. The scales are somehow different. What is heavy here is light there; and what is light here is heavy there; it is extremely difficult to know. The only way this can be done, is to somehow visualize the great rocks of the Phaedriades which dominate the theatre, and to tune one's ear at a distance to the mountain echoes and the open spaces which are there. It is not easy to do, but it is fatal if one makes a mistake. I feel that the committee is judging rightly for Athens, but wrongly for Delphi,--I will not make the change." The member went away hardly concealing his chagrin. But after the first performance of the play in Delphi, he came to me, again as spokesman for all the others:

"You had been right. How had you known?"

"I had not known, I said, I had only felt. That is all I am good for."

The Exhibition of Handicrafts was also much easier. The peasants had all *learned* to send their things without selling them beforehand. Mme. Nazou took the chief responsibility.[1] Angeliki was still directing the whole thing.

The Games again promised trouble. The same Director of Athletics in the Ministry of Education was again making promises, but not with quite such a good grace as before. One day I spoke of it to a friend who was a member of Parliament.

---

[1]　[Ed. What reads like a gnarled sentence at this point becomes clear with the deletion of two words that were inadvertently left in the text. -J.P.A.]

"Why don't you ask," he said, "for all the athletes in the army? Go to the Minister of War."

This seemed too much for me to do alone, so I asked Mr. Benakis to get the whole committee together, and ask for an interview. He did this, and we all filed into the Minister's room. Mr. Benakis started to tell about the Delphic work; but presently the Minister interrupted him: this time it was Mr. Sophoulis, whom I had never seen before.

"The Army knows," he said, "what Anghelos and Eva Sikelianos have done for Greece. She had only to appoint a time with me, and come to tell me what she wants."

I was both embarrassed and overjoyed. Again the army! Why?

When I went to see him there was nothing he did not give. Athletes, soldiers, tents, nourishment, traveling expenses, everything for a month! The army took over the whole responsibility of the Stadium. As I was leaving the Minister's office he said to me:

"Wouldn't you like some horses?"

"Yes," said I, "I would."

"I will send you," he said, "fifty good ones."

And he did.

About two months before the Festival, Mr. Benakis came one day to see me, and said that he felt that the Festival should be postponed until the following year.

"It has all been too hurried," he said. "There has been no time for propaganda abroad; in fact, it has hardly been announced. The travel bureaus are interested, but they can do nothing; they need at least a year ahead. And then," he went on, "we could have boats come in to Itea, perhaps one from each country; and, with the excellent press notices of the first Festival, it would be a sure thing to make the second not only pay for itself, but come out with considerable surplus."

I knew that this was all true. But I was on the wave of accomplishment. It was extremely fascinating to have all Athens working feverishly for a given date. Everyone was keyed up. Could I let them down, and expect to find the same conditions again? I felt sure of the play then; and that kind of sureness seemed to me too fragile a thing to gamble with. The long dreary year in America made what I actually had in Athens seem very precious. Would all these people ever be the same again? Would I myself be the same? I could not tell. But I chose what seemed from the artistic point of view the least danger. I told Mr. Benakis that I would rather not put it off. The result of this was that the Guarantee Committee, after three series, of three days each, (at the first Festival we had had only three days in all) came off with a very small deficit. Our own remained the same as before.

When the time was quite near, Mr. Benakis said he was very anxious to have *Prometheus Bound* repeated. Everyone wanted to see it again, he said, and it would be better to have two plays instead of one. I myself dislike repetitions. I have no longer any feeling for a play I have done before, unless I could begin over again with another interpretation: new costumes, new music, everything different. This is because in presenting a play, one learns a great deal; and it is exasperating not to be able to apply it. We did it, however, as nearly as possible as it had been before, except for the stage-setting which was done this time by the architect, Mr. Kontoleon, who made a very simple, stylized design, appropriate for both plays. Presently it turned out that Mr. Psachos had an orchestral score for the new play, and again wanted a hidden orchestra.

I was horrified.

His music was good. The whole chorus knew it perfectly. They needed nothing but a few flute notes to give them the key. Why spoil a thing which was clean, with vague orchestral murmurs? However, I was still, psychologically, if not actually any more, the pupil of Professor Psachos. Again I accepted what he wanted. Mr. Kontoleon believed that, with certain acoustical appliances, the difficulties we had experienced before could be avoided. But, at the first rehearsal in Delphi, we were in the same situation we had been in before, only worse. Mr. Oikonomides, who was again leading, could hear nothing. For the *Prometheus* we went through the same dangerous pantomime as before, and I let it go at that. But for *The Suppliants*, which was a larger chorus, with much more complicated movements, the result was pandemonium. Nobody could get in time with anyone else. Evidently the Greek Theatre was not to be bamboozled into accepting modern methods. I was disgusted, and very anxious, with everything going [w]rong[2], but I was also secretly delighted. Perhaps I could now move a step toward my own conception of the theatre.

After this first trial I took Mr. Oikonomides aside. Could he arrange the score for two harps and a few wood-winds, leave out all the other instruments, and bring these few out to the edge of the horse-shoe where he could see, and hear the chorus, and follow them in what they were used to doing? Mr. Oikonomides was delighted. He arranged the score that night; and the next day we placed his little band right under the parapet of the auditorium, exactly in the centre, and they could be seen only by the first two or three rows of spectators. We started rehearsing in the early morning to avoid the great heat; and from the first moment it was perfect. Everyone felt free and happy; and we had almost finished the play when Mr.

---

[2][Ed. 'Strong' in the original. -J.P.A.]

Psachos arrived. When he understood what we had one, he refused absolutely to admit the change. He was rather angry. But so was I. I said that if he insisted on his hidden orchestra I would give up the play, and the whole Festival, rather than ruin his work and mine. He turned on his heel without another word, and left the theatre.

I have never seen him since.

It was, I think, this complete freedom of everybody who was in it which made *The Suppliants* so remarkable. Mr. Oikonomides sat there, leading his little orchestra, following the sometimes erratic tempo of the girls with a smile on his face. He had been cooped up in a terrible dungeon, and now he was in the daylight, and could see the play. I had not wanted so many instruments, but at least I had gotten rid of the strings; and, above all, the girls were free and joyous because they were rid of the bug-bear of a hidden orchestra. There was no constraint; and the play seemed to move, as it were, by itself, organically. I think, if I ever had to produce *The Suppliants* again, I would not mind doing it exactly as it was then. Only, perhaps, I would then have just a single flute, on the stage, as part of the chorus. That would at last be right.[3]

While we were still in Athens, Mario Meunier had been the first of the French critics to arrive. He saw rehearsals there and rehearsals in Delphi, and all four performances. He must have seen the play about twenty times. At the last performance for the peasants, in the packed theatre, with all the mountain behind black with people, tense and silent, he was sitting next to me. Suddenly in the middle of the play, I realized that he was sobbing. I looked, and his face was wet with tears.

"What's the matter, Mario?" I said.

"I shall never see *The Suppliants* again," he answered.

Gabriel Boissy, with most of our old friends, had arrived. And what is one to say about these critics? They really were not critics in the usual sense. They told us our faults, but they did it in a spirit which was not critical at all. It was almost as if they had forgotten their function, and had become visionaries like ourselves. And one wonders: Was this extraordinary response, this almost apostolic mission of the Press, in regard to Delphi, due to the fact that we ourselves were ultimately concerned with the play? It was not an end in itself, but an instrument, used consciously, to reach a goal infinitely beyond. Of course, in

---

[3] Right at least for that play. But other plays need other instruments. Or again, one might have two flutes, changing of course the arrangement of the chorus of an antiphonal effect; or one might have flutes, one for each group. But in all cases, the flute or oboe, or any instrument used, should be on the stage, and active, a leader of its own group. Therefore other capacities are required in a Greek play from those which flute-players now possess. They should also be good dancers.

the meantime, many had become familiar with the Delphic Plan through Anghelos' writings, his speeches, his correspondence. When they all arrived this time it was clear that they had not come only for the play; it was as if they understood the ultimate object, and as if their hearts were fired, as ours were, to reach beyond the immediate phenomenon which was the play. And, as a matter of fact, they did reach beyond.

During the preparation, Anghelos and I had been deeply concerned because we could do nothing to advance the founding of the Delphic University. We had hoped to bring from many countries,--and by that time we knew better who they were, "non-attached," the men-of-good-will, the "Overseers", the *Epoptai*, to form Summer Schools every year (connected with local Greek Games and exhibitions, and with a Festival every three years) which, little by little, would have formed a permanent Nucleus, a first bulwark against dogmatism and fanaticism all over the world. We were not able to do this. The committee was not interested in anything but the Festival. This was not their fault. They had not undertaken to do anything else. But owing to this limitation, we were surprised to find that, in spite of this, the objective itself seemed to be moving. The play was no longer the main subject of discussion, as it had been the first time, (although undoubtedly the second play was better than the first) but everyone was talking about the Delphic Idea. It seemed to have a life of its own. The intellectuals who were there gathered together, round the large table in Anghelos' study, and drew up resolutions concerning the advance of the whole Delphic Plan. It was as if the seed sown at the first Festival had really grown out of the earth, and blossomed by itself.

Was it on account of this that the future shaped itself as it did? In Athens everyone was full of plans,--but I was soon disillusioned. The Minister of Education said to me:

"Why are you not pleased; why do you hesitate? You have the Government back of you. We will do anything you suggest to make the Festival permanent, but we cannot tolerate what you call a spiritual centre. You will have to separate the two things."

I told him that the outer success of the Festival, in which he was interested, had an inner reason; that I never could have directed the plays as I had unless something beyond the plays had kept me going; that what he was asking for would soon degenerate into a sort of commercial *Oberammergau* which did not interest me in the least; and that the mere fact that he was forbidding us to form an Educational Centre made it seem as if one side of the Delphic Plan had advanced in disproportion to the other side, and as if we were then called upon, in order to save the Plan at all, to let the Play wait until it would no longer be in danger of being reduced to a mere show.

"In short," and I ended my speech, "if I do not separate these two things, what are your going to do? I am not a ballet-master."

Anghelos and I went together to see Mr. Benakis. He repeated almost verbally what the minister had said: The Committee was back of us; they were anxious to go on; we had all the elements to make the third Festival a financial success; we could pay the remaining debts of the first Festival, and all of us would have profits instead of deficits. We knew this, but we suggested our original reason for undertaking to organize the thing at all. We wanted to found a Spiritual University, and make Delphi worthy of its great tradition. Would the Committee help?

At the mention of our ultimate goal Mr. Benakis became quite angry. He would not hear of it. He said we must separate these things. So we thanked him for what he had done, and took our leave.

We were struggling again, as we had after the first Festival, for the completion of the Delphic Plan. The performance of great drama had done its work and done it well. Again it had set moving the spirit of Upward Panic. But the artistic success of the second Festival, much greater than it had been the first time, made the next Delphic step more than ever important. The very insistence of the Greek Government, and of our patrons in Athens, that we continue the play for its own sake showed clearly enough that the Means was in danger of becoming an End. The time had come when the Delphic work had either to stop, or be debased.

There were one or two more events connected with the second Festival which I shall record. Things had quieted down. I was living in a little suburban house with a large garden. Life was peaceful. One day a knock at the garden gate: it was an officer who had been sent down from Thrace, twenty-five hours journey, by General Vlachos, Commander-in-Chief of the Greek army on the borders of Thrace and Macedonia. Would we come up to Thrace? Would we lend all the equipment of the Delphic Stadium? And would Anghelos speak to the officers of the border forces of Greece? The army wished to institute games in our honour.

Again the army! And, as before, with complete spontaneity. We did not know General Vlachos, nor the officer who had been sent to invite us. What, for them was this unpredictable, irrelevant attraction of an impetus which seemed, on the surface, contradictory to their very reason for living? Delphi is engaged in an effort to make peoples see each other, cross national borders, with love in their eyes. The army is dedicated to the propagation of fear and distrust, to constant practice in the efficacy of destruction. Nevertheless, from the very beginning, the army was the only organized unit in Greece which responded with lightning rapidity to the Delphic Idea. It was as if it were already part of their inner consciousness, it was like love at first sight. They never questioned, they never considered pros and cons, they simply acted. This action was so spontaneous, so impersonal, and from so many different quarters, that one is tempted to seek for reasons beyond the phenomenon. Perhaps it is this: All men in the military profession think differently about death from almost all other men. Death is to them not a thing to be avoided, or warded off as long as possible, but a thing to be instantly accepted, even sought after at given moments. Violent death might almost be called their object in life; at all events, it is always a contingency in their inner consciousness. This being so, they are less prone than others to become entangled in little considerations, and are, in a way, "unattached," because they have transferred their attachment from personal advantages to a larger unit which is the "country"; and although this unit is still too small, it is nevertheless an ideal, for which members of the army are living regardless of death. This makes them potentially eligible for a larger "non-attachment".

Moreover, military men who have had the experience of war, and many of those who have not, have usually had enough of it. They are probably the most absolutely tender people in the world whenever they have a chance to give their tenderness free play; that is to say, whenever their duty and their dignity do not stand in the way of it. But though duty and dignity are both minor virtues, they are still virtues, and they fit a man better for passing on to the major virtues than no virtue at all. So far, what has been said is true, probably, of the military men of all civilized countries. But, in Greece, there is another characteristic, relevant here, which is probably unique.

In the Oxford Dictionary, the word "psychiatry," is defined as the treatment of mental disease. Will it ever become the treatment of mental health; or rather, will someone invent a new science, and a new word, and call it perhaps "psychohygeia", a search for the innate health, not so much of individuals (that is already being followed, in a way, by certain quasi-religious sects) but rather the search for subconscious health and intelligence in nations? In regard to Greece, this would be a particularly interesting study. In the present context what concerns us is the fundamental lack of fanaticism of the Greek people. I do not know whether this has ever been studied, or even observed, but it is a significant asset for the world in general, which might be put to better uses.

The religion of Apollo (by which I mean the history of the Delphic Sanctuary) is the only one in the history of Europe which was completely innocent of military aggression, and also of domineering priest-craft; and it surpassed the non-fanaticism of India in being positively educational all along the line, and definitely seeking for world unity beyond national boundaries. The Greek Orthodox Church, also, has been, and is, more free than other Christian churches from narrow fanaticism. One can go today into an Orthodox monastery during lent, when all the monks are fasting, and the abbot will ask, soon after his first greetings: "Are you fasting?" If one says, "Yes," then one eats what the others are eating; but if one says, "No," why, then he will go out and order a chicken to be killed, or, if one is with a party, he may order a lamb to be killed for his guests. In any case, there is never a trace of disapproval, or of the "I am holier than thou" sort of thing; and it is true all along the line.

The Greeks are not fanatical: they are far too intelligent (another sub-conscious characteristic which might be studied) and if, on the surface, they occasionally seem to take sides somewhat violently, it is probably not more than skin deep. They are easily brought back to mental balance by their own striking gift of irony, which was invented by themselves many centuries ago, which is still in their blood, and has often led them to disaster, but more often has brought them back, or kept them balanced, in a keen estimate of the world around them. But there is a point where irony ends in the Greek character: Give them an objective which satisfies their intelligence, and then their enthusiasm, courage, and their loyalty come to the front: and this is a combination which is enduring and unshakable. In short, the Greek people have a few subconscious Apollonian characteristics, the most significant being their unusual ease in understanding abstract concepts about human solidarity.

This, considered along-side of the scattered roots of Greek culture among European and American civilization, (which make Greece a sort of mutual possession, or common hearth among warring, or potentially warring nations) leads one to feel that Greece, today, comes nearer than any other country to being something more than itself. That is to say, that to be a nationalist in Greece binds one, almost irrevocably, to being also a super-nationalist. It was this super-nationalism of the Delphic Effort which made the officers of the Greek Army immediately feel at home, and it was the more interesting because, on their part, it was entirely unconscious. As military men, their acceptance of death as a constant contingency had already separated them from small personal ambitions, and made them attached to Greece as their only ideal. But something sub-conscious in themselves, which may have been very powerful, connected Greece with something beyond Greece. They instantly recognized the Delphic Effort as being profoundly Greek. There was nothing in it which was contrary to their duty, or to their dignity: their long-suppressed kindness had a free hand. It was as if they had found their own. They did not know that super-nationality is a profoundly Greek characteristic which once had been consciously developed, and might be again (and this was the subject of Anghelos' speech to all of the officers of Thrace and Macedonia who had been ordered to attend) and that this is today one of the things which makes Greece worth fighting for, and worth dying for.

The following year the same thing occurred again. A knock at my garden door; another Greek officer sent from Thrace as before, only by another Commander-in-Chief, whom, this time also, we did not know. Again the Greek army! Would we again come to Thrace? Would we lend the equipment of the Delphic Stadium?

"But this time," the Lieutenant said, "it is not only a few army officers who want it. This time the whole people of Thrace are waiting for you."

Would we therefore, beside the athletic games of the year before, also give a play? They were asking, in short, for a repetition of the Delphic Festival on the borders of Thrace.

Anghelos was standing silent during this request. He was looking at a little picture which was on my desk. It was the beautiful vase in Berlin, with Orpheus among the Thracians. He said nothing during my answer: I could not prepare a play so quickly, I was saying, and many other such excuses. Suddenly Anghelos looked up: If they would give him a week's time, he thought he could give us a play which would not be so difficult for me to produce as an ancient tragedy. During those few moments, the words of the Lieutenant were resounding in his consciousness.

"The people of Thrace are waiting for you."

Thrace, the home of Orpheus! Thrace, the border of Greece! The land where someday the Greek people would again battle with their neighbors in destruction, or, somehow, reach beyond destruction into love. A Festival in Thrace, wished for by the officers of the army, and *the whole people*, he had said, of *Thrace*!

The result of this was that, in six mornings, Anghelos wrote *The Last Orphic Dithyramb*, or, *The Dithyramb of the Rose*. Circumstances prevented our presenting it in Thrace, or even going there. But if the whole Delphic Effort had accomplished nothing else up to now, or, if it never accomplishes anything further in the future, this poem is enough.

In 1933, Greece, like other countries, was making an effort to increase the sale of home-products at home, and also abroad if possible; in short, to increase exported, and reduce imported goods. A committee was formed in Athens to further this purpose, and I was asked to join it. At the first meeting there were quite a number of men, and a few women, active and distinguished in the social life of Athens. It soon became clear, when they started talking, that their effort was centered around the belief that, to become commercially successful, the "backward" countries, of which Greece was supposed to be one, should imitate modern industrial methods as quickly as possible. I suggested that the markets of the world are glutted with factory products which tend, everywhere, to be similar to each other, and that in most countries supply exceeds demand, which creates a wide-spread problem of unemployment: therefore why burden Greece with a kind of distress from which it is almost free? But also that even if this problem of unemployment should, in one way or another, be universally solved, the situation in Greece would still remain unsatisfactory. In Greece, we have certain assets which do not exist in other countries, and the propaganda in which the committee was then engaged would go far to destroy its best chances for commercial success. On the one hand it is a country whose history, climate, topography and archaeological remains attract a class of tourists who are apt to be the pick of intelligent travelers. On the other hand, Greece is still a nation of craftsmen, capable of producing a great variety of objects which cannot be made in other places, and which intelligent travelers like to buy. This was triumphantly demonstrated at both Festivals. But to gradually force the Greek people, who are highly individualized, to become a nondescript hoard of factory workers, would, in the end, destroy the local and human spirit which Greece still possesses, leaving nothing but a few ancient ruins for strangers to see, and destroy at the same time the present capacity of the Greek people to produce objects which these same strangers like to buy. The policy they were advocating would throw a great quantity of commerce into foreign hands; many things which the peasants now make for themselves or do without, and which Greece cannot manufacture so cheaply, would be sold by foreign merchants, with a considerable loss of Greek capital. We cannot compete with these foreign countries on their own ground. But also, they cannot compete with us on our ground. Why not leave to them their great quantity of good; and leave them their social problems to settle as best they can, according to any one of many cure-alls now advocated? But we do not need these cures, any more than a man with a headache needs to have his leg amputated. And why not invite all these nations to come and see our QUALITY in work, and also our freedom from "mass psychology"?

I suggested, as a good beginning, that the committee employ a few spinners and weavers to make stuff: linen and silk for the summer, wool for the winter: that they themselves start wearing truly Greek products, first in the street, and then in their houses, and that they demonstrate, to themselves and to others, that these materials are more comfortable, more lasting, more easily washed and more beautiful than anything any factory can produce. In short, I suggested that they use their social position to make better things the fashion instead of worse, and I tried to show that in the matter of quality, for which there is still a demand in the world, Greece could soon have a monopoly which it would take any other country some time to rival.

But I was talking to deaf ears. The only result of this effort was that (with money which, according to my suggestion, would have been spent in building a few hand-looms, and in employing a few spinners and weavers to produce a stock of good materials) the committee ordered and installed an electric sign, so huge that it covered the whole side of the beautiful hill of Lycabettos: "BUY GREEK PRODUCTS". And it flared every night, effectively changing Athens into Broadway.

Perhaps the ugliness, actually and ethically, of this electric sign was one of the reasons which made my thoughts again turn to New York. But there was also in my mind the same obsession, then about six years old, of rattling plates, and wheels and steamboat whistles. Perhaps, after all, not by lectures, or appeals to individuals, but just by myself, I could find a way to start the Delphic work again. Anyway, I could try.

CHAPTER 18

America

Before leaving Athens I received a request for an interview from an American about whom I knew nothing. He showed me an announcement for the coming season of the "Greek Theatre, Griffith Park, Los Angeles", and pointed out his own name: "Ed. Perkins, Managing Director". He had come to Athens to engage some Greek singer for his Season, and, while visiting the Acropolis, he had seen a great crowd of people in the street below, all moving in the same direction: his curiosity aroused to know where they were going, he had come down from the Acropolis and followed them round a turn in the road. There he saw great throngs of people sitting along the slopes of a hill which flung out two arms, embracing at its base a round wooden stage. Evidently something was preparing which all these people were waiting for; so he waited too: and presently he saw a performance which I was directing of *The Dithyramb of the Rose*, the play which Anghelos had written for Thrace.

The way this performance came about was as follows: During the great inroad of refugees who fled from Russia and Turkey in the years 1922 and 1923 there arose for Greece an overwhelming problem of housing nearly half again the actual population of the country. One result of this difficult crisis was that settlements of minute houses appeared almost overnight on some of the finest archaeological sites in and near Athens. I had watched this process with some concern on the near side of the Acropolis, but this concern became active anxiety when I saw these encroachments reaching into a place on which I had long had my eye as part of a future plan of my own for Athens.

As the danger of its permanent loss was becoming acute, I went one day to the Archaeological Department of the Ministry of Education and begged certain members to come with me and look it over. On the way they agreed with me that Athens, where great drama was born, had now no proper place where an ancient tragedy could be performed. In the great Theatre of Dionysos the archaeologists themselves forbade any assembling of people, and rightly, because the ruined seats are no longer safe for such usage; and the Theatre of Herodes Atticus, being Roman, is inappropriate for the production of a Greek play. On arriving at my goal I showed them that this slope on the hill of Philopappos is even more ideally situated than the Theatre of Dionysos itself, because the ancients, anxious no doubt to be on the very slope of the Acropolis, chose a place where only the back of the theatre is protected by the wall of the citadel, whereas, in my hollow, a theatre could be so built that the mountain would embrace in on three sides, while on the fourth side there would be a view similar to that from the ancient theatre, and that, in relation to the sun, this emplacement would also be the same.

I showed them the refugee houses which had been built recently, and referred to the expense for the State which would be involved in removing a far greater number of these later on; whereas, if a law were passed at once dedicating this site to the erection of a theatre, this danger would be averted. The place would then continue as it already was, a public park; and eventually, when the time came, there would be nothing to prevent the building of a new Theatre for Athens, which should be a reproduction of the great Theatre of Epidaurus, whose ruins have never been degraded by various Roman adaptations.

Of course, funds for such a plan would not be immediately available, but if the preservation of the site were once assured, we might calculate afterwards the cost of a theatre for an audience of fifteen, or twenty, or a hundred thousand people, and ask for contributions from all over the world which would each cover the building-cost of one seat or more, and allow to each contributor the honour of having his name and country of origin carved in beautiful archaic letters, which would form decorative lines of inscriptions around the base of each row of seats, with lettering similar to that on the Cyclopean Wall supporting the terrace of the Temple of Apollo along the Sacred Way in Delphi.

The archaeologists agreed to this in a general way, and saw the necessity of immediate action in regard to saving the site from further encroachments. So they asked me, in order to draw the attention of the general public to this necessity, to give a play there, and thus to demonstrate the beauty of the site, its naturally fine acoustics, etc.

I chose *The Dithyramb of the Rose* which I had longed to do ever since circumstances had prevented our performance in Thrace. For the play I built a round dithyrambic stage of wood; and for this audience, pillows, and that was all. Over fifty thousand people saw this performance; and, among others, the tourist whom I have mentioned. He sought me out afterwards, full of enthusiasm about the play which he had seen by chance. He seemed in fact extremely excited about it, and immediately proposed that I come to California to found a school of Greek Drama. This proposal suited me well enough, as I had already secretly decided to return to America, and I preferred to have some definite goal on arriving there. Mr. Perkins offered to draw up a contract with me, which I accepted, and he wrote it out one day in the lobby of the Grande Bretagne, where we both signed it. After that he was returning to America, and asked me to follow on as soon as possible, letting him know the date of my sailing, so that he could have someone meet me on the dock.

Before going he begged me to lend him some of my press-books, because it would be necessary, he said, to have them when he arrived in order to start things going. He was insistent about this, and finally I let him have them, and off he went.

Not long after this I also left Athens for the reason which I stated above, and, about ten days before starting, I sent a cable to Mr. Perkins announcing the name of my ship, and the date of my arrival in New York. I expected to receive an O.K. on this before sailing, but nothing came. Arriving in New York I looked for some person on the dock to meet me, as had been promised, but there was no one there. Only Kitty Heyman, who had happened to hear that I was coming, had graciously come down to greet me. There was also no word for me at the address I had given. I sent a telegram to California and waited over a week for an answer which finally came by mail, in which Mr. Perkins explained why the school could not begin immediately. I consulted a lawyer, only to find out, of course, that the contract I had signed was worthless. From that day to this, that is, for about eight years, I have nothing from Mr. Perkins. And he still has my press-book.

So there I was in America for the third time since I had first settled in Greece. During my first trip I had been married. My second was my lecture tour, and from that I had returned with mixed impressions. I had realized, on the one hand, that if many people had heard me speak, they were drawn to my lectures more by curiosity than by any active interest, and that no spontaneous sign of collaboration had been given me; but on the other hand, I had left with a lasting feeling that true understanding of my objective was just around the corner and that I simply had missed getting in touch with it. This third time after the crumbling of the California contract, I had no plans at all. I had nothing but the knowledge that after all I am American, and that most certainly the work I had done, and the ultimate vision of the work's function in the world were of the very essence of American idealism.

Over a quarter of a century had passed since the days on Kopanas when the Delphic Idea had become for me a central pivot which gradually drew all other manifestations of life into its orbit. In the meantime, in 1927 and 1930, this Idea had become, in part, a reality outside of my consciousness. Many currents had come together, and their meeting had formed a spring of clear water where one nation could quench its thirst. Clear currents from other nations also were flowing towards it, to add volume and power to the vein which had been opened. It seemed that together they could quench the old thirst of the world: Among Peoples let there be Peace.

But only a part of the Delphic Idea had become a reality. The more important part, which this beginning was to lead to, had lagged behind our artistic achievement. The founding of a Neutral Centre, outside of politics, where non-fanatical education could build first a watch-tower, and finally a University, using Science and Art as its medium to guide men toward the realization of the three human ideals: Education, Economy, Justice: for this we had started the work, and for this we had stopped it.

Three points we had gained with our three-sided program. It was certain that the Drama, the Athletics and the Handicrafts in Delphi had all three proved their efficacy as means to the given end. In the history of the modern stage, no single performance of a play had ever awakened such enthusiasm in so many places: and none had been so widely accepted as a means to guide a nation, and perhaps the world, to a realization of its own highest hopes and beliefs. The Athletic Contests had turned this activity back into its original and proper channel; not a few professional athletes, but a nation of individuals with body and soul balanced in beauty and goodness. And the Economic aspect of the work had also won its spurs. Concerning this last, I will cite the opinion of Mr. Maximos, formerly Director of the National Bank of Greece, and at that time Minister of Finance. Mr. Maximos said to me just before my departure for America:

"Concerning the dramatic performances, that is not my specialty, and I cannot speak with authority; but as a financier, I consider the Delphic work the most important thing in Greece; it is perhaps the only thing which could balance the Greek budget."

Here were facts, here were deeds. But to awaken a tourist interest in Greece, and stop at that, or even to bring the peasants from dire poverty into plenty, seemed a poor goal to work for when at any border land of any nation fear and terror alone are alive. What did Art matter, and what did ease and plenty matter for Greece or for any nation when, after all, the chief objective for everyone of us is to murder or be murdered? Before starting the work in 1925, Anghelos had made it perfectly clear that the Festival was not an end in itself, but a means to an end.

If we had proved that great tragedy can still fulfil its original function, which was to lift men's consciousness above their petty discords, purify them, as Aristotle said; if we had shown that it can still make men spiritually clean toward each other; and if we had made one nation conscious of its own creative power all along the line, this advance must not become an end in itself, but must be made a stepping-stone on the mountain whose many paths lead to one summit: to Charity, which is love. It was on this rock that we struggled and fell.

Greece must not use its ruins only for tourists; its intelligence and its dexterity only for money; its art only for art's sake; but these values, once rediscovered, must instantly be used for the greater goal: the spiritual unity of the human race. We believed, and still believe that the number of those who are with us in heart is great: great enough to conquer the monstrous Python that has us all now in its coils. Why are they silent? Why have these deeds been fruitless?

During and after the last Delphic performances, my vision of Greek drama took another turn. In the *Prometheus Bound* and in *The Suppliants*, I had directed two plays with choruses with women. This, by the mere force of events, led me to imagine what a Greek play would be like with a chorus of men. I had succeeded in making my Oceanides and my Suppliants the vital centre of the play, in fact the protagonist. This inevitably led me beyond itself toward a greater possibility. I knew that those plays had been only suggestions of what might be. My girls had been noble and beautiful, but they themselves would also feel that they could be still better, and the road toward this goal of "still better", both for men and women, seemed then to point another way. The beauty and magnificence of men's voices, the power and dignity of their gestures, became an obsession. I felt that with a chorus of men I could really produce a Greek play.

Arriving in America again I was weaned from expecting help for my main objective from any individual or any institution. Or not quite that, because I still felt sure that there are in America people who would help the Delphic work if they knew about it, and institutions, too. But I was entirely weaned from the idea that I myself could do anything about it. So one of my hopes in coming again was to get a chorus of men, and give the greatest of peace plays: *The Persians* of Aeschylus. My problem was to get fifty men together and teach the chorus, that good actors would want to be in it. I thought of college settlements where I knew that they had classes of drama. Could I not, in one of these places get a group together? I tried several. But in each I found that the individuals who came to my classes were never twice the same. I gave my first lesson over again for new faces each time I went. They seemed to be a moving population, almost like people in the street. I thought of Summer Schools in colleges, and several of these invited me to come and teach. But through correspondence I learned that these also harbour a moving population: three weeks for one group, and then a new group for three weeks. There seemed to be no permanence in teaching the poor.

After several efforts of this kind I put aside my hope of getting a group of men, and

I accepted an invitation from Smith College to direct their Senior Class play. I chose *The Bacchae* of Euripides, which, the following year, I also gave at Bryn Mawr. Each of these experiences was pleasant as a pastime, but unsatisfactory as a play. In neither of these colleges do they give credit for work in the drama, therefore any time given to the play is stolen by the students from the all-important objective of acquiring a degree. It is wonderful, under such circumstances, that even a scratch performance of such a play as *The Bacchae* can be accomplished. Nevertheless, such an effort is demoralizing. It puts the drama on the level of "recreation" in the modern sense, whereas it should, and could be, Re-Creation.

After this I heard of the foundation of the Federal Theatre. Here, I thought, will be an opportunity to obtain a chorus of men. Blanche Yurka urged me to try it; and she arranged a meeting with the Director of the New York branch of the W.P.A. Theatre. Mr. Barbour asked me to come on the "Project" and found a department of Greek drama. I told him I would need fifty men for my chorus, five actors, and one actress; also threads for my loom in order to weave the costumes, and two weavers whom I would train myself. That was all. Mr. Barbour's answer was not once encouraging: he himself, he said, was sitting on a keg of dynamite and did not know when it would blow up. But anyway he asked me to try, and I decided to risk it. After a long wait, a group of fifteen men were assigned to me. These were tap-dancers, a few vaudeville stars, circus riders, etc., several of them were sick, and not a few were drunk. They were all indignant, in fact in a state of revolt at having been put in a Greek play. They considered it girlish, and beneath their dignity. The situation was so bad that it was interesting. If these people could be convinced, anybody could.

So there I stayed and worked with these furious human derelicts. Other indignant tap-dancers and actors were gradually added to my group, but by that time the first ones had become my partisans, and made fun of the impotent rage of the newcomers. After some months there were about forty men who were singing and dancing simultaneously all five of the great choruses of *The Persians*. The sound of them was magnificent, and the looks of them was rather good considering that many were half decrepit. As soon as the thing got going they forgot all about their fury, and finally became equally violent in their effort to keep the group together whenever the unpredictable policies of the Federal Theatre tended to break it apart. This was a satisfaction. But it was the only one which this institution vouchsafed me.

During all this time there was no sign of life from the heads of the Federal Theatre. I frequently wrote letters; so did the group, with all their signatures. We asked for an audition. But the General Director of the whole Project in Washington never came, and the Director of the New York section never came. The only word I had from Mr. Barbour about this play was a message through some subordinate that he would not sanction the purchase of threads for the weaving of the costumes. It was, I was told, too expensive. (Five hundred dollars was to have been the cost of costuming a whole Greek tragedy). But, at the very time of my application, the Federal Theatre was mounting another play, just opposite to where I was rehearsing. The cost of this play was a hundred thousand dollars, so the story went, and the name of it was *Horse Eats Horse*. So the refusal to buy my threads was all the notice *The Persians* ever received after more than nine months of work.

About a month before Christmas, a hurry call came to me from one of the sub-directors; would I write and teach the music for a Christmas play? They wanted certain psalms of David, a few passages from the prophets, and a few from the New Testament. This I found interesting, because it gave me an opportunity to apply the Greek method in music to a religious context. I wrote a number of things very quickly, and started to teach them immediately. Before Christmas they were ready, and sounded well. But in the meantime there had been some difficulty with the author of this play, and the whole thing was called off. The directors also never heard my Christmas music.

After that, another sub-director came one day, and took away my best singers: "borrowed them" as the phrase was, "for a few days". I never saw them again. This same sub-director gave me a few more tap-dancers, and thought I ought to be satisfied.

I did not have the courage to start teaching the great Aeschylean choruses all over again, especially as there was no way of weaving the proper costumes; so I smashed *The Persians* which no one had seen, and started to direct a comedy of Aristophanes. This also interested me, because it was an opportunity to apply the Greek method in music to a context which was very gay. I decided to do this play with modern clothes, as this seemed within the capacity of the Federal Theatre; and then, by changing a few proper names, and also a few allusions, to modern equivalents, the thing became extremely funny, and amazingly up-to-date. The music had jigs, drinking songs, and so forth, which were fun to write. This comedy fell quickly into shape, and again I asked for an audition. This time the directors of the Federal Theatre responded, from Washington and from New York. On different days they both saw a "run through", and both expressed enthusiastic approval, with promises of collaboration in all details which needed their help.

Everything seemed swinging toward realization: but it was only a few days after this that I received my dismissal from the Federal Theatre, with no reason given. I have never understood why they asked me to come into it; why, having me in it, they never came to see the tragedy I had prepared, not the Christmas play they had asked for; why they finally came to see my comedy and like it, but dismissed me immediately after. It seemed a year and a half in which I had been dealing with situations that had no connection with ordinary logic, and among people pulled this way and that by invisible strings, and all of them afraid of each other. Time lost: and yet not lost: for my debt to the Federal Theatre is great. Before going into it I had dreamed of a chorus of men, without being sure that I myself could direct it. But that first day of my encounter with a furious group who were against me, and all the months that followed, with new antagonists often struggling in, forced me to create a technique which made even tap-dancers keep their feet quiet. It gave me certainty instead of a vision of what a Greek Chorus can be.

Soon afterwards, this certainty developed into a plan. My greatest difficulty in the Federal Theatre, but also with the women's choruses I had trained before, was a general disbelief in the possibility of the human organism doing more than one thing at once. It seems to be very difficult for those trained in any of the theatre arts to imagine that they could add another form of expression to the particular branch of dramatic art to which each one has been accustomed. In short, singers are afraid to dance, and dancers are afraid to sing. But there are people in the world who know how to do both, and still do it habitually. And these are the modern Greeks. Even in America, where the difficulties of competition force them into inhuman drudgery, they all met habitually in order to dance. And although many of them have now formed the habit of dancing with bands of music, there are still some who sing as they dance, just as they do in Greece. I think that they are the only men who, as a nation, are not somewhat ashamed of dancing. And their dancing has an upward swing to it, dignity and spirit, which are lacking in American dancing. These people would be proud to produce a Greek Tragedy. However, the Greeks in America are hard workers, often barely sleeping from their toil, and most of them could not give the time to produce a Greek play. A subsidy would be required to make this possible. But there are also Americans of this type, who are struggling in the daytime for a living, and afterwards at night-schools for an education. Many of these fell under the generic title of "Greeks" which is independent of time and place. Such men I hoped to get together for work on *The Persians*, and also, perhaps, on *The Peace* of Aristophanes, feeling that when a Greek tragedy and a Greek comedy were ready, they would work their own way to various American Universities: and that with such a cast of Greeks from any nation, the plays, after a tour in America, certainly would be seen in Greece: perhaps at a third Delphic Festival. Here would be a way of joining together not only nations but continents.

In the early spring of 1938 I gave a lecture for a Greek society called Philiko, and I announced my intention of teaching *The Persians* of Aeschylus to anyone who wished to come and learn. A few came, also a few personal friends of mine, but not nearly enough to found my great chorus of fifty men. I could of course go on with those few, and gradually others would have come; but this time I was doubtful about my own confidence in going ahead. All my work in the Federal Theatre has been wasted in this way, and only four people had seen it: Harl and Leo Cook, Helen Hyde and Peggy Murray.

I regretted afterwards that I had not invited a number of people to see it before I broke up my rehearsals for *The Persians*: or that I had not at least had records made of the singing: because the actual swing and grandeur of a Tragic Chorus are Dead Sea fruit when expressed in words. No one has ever seen one, and therefore no one imagines what it is really like. So there I was at the beginning again, just as if I had never directed a Greek play.

Was it this outlook that discouraged me (for all disease is a kind of discouragement), or was it the long exasperating fatigue of the Federal Theatre? Anyway, fate overtook me; and all my plans came to a standstill during a prolonged siege of double pneumonia.

CHAPTER 19

Thing-In-Itself

There are perhaps few conditions as blissful as the first stages of convalescence. One is far too weak to hold a book, too weak even to be exasperated that one cannot hold a pencil and record the thoughts that pass so smoothly through one's brain. These thoughts centre round recent occurrences, but they also rest easily on distant ones, so that essential correspondences are preserved, but time which had intervened between them is anticipated.

The sweep of the men's voices in *The Persians* was present. Why, I wondered, was the world so far away from the power and beauty of this kind of singing? Why are they not enthralled by it as I was the first time I heard Penelope sing? Is there any basic principle which separates their consciousness from its acceptance, and so makes their ears deaf to the sound?

At the same time, Courtlandt's voice, his voice when he was about fourteen, was speaking about music.

"It stands alone, quite cut off from all the other arts. In it we do not recognize the copy or repetition of any Idea of existence in the world. Yet it is entirely and deeply understood by man in his inmost consciousness as a perfectly universal language...It is entirely independent of the phenomenal world, could to a certain extent exist if there were no world at all, which cannot be said of the other arts...All possible efforts, excitements and manifestations of will, all that goes on the heart of man may be expressed--but always in the universal--always according to the thing-in-itself, (expressing) not the phenomenon, but the inmost soul as it were, the phenomenon without the body...The composer reveals the inner nature of the world, and expresses the deepest wisdom in the language which his reason does not understand."

Courtlandt was not quoting Schopenhauer verbally, he had not read *The World as Will and Idea* at that time; he had heard someone talking about it, probably Louis Breitner; but he was extremely excited in repeating the sense of it:

"Music is the greatest of the arts because it is the most disconnected from the phenomenal world: because it is a universal language: because the musician is directly inspired from a region beyond all human reflexion and intention, where he comes in contact with the inmost kernel which precedes all forms, where even his own reason is in abeyance."

And he concluded:

"It is therefore the most spiritual, the most powerful, the most universal of the arts."

In listening to him so many years ago, I had been sure he was right. I did not need persuasion. His own existence was enough. How, otherwise, did music pour through him with no apparent volition on his part? I was immediately a believer without ever having doubted.

But there, in the hospital, I also heard Goethe talking to Eckermann:

"A particular event becomes universal and poetic by the very circumstance that it is treated by a great poet...The poet should seize the particular; and he should, if there be anything sound in it, thus represent the Universal."

And I heard Professor Psachos talking to me:

"Greek music is subordinate to language. It has always been considered, both by the ancients and by the Orthodox Church, as having properly no independent existence. Its function is to enlarge and enhance the word, to make the greater meaning and emotion inherent in the word distinctly comprehensible in very large churches, or in the open air."

Somehow it seemed that Goethe and Psachos were saying the same thing, and that in theory they were diametrically opposed to Schopenhauer. And I remembered a passage where the latter was explicit in condemning any relation between meaning and words and music; where he maintained that because music is universal in itself all localized experiences of life, interrupting the spontaneous flow of music, are a mere intrusion:

> It must never be forgotten...that music has no direct but merely an indirect relation to them [i.e. pleasure, pain, etc.], for it never expresses the phenomenon, but only the inner nature, the in-itself of all phenomena, the will itself. It does not therefore express this or that particular and definite joy, this or that sorrow, or pain, or horror, or delight, or merriment, or peace of mind; but joy, sorrow, pain, horror, delight, merriment, peace of mind themselves, to a certain extent in the abstract, their essential nature, without accessories, and therefore without their motives. Yet we completely understand them in their extracted quintessence. Hence it arises that our imagination is so easily excited by music, and now seeks to give form to that invisible yet actively moved spirit world which speaks to us directly, and clothe it with flesh and blood, i.e., to embody it in an analogous example. This is the origin of the song with words, and finally of the opera, the text of which should therefore never forsake that subordinate position in order to make itself the chief thing and the music a mere means of expressing it, which is a great misconception and a piece of utter perversity; for music always expresses only the quintessence of life and its events, never these themselves, and therefore their differences do not always affect it. It is precisely this universality which belongs exclusively to it, together with the greatest determinateness, that gives music the high worth which it has as the panacea for all our woes. Thus, if music is too closely united to the words, and tries to form itself according to the events, it is striving to speak a language which is not its own. No one has kept so free from this mistake as Rossini; therefore his music speaks *its own language* so distinctly and purely that it requires no words, and produces its full effect when rendered by

instruments alone.[1]

This is the very antithesis of the Greek idea of music. To them poetry, the word, is the central creative power, and music exists only to convey and enlarge its meaning and its rhythm. Perhaps ancient poets often composed the poems and the melody simultaneously, but even then the word predominated. "And shall we say," asks Socrates, "that melody and rhythm depend on the word?" And the brevity of the answer precluded discussion: "Certainly."[2]

The Greeks were not afraid of the close encounter of real life and art. They felt in the word the power to exalt life to its highest expression; and for them music became the bridge uniting the poet and his hearers, uniting also all the arts in the stupendous creation of drama.

So Schopenhauer's theory is an axe which splits apart the musical worlds with an ever-widening space between them. To modern musicians the phenomena of life do actually seem unworthy of their own highest artistic achievement.

Two philosophies of life, two approaches to Art. One is the conquest of soul by denial of body; the other is the simultaneous elevation of body and soul through the intervention of spirit; that is to say, through the poet. Schopenhauer represents music as a means of drawing people toward an abstract state. All of the objects and feelings and details of life are under a ban. It is like going to church, which undoubtedly elevates the devoted to a better state while he is there, but leaves him little or nothing which connects with every-day-life when he comes out. It is a thing which touches man's life at a tangent, but can never describe the full circle of his experience. He hears it and is exalted: but at the end of church, or at the end of a concert, his life is as empty or as desolate as before. The Universal reaches out to him, or he to it, obtaining a momentary contact, as a prisoner might see the sunlight through iron bars.

So, lying motionless, without strength to move at all, I tried to formulate the relation to life of these two kinds of music. Certainly Bach, and his predecessors, and his successors,

---

[1] [Ed. See A. Schopenhauer, *The World as Will and Idea,* tr. R.B. Haldane and J. Kemp, (Garden City, N.Y. Doubleday & Co., Dolphine Books, 1961), pp. 272-3. I have restored the text of the passage by comparing it with the translation in Eva Palmer-Sikelianos' MS. Her text mentions Schopenhauer by name and gives the title of the work. Elsewhere in the MS she also gives the names of the translators, Haldane and Kemp. -J.P.A.]

[2] *Republic* IV. [Ed. I suspect this is the author's own free translation. Only the title of the Plato's work is cited in the MS. It may be that the paraphrasing is from *Republic* IV, 441e-442a: "Socrates -Does it not belong to the rational part to rule, being wise and exercising forethought in behalf of the entire soul, and to the principle of high spirit to be subject to this and its ally? -Assuredly. -Then is it not, as we said, the blending of music and gymnastics that will render them concordant, intensifying and fostering the one with fair words and teachings and relaxing and soothing and making gentle the other by harmony and rhythm? -Quite so." (Tr. Paul Shorey). -J.P.A.]

have given to the world the quintessence of life through music.[3] They have done this so often and so magnificently that no other art in modern times can be compared with their achievement. Through the development of modern harmony they have created a medium which, as Schopenhauer points out, is eminently suited to compositions expressing abstract emotions. In fact, properly, this medium cannot express anything else, and Schopenhauer's dislike of voices combined with orchestras is an exhibition of innate good taste, which seems to have been adhered to instinctively by almost all of the great composers, whose significant compositions are for instruments alone. For whether the words of operas be meaningless, as in Rossini's music, or meaningful as in Wagner's, it is all one.[4] In any case it is impossible to understand what they say. In one kind of singing there will be trills and roulades for those who care for them; and in the other kind there will be immense human effort to dominate an overwhelming accompaniment; in neither case can there be anything dramatic. The applause is always for individual performers. The emotion of an audience never has any relation to the words of a poet. There is no reason for a human voice in opera except to exalt individual talent. Schopenhauer is right.

From the point of view of modern music, Schopenhauer is right all along the line. It is as he says. The other arts are separated from music, except in opera, where nothing organic unites them; and life, that is to say life "with its accessories and motives" is an outcast from the great hall of glory where tremendous harmonies swell. How then, over against this established magnificence, shall I dare to recall the voice of a peasant woman that I heard once in a high mountain village? She was mourning for her husband who lay dead before her, and her lamentation had risen into a song. Was it an improvisation, was it as old as the Greek people? I do not know. But whatever it was, it was *her* song, *her* grief, *her* husband, *her* life destroyed, *her* children, *her* fields, *her* house abandoned. Amid verses describing all the aspects of her loss, there was the refrain, always the same: "George, my George!" In Greek the name was musical and added to the intensity of the personal distress

---

[3] The predecessors of Bach, as far as the use of polyphonic music is concerned, might trace their descent from India and Egypt and China.

[4] Wagner wrote his own librettoes - poems, one might better call them - and he wrote them before, sometimes quite a while before he started the instrumental and vocal parts of his operas; thus proving the predominance in his own mind of the meaning he wished to convey. To this extent he was right in considering his own work directly derived from Greek Drama. Schuré was also right to this extent in his estimation of the Wagnerian music drama. (*Le Drame musical* by Edouard Schuré). But both of these great men were separated from the Greek tradition by the intervention of the tempered scale, which, in their time, was firmly established. Wagner did not know, nor did Nietzsche, what Greek tragedy really was. So he fell inevitably into the fatal artistic error of combining great orchestras with human voices, and made his operas, through the very grandeur of his musical invention, an unsurpassed torment in the history of tragic art.

of the singer.

Here was a glaring instance of Schopenhauer's "utter perversity": music used to express the phenomenon, the upstart emotion of one human life. Yet this woman was doing precisely what Goethe had laid down as an axiom of great art. She seized the particular event, and, the intensity of her grief assuming for a moment the function of a poet, she actually did represent the universal agony of the world to us who were listening.

But, facing the immensity of musical achievement, my refrain kept coming back as in the woman's song on the mountain. How shall I dare to raise this incident, or any number such, to say that though music may and does represent the Universal, there is another kind of music which approaches life from another point of view, and which, through the Particular, knows how to reach the Universal?

Cutting across this question, which my mind is used to, as a sort of constant residuum which remains underneath the passage of other thoughts and events, another question suddenly faced me: Why did the Greeks reject polyphonic music? With other nations around her who were tending toward fuller instrumental expression, why did Greece stand out deliberately and aggressively against it? Why should the nation which did this be precisely the one that seems to have cared more, thought more, written more about music than any other until modern times? We know well what they lost by their rejection of musical instruments, excepting only the lyre, and of the simultaneous sounding of many notes which today is called harmony. But what did they gain? What were they trying to do in their system of education which so jealously guarded the nation against the intrusion of foreign, to them barbaric, musical forms?[5]

[The flute was an Asiatic instrument which the Greeks accepted only after considerable opposition: and, at first, only to indicate to the chorus a change of mode. The reason for their somewhat fanatical preference for the lyre is obvious: with it they could sing, whereas, with the flute, words were ousted by the thing-in-itself. This approach to the ancient quarrel between the flute and the lyre throws a new light on several ancient legends. The myth of Apollo and Marsyas, for instance, has been cited repeatedly to show the innate cruelty of the Greek nature because, after the strife for musical supremacy, (the God playing the lyre and the Phrygian the flute), Apollo, having won the victory, had Marsyas flayed alive. But Marsyas was a hairy satyr, with ears and tail of a horse, whose music and dancing were the throb of the generative powers in nature untouched by any light from the mind. He played the flute and danced because melody and rhythm are sufficient to release the whole pent-up sensual impetus of man.

If this myth could be dated, we would possess a key to the mysterious excellence of the Greeks.

---

[5] [Ed. At this point the MS showed a footnote inserted in the manner of a long textual addendum. Since the content is directly related to the main theme as a special comment on the meaning of certain Greek myths that refer to the role of musical instruments, it seemed logical to move it into the body of the text and print it within brackets. -J.P.A.].

Certainly we would know when the Dorians first dared to subjugate music to the power of the word. For Apollo's musical victory over Marsyas was, first of all, a victory of poetry over the other arts: that is, it gave to poetry the chance to use the other arts: melody, rhythm, dancing and singing, to make its own excellence completely manifest. Apollo upheld the superiority of the lyre over the flute because with that instrument he could sing: and thus express, not only the intoxicating power of movement which soon ceases in man's soul when movement is done, but also the Meaning which all could understand, and which would remain afterwards with his people, and gradually awaken them to the consciousness that they too could become creators.

Thus Apollo's victory was a commemoration of the passage from hairy crooked-limbed satyr to straight-limbed, smooth-skinned man; and also a foreshadowing, for all mankind, of the balance between intellect and emotion which he, as god of radiance, had attained. So Apollo, with his chorus of Muses, who were all the other arts, having bound them in this powerful alliance of poetry, music and dancing (capable thus of braving and eventually conquering the blindness of his own nation, and of all nations), was indeed a personification of that Sanctuary which established broad and noble institutions, drawing together men consumed with hostility toward each other, and which led them, through the order and radiance of Apollonian rhythm, to awareness of life where savagery could be surpassed.

The same meaning is evident in the Septeria, the dance of Apollo and the Python, which always opened the ancient Delphic Festivals. Here Apollo represents the Dorian mode in music, and also the lyre; whereas the Python stands for the Lydian mode and the flute.

And we also have the story of how the goddess Athena tried playing the flute, but threw it away in disgust because it puckered up her mouth.]

Here my own belief spoke out clear: the ancient Greeks were seeking consciously to produce a perfect type of man; and to them this meant, not a man highly developed in this or that particular faculty, but a man in which highly developed faculties would balance and support each other. And Plato's trend of education was the answer. The beautiful words came back to me; Athletics, mathematics, music. We have borrowed them in English, and French and German and Italian and probably in most other European languages. But what do they mean to us: and what did they mean in Greek?

A Greek athlete, in order to be crowned as victor in the Olympic Games, or in the Pythian, or the Isthmian, or the Nemean Games, had to excel in what was then called the Pentathlon: a series of athletic events (running, jumping with weights, disk-throwing, javelin-throwing and wrestling) chosen because they brought into play various muscular capacities which together led to a harmonious balance in the human body. For them an athlete could not be a specialist. And these men sang while performing their very vigorous Pyrrhic dances, and they also sang in their choral contests, when every village, or every deme of a city would send their fifty men and also fifty boys to compete for a choral prize; and the word "chorus" is also Greek, and means a dance; and to them singing and dancing were almost always simultaneous. This requires a kind of strength which no modern athlete could boast of; so that a runner of today, or a tennis champion, or the captain of a football or baseball team, or a wrestler, would not be considered an athlete at all. For them it would be a contradiction in terms to speak of an "athletic heart" which, today, means a heart overstrained and enlarged by exaggerated use of one set of muscles. The Greeks created this beautiful word along with its true value, and they have not lost it; for still, in modern Greek, the word "athlete" has a heroic swing.

"Mathematics" and "music". I remembered pouring over these words and their derivatives in Bailly's dictionary, fascinated by what they reveal.

Mathesis (μάθησις) means the process of learning, of instructing one's self; the faculty of intelligence; knowledge, instruction, science.

Mathema (μάθημα) means study, science, learning; and, in the plural, mathematical sciences (arithmetic, geometry, astronomy).

Mathematikos (μαθηματικός) means: one who devotes himself to study, (arithmetic, geometry, astronomy and mechanics).

The verb *manthano* (μανθάνω) means: to learn, to study, to instruct one's self; in the past tenses, to have become accustomed to, to have acquired a habit; to perceive, to remark, to understand.

The first meaning of all these words is study, science, learning; in two of them, arithmetic, geometry and astronomy are secondary; and the verb is never limited to what we call mathematics. In short, to the Greeks, this word signified learning in general: science, intelligence, understanding in general. In modern Greek the word *mathema* means a lesson of any kind, and *mathetes* means a student or disciple.

The word *Mousa* (Μοῦσα) means Muse, of whom there were nine, who personified all the arts. Its second meaning is science, art; its third song; its fourth persuasive speech. In no case does it signify what we call music.

Mouseion (μουσεῖον) is a temple of the muses, a place where poetry and other arts were practiced, a school. Our word Museum, a place where anything of value is collected and exhibited, is rather near to the original meaning; only a Museum is a place for preserving things past, whereas a Mouseion was rather a place for creating future works of art: more like a school.

Mousikos (μουσικός) from which our word "musician" comes, is one who excels in poetry, or any of the arts. It also means one who has general instruction.

Mousodonema (μουσοδόνημα) means poetic transport.

Mousoleptos (μουσόληπτος) one inspired or possessed by the Muses.

Mousomaneo (μουσομανέω) to be passionately devoted to the arts, poetry, music.

Mousomantis (μουσομάντις) one who predicts the future through songs.

Mousopneustos (μουσόπνευστος) one inspired by the Muses.

Mousopoios (μουσοποιός) one who composes in verse, or who sings in verse.

Mousopolos (μουσοπόλος) one who cultivates the Muses, a poet.

Mousourgeo (μουσουργέω) to do the work of a poet or a musician.

Mousophiles (μουσοφιλής) a friend of the Muses.

Mousoo (μουσόω) to instruct according to the rules of art; to have cultivated taste, to put to music.

I thought of these beautiful words, and how, one after another they show that what we call "music" meant first: all the arts; then it meant poetry; and finally, poetry and music together; it never meant just music by itself.

So, through the derivations from Athletics, Mathematics and Music, it is clear that the Greek curriculum was immensely broader than ours would be if we reduced education to what we now mean by these three words. The first meant harmonious development of the human body; the second, instruction in all forms of knowledge, especially science; and the third meant practice in all the arts, especially poetry. The immediate objective of the Greeks in educating their youth was to make the thing learned become not merely a mental concept in the students' mind but also a part of his inner consciousness; and, in accomplishing this, they obviously had a way of their own. If, apart from the study of poetry, the learning by heart of Homer and other poets, such subjects as history and science were also taught in verse, and if the oracles of the gods were always expressed in poetic language, one may conclude that they considered rhythmical language a better help to memory than prosaic statements. But this does not seem to have been enough to satisfy them. How can even poetic speech become more impressive, so that all the faculties of man will seize on its implied truth? This question they may not have asked consciously, but it makes no difference whether they did or not: because they acted, and acted energetically on the only possible answer. They sought to enhance the words with melody; and, in order to make this really effective, to develop melody greatly, and make it express all the shades of meaning and emotion which words may contain; but also to take advantage of the powerful accents or words,[6] so that their rhythmic beat would remain an integral part of the consciousness; and, above all, to so construct this melody that the sound and meaning of the word should never be lost to the listener.

---

[6] I wish that modern Hellenists would study Byzantine music. For so they might end the tiresome quarrel about accent and quantity in the Greek language, understanding then, as they certainly would if they were familiar with this great musical system, that these two foundations of the Greek language are not mutually exclusive; they are merely musical.

Thus the reason for the Greek attitude concerning music was their desire to convey, in the most vigorous manner possible, the ideas which their intelligence considered the most excellent. For this purpose they dared to subjugate that art "which stands alone, "which is connected with the inmost nature of the world and our own self", which is "stronger, quicker, more necessary, more infallible", which is "instantly understood by everyone"; which gives "the inmost kernel, or the heart of things, and precedes all forms."[7]

In short, they knew, as Goethe said, that "the poet should seize the Particular; and should, if there be anything sound in it, thus represent the Universal." The Greek educators did this in the most effective manner by "making music subordinate to language: its sole function being to enhance the word, and make its greater meaning distinctly comprehensible." In this way they went far beyond Walter Pater's saying that "all art tends toward the condition of music",[8] for they made all life tend toward the condition of music. There is not a circumstance in life, from birth to death, including all forms of labour, all forms of amusement, all forms of sorrow or despair, but which could be, and habitually was intensified or alleviated by this use of music. Instead of its being, as it is today, a tangent, touching occasionally the circle of man's individual life, (and this in no way changed by an even continuous performance of radio music for twenty-four hours a day: because this can never be connected with the personal life of the hearer). Music, for the Greeks, really did make every manifestation of life musical, describing the whole circle of his experience with infinite variety. The variety of it is certain; because, although we have very few fragments of ancient music to judge by, the method imposes variety, since a change of word, or accent, or meaning, necessarily imposes a change of tune. Also, to people brought up from childhood in the practice of this Method, almost anybody would be able to compose himself. (This is still true today in parts of Greece which have not been influenced by European music, but these places are rapidly growing fewer.) So all personal experiences, and all thoughts and emotions could, if they wished, be used as impulsions toward personal creation. Anyone could, and did, lift his own humdrum life to the level of the Universal, the Thing-In-Itself, not by debasing and denying that life, but by carrying it along to the heights.

---

[7] [Ed. The phrases are Schopenhauer's. *op. cit.*, Bk. III, Section 52, pp. 267, 274. -J.P.A.]

[8] Walter Pater, *The Renaissance*. [Ed. Essay on Giorgione. Only the author's name and the title of the work in the ms. The passage is slightly altered, perhaps because Eva Palmer-Sikelianos is citing from memory. The essay to which she refers is actually titled "The School of Giorgone." The passage reads as follows: "All art constantly aspires toward the condition of music." (Random House edition, The Modern Library, p. 111) -J.P.A.]

The dramatic possibilities of all this are evident; and therefore also the advantage which would be gained by an application of this Method to some of the contemporary forms of drama, entirely apart from the question of reproductions of Greek plays.

Above all, this study clarifies the Greek attitude toward life. The perfectibility of man did not depend, for them, on the development of particular faculties, but on the high development of all faculties which would balance and support each other: the simultaneous elevation of the whole of man, tending toward the condition of personal creation. To them "Be ye perfect" meant "Be ye creators", as probably also it did to Christ.

Greek education, whatever else it did or did not do, came much nearer than any other ever has to producing, in every kind of human activity, a race of creators.

If their musical method had any bearing on this phenomenon it is worthy of more serious study than it has so far elicited.

CHAPTER 20

The Treaty of the Two Great Gods

Still motionless from weakness, other correspondences passed through my mind, annihilating time. Emerson was present, and Dionysos, and Apollo. By turns the two gods were projecting thought into Emerson's brain. Apollo spoke first:[1]

> Poets should be law-givers; that is, the boldest lyric inspiration should not chide and insult, but should announce and lead the civil code and the day's work. Poetry and prudence should be coincident.[2]
>
> The highest end of government is the culture of man; and if man can be educated, the institution will share their improvement. There is a great and responsible Thinker and Actor working wherever a man works.[3]
>
> A man is a method".[4]

Emerson retained these phrases in his mind, but suddenly Dionysos broke in:

> Behold I am born into the universal mind. I, the imperfect, adore my own perfect.[5] There is one mind common to all individual men. Every man is an inlet to the same. Who hath access to this universal mind is a party to all that is or can be done. Man lies in the lap of immense intelligence. When he discerns truth, when he discerns justice he does nothing of himself, but allows a passage to its beams. The soul is. Under all the running sea of

---

[1]   [Ed. Emerson does not use Dionysos and Apollo as *dramatis personae* or as interlocutors. As the author recuperates from her illness, she recollects and recreates imaginatively thoughts of her own about Greek divinities and parallel reflections of Ralph Waldo Emerson (1803-1892). No edition of Emerson' works and no reference to page in any of the footnotes are cited. This explains the omissions and inaccuracies in the text. Often phrases from different essays are brought together without explanation. I thought it helpful to the reader to add in the footnotes the exact title of the essays from which materials are cited and also give the corresponding full text. I have used an easily accessible edition: *The Complete Essays and Other Writings of Ralph Waldo Emerson*, edited with a biographical introduction by Brooks Atkinson. The Modern Library, New York, 1940. -J.P.A.]

[2]   [Ed."Prudence," p. 242: "Poetry and prudence should be coincident. Poets should be lawgivers; that is, the boldest lyric inspiration should not chide and insult, but should announce and lead the civil code and the day's work. But now the two things seem irreconcilably parted." -J.P.A.]

[3]   [Ed. "Politics," p. 425: "Truly the only interest of the consideration of the State is persons;..property will always follow persons;..the highest end of government is the culture of men;..if men can be educated, the institutions will share their improvement and the moral sentiment will write the law of the land." -J.P.A.]

[4]   [Ed. "Self-Reliance," p. 153: "Let us affront and reprimand the smooth mediocrity and squalid contentment of the times, and hurl in the face of custom and trade and office, the fact which is the upshot of all history, that there is a great and responsible Thinker and Actor working wherever a man works; that a true man belongs to no other time or place, but is the centre of things. Where he is, there is nature." Also, "Intellect," p. 295: "Each mind has its own method." -J.P.A.]

[5]   [Ed. "The Over-Soul," p. 227: "Behold, it saith, I am born into the great, the universal mind. I, the imperfect, adore my own Perfect. I am somehow receptive of the great soul, and thereby I do overlook the sun and the stars and feel them to be the fair accidents and effects which change and pass. More and more the surges of everlasting nature enter into me, and I become public and human in my regards and actions. So come I to live in thoughts and act with energies which are immortal." -J.P.A.]

circumstance, whose waters ebb and flow with perfect balance, lies the aboriginal abyss of real Being. Essence, or God, is not a relation or a part, but the whole.[6] The simplest person who in his integrity worships God, becomes God; yet forever and ever the influx of this better and universal self is new and unsearchable. It is the doubling of the heart, with a power of growth to new infinity on every side.[7] The way of life is wonderful, it is by abandonment. The rich mind lies in the sun and sleeps, and is nature.[8]

These words also remained engraved in Emerson's consciousness; but the two gods did not reveal to him the inner relation of these things they had been saying. They did not tell him that they had opened the doors of two different aspects of man's nature, or that they themselves, the great potential enemies in man's being, who so often had tortured him through their contradictory counsels, had now come together and signed a pact, a Treaty: to teach man how to follow the wisdom of both gods, and so advance toward his own perfection.

So Emerson did not know that these sayings he had heard are inherently different, and are not interchangeable. He therefore recorded them some here, some there, in any essay he happened to be writing;   on Prudence, Politics, History, Self-Reliance, The Over-soul, Compensation, The Poet. He did not even remember the names of the Two Great Gods who had spoken to him, but scattered their sayings here and there, wherever he thought they would fit. So, in his philosophy, there is nothing distinguishing which is which. Indeed, there is hardly an essay in which these two gods do not work more or less at cross purposes, and sometimes in direct contradiction to each other: as for instance, in the essay on Self-Reliance in which he says: "Thy lot or portion in life," said the Caliph Ali, "is seeking after thee: therefore be at rest from seeking after it."[9]

And then, less than a page below: "In the Will work and acquire, and thou hast

---

[6] [Ed. "Compensations," p. 185: "There is a deeper fact in the soul than compensation, to wit, its own nature. The soul is not a compensation, but a life. The soul *is*. Under all this running sea of circumstance, whose waters ebb and flow with perfect balance, lies the aboriginal abyss of real being. Essence, or God, is not a relation or a part, but the whole." -J.P.A.]

[7] [Ed. "The Over-Soul," p. 275: "Ineffable is the union of man and God in every act of the soul. The simplest person who in his integrity worships God, becomes God; yet for ever and ever the influx of this better and universal self is new and unsearchable... When we have broken our God of tradition and ceased from our god of rhetoric, then may God fire the heart with his presence. It is the doubling of the heart itself, nay, the infinite enlargement of the heart with a power of growth to a new infinity on every side." -J.P.A.]

[8] [Ed. The note in the ms. cites only the titles of the essays "The Over-soul," "History," "Self-Reliance," "Compensation," "Circles," "Spiritual Laws." -J.P.A.]

[9] [Ed. "Self-Reliance," p. 168. -J.P.A.]

chained the wheel of chance."[10] How can anyone, taking Emerson seriously, know how to act on life with these contradictory counsels following each other? Is one to wait in a meditative attitude for one's portion in life, or is one to rise and actively seek it?

The reason why this hiatus in the teaching of Emerson is not evident to most of his readers, and was not evident to him, is that they are not grappling with any immediate problem concerning the *application to life* of abstract principles, but also, neither was he. Or it would be truer to say that any such effort which one can observe in his followers is feeble and ineffective, confined to the personal problems of individuals, and therefore is lacking in the broad sweep and the excitement of noble accomplishment which might be persuasive to a nation. Emerson writes very stirring sentences, and people reading them may be deeply impressed, but neither he nor they are called on to put what he says into immediate practice. Whether one believe it well to work and acquire, in order to chain the wheel of chance, or to be at rest from seeking through assurance that one's portion in life will materialize anyway, makes no difference; one is not called upon to prove it one way or the other. And so this teaching, however stirring one may find it, does not really touch life except, sometimes, at a tangent. It cannot describe the circle with its myriad points; and real life is again an orphan, desolate, except for disconnected and irrelevant moments of inspiration.

Like Carlyle, Emerson knew that "Man will not only be a spirit, but is one." Yet though both realized instinctively the fundamental unity of man's spiritual and material activities, neither of them clarified the differences involved in attaining this unity. Going down into a valley is a perfectly legitimate exercise, whether for human legs or for the human soul. Only the soul should be aware of its direction, upwards or downwards, just as human legs are aware. It is one thing to fall back inertly into the "mind common to all individual men," and it is another thing to make one's own mind a vehicle for the outward expression of the Universal Mind. These two processes require a different technique in actual experience, and both are weakened by lack of awareness of direction. By this lack of awareness Western philosophy is often blurred.

But Apollo[11] is never blurred. He knew that "man lies in the lap of immense intelligence" and that there is "one mind common to all individual men, and that every man is an inlet to it"; he knew that "under the sea of circumstance lies the aboriginal abyss of

---

[10] [Ed. "Self-Reliance," p. 169: "In the Will work and acquire, and thou hast chained the wheel of Chance, and shall sit hereafter out of fear from her rotations...Nothing can bring you peace but yourself. Nothing can bring you peace but the triumph of principles. -J.P.A.]

[11]   Here, and elsewhere, in using the name "Apollo" I am referring to the Delphic Sanctuary.

Being" and that "the rich mind lies in the sun and sleeps, and is nature."

But the poor mind can do the same thing. And whereas the rich one will awaken with the generosity of God's word flowing from his lips, with his heart afire to bring the whole frozen world to this blessed inexhaustible warmth which has filled his whole body, toes and fingers glowing with the heart's blood which he calls God's; the poor mind may simply go on sleeping. He may remain in a lethargy and never wake up, or he may awaken and find this same inexhaustible warmth flowing, not into his heart and his mind and from there to his lips to declare God's glory, but into his sexual organs, or into his pent-up hatred and vengeance toward mankind. Man is a shell giving shape to the sea which flows into it; a reed through which the breath of life passes, and with this supernal wind man is free to create harmony or discord. He is a transmitter over which a mighty current passes to bring light or destruction to the world.

This was Apollo's problem. He had received the other god in his Sanctuary, knowing that the "abyss of real Being" is beyond the power of both gods and men; he had given him away in his own Temple for half of the year, to enrich the lives of all men through the influx of this "one mind common to all men." But this influx can debase and destroy, as well as create and exalt.

How make this shell worthy of the inrushing sea; how produce harmony with this great wind in the reed instead of discord; how make mankind lift this power he had unchained toward his, Apollo's sunlight, and not rush with it into abysmal darkness?

Apollo was not dealing with individuals. If he had been, there was a method at hand, in India, which he, as god of prophecy and divination, knew well. "Seeking solitude, eating little, with speech, mind and body controlled; free from vanity, violence, pride, lust, wrath, avarice, without desire of possessions, full of peace, reach union with the Eternal."[12] But Apollo was dealing with a nation. His mind was as swift as his own sunbeams; and the one-by-one method, with so many reeds out of tune, was too slow. He had to shape so many bodies, so many minds and spirits to be worthy swiftly, by thousands.

Apollo did not have jurisdiction over the whole policy of Greece, foreign and domestic; but in one highly important branch of government his power was absolute: the education of the Greek people was entirely in his hands. In this one direction in which he ruled supreme, Emerson has recorded his words exactly.

As the eyes of Lyncaeus were said to see through the earth, so the poet turns the world to

---

[12] *Bhagavad Gita.* [Ed. Only the title in the MS. -J.P.A.]

glass, and shows us all things in their right series and procession. For through better perception he stands one step nearer to things, and sees the flowing or metamorphosis; perceives that thought is multiform; that within the form of every creature is a force impelling it to ascend into a higher form; and following with his eyes the life, uses the forms which express life, and so his speech flows with the flowing of nature. This is true science.[13]

It is not meters, but meter-making arguments that make a poem: a thought so passionate and alive that, like the spirit of a plant or animal, it has an architecture of its own, and adorns nature with a new thing. Not with the intellect alone, but with intellect inebriated with nectar.[14]

The poet is the person in whom these powers are in balance, the man without impediment, who see and handles that which others dream of, traverses the whole scale of experience, and is representative of man, in virtue of being the largest power to receive and to impart.[15]

The poet knows this doubling of the heart itself, nay, this enlargement of the heart with a power of growth to a new infinity on every side;.. for he has become porous to thought, and bibulous to the sea of light."[16]

All of this is purely Apollonian in spirit; it is radiant as a Doric temple; it gives one the very essence which went to form that inimitable entity which we call Greece. Why then did this masterly understanding of Emerson's remain sterile; why have the American people, with such a prophet in their midst, become steadily more prosaic ever since his time, as if they had never heard these stirring words?

I have said the answer. Emerson was not concerned with *the application to life* of these, or any other abstract principles which he sought to teach. He believed it sufficient to express them in writing, and there his mission ended.

But Apollo was concerned with the broadest and swiftest dissemination of these truths. For him it was not enough that Homer, or Demodokos, or any other rhapsodist, sing the exploits of heroes in the halls of the rich; and poets were to him pre-eminently those individuals "who stand among partial men for the complete man, and apprise us, not of their own wealth, but of the common wealth."[17]

Apollo had his language, and he had his poets; but how could their word be transfused into the consciousness of each one of his people? How could this "better perception" of the poets, along with this "doubling of the heart" become the heritage of each

---

[13] [Ed. From the essay "The Poet," p. 329. -J.P.A.]

[14] [Ed. "The Poet," p. 323. -J.P.A.]

[15] [Ed."The Poet," p. 321. -J.P.A.]

[16] [Ed. "The Over-Soul," pp. 275, 274. -J.P.A.]

[17] [Ed. From "The Poet," p. 320, with slight changes. -J.P.A.]

individual in his whole nation? He had seen that genius, however transcendent, may be neutralized and destroyed by the evil intentions of a single man. He had seen how, while the godlike power of Orpheus was guiding his people:

> Thousands followed him, they know not why themselves
> Nor know it to this day. But as when the sun
> Begins suddenly to melt snow upon the mountains
> And in the rivers ice.
> The liberated waters rush forth in cataracts:
> Thus scarcely were his lyre and his voice
> Heard among the people than behind him thronged
> Vast crowds. And as the rivers,
> If once they spring forth toward the sea
> Can never more turn back, nor stay their course,
> Thus the crowds followed him."[18]

But he had also seen his people left empty and desolate again when their godlike leader was torn asunder, and all his works destroyed. How could he write the words of Orpheus, or any truly great word, in all their hearts, so that no tyrant could again betray them?

That was the undertaking of Apollo: to find a medium which could span the chasm between the lethargy of mankind, or even between their blind enthusiasm and the actual meaning of inspired language. How make their own brains work intelligently, each one by itself? How carry the true meaning into their inner consciousness? This was his problem: the education of his whole people with heart and mind at one.

To do this, he chose the only effectual means: he called in the other god, so that the poets' word might throb in the heart's of his people as an earthquake vibrates through the geological faults of the earth. He dared to subjugate music to the word, and to exalt the particular joys or terrors of each man's life, that they become a means of commanding access to the "abyss of real Being." With this goal ahead, to lift the whole man, the whole nation to an awakened consciousness of the "Universal Mind", he ordered his poets to gather his people together and teach them poetry, enlarged by music, and completed by dancing. There were to be choruses: choruses of young men, of old men, of boys; Choruses of women and of girls. All over Greece there whould be choruses: choruses and athletic contests. But above all he ordered them to recreate in dithyrambic form the whole tragic myth of the other god: his miraculous birth, his tragic slaughter by the Titans, and the sacred resurrection of

---

[18] Anghelos Sikelianos, *The Dithyramb of the Rose*. [Ed. Greek text in the first edition, Athens, 1932, p. 13, lines 14-25. The translation is Eva Palmer-Sikelianos's own translation. -J.P.A.]

Dionysos.

Herein lies Apollo's immense superiority and effectiveness as an educator. Emerson wrote about "intellect inebriated by nectar", but actually he never inebriated anyone in his life, whereas this is exactly what Apollo did. With the sacred legend of the "other god" he made his whole people drunk with what Matthew Arnold used to call the "passion for perfection."

The constant objective of the Delphic Sanctuary was the perfecting of man, and this presupposed the constant and harmonious interaction of the Two Great Gods. The action of Apollo in ceding his temple for six months of the year to the other god is symbolic of the necessity under which the majority of men labour, of doing one thing at a time. Though Dionysos be "the one mind common to all individual men", and though Apollo be the medium for all outward expression of this universal mind, though they be inexorably bound on this earth one to the other, as body and soul are bound while we live on earth. Nevertheless, when, with the winter months, Dionysos returns to the Sanctuary, Apollo departs for his yearly journey to the land of the Hyperboreans who live beyond the snow-bound regions of the North, and the two Gods only touch hands in passing: they do not dance in the same place at the same time.

There is, however, in man's nature, the possibility of complete simultaneous manifestation of these two powers. This occurs when Apollo has already shaped the shell and made it worthy of the inrushing sea; when he has so whittled the reed that true harmony can breathe through it; when it becomes, as Emerson says, an "unobstructed channel"; and when the body of man becomes capable of receiving the spiritual light, with sufficient strength to transmit its radiance to the world. But this shaping of the shell, this whittling of the reed, occurs before birth. Then the poet is born. The creature who in Greece was Poet, Musician, Dancer. And it is he who can transmit to others, in a lesser degree, the wisdom of following outward objectives to perfection, but knowing always that each attainment of outward perfection, though it be as long-lasting as the great Pyramid of Egypt, is to its creator a transitory thing, nothing but a stepping-stone of ascent

> on the numberless sides
> Of the Mountain, the many which become One.[19]

But to those who are behind, these temporary objectives become models greater than themselves, and so raise them also a step on the Mountain.

This is the wisdom of Apollo the most dangerous no doubt which has ever been taught

---

[19] [Ed. *The Dithyranb of the Rose*, lines 23-4. -J.P.A.]

to man. Dangerous because at each stepping-stone man risks his own pride of accomplishment. In each changing season of his life he cannot always see to it that the Two Great Gods touch hands in passing; and so his last landing-place becomes for him a goal. And the higher he climbs, the more dangerous the fall. For the price of the "Olympian Gift of Holy Symmetry" is to know that there is no end, that every attainment is only one step higher on the Mountain, and that the mightiest creation, when once completed, is for the creator a thing of the past. It no longer concerns him, except insofar as it has opened his eyes and prepared his hands for the next task which is ahead. It belongs to others.

This is the test of the creator; and his secret enemy is inner exhaustion, the aching desire to rest on his accomplishment among the bleak rocks which he has reached:

> And I sighed so profoundly that my sigh became the
>   very staff and prop of my heart;
> And I said: 'What matters it if thou are alone! Now that
>   the summit is far, what else remains for thee but to climb?[20]

There are few who have this courage. One's own accomplishment brings the strong yearning to keep Apollo bound to the deed which has been done, to keep the summer which is passing around us. It is difficult then to let Apollo go back to the Hyperboreans, and to receive Dionysos again in the winter months: to let the "sea of oblivion" rush in. Yet that is the only way to climb higher on the Mountain. "We cannot let our angels go. We do not see that they only go that archangels may come in."[21]

Greece herself did not resist this temptation. There came a time when, through fatigue, she rested on her own accomplishment; then her strength became grace and prettiness, and her flawless intellect fell into the easier path of sophistry. Nevertheless, though Greece herself once fell from exhaustion by the wayside, she then already had built a bridge for the feet of those who believe that each man can and must become intelligent; that each man is, and must be, at once a member of an earthly and a member of a heavenly order. Archaic Greece is the Bridge.

---

[20] Anghelos Sikelianos, *Dedication*. [Ed. Greek text in *Lyrikos Vios*, Vol. III (Ikaros), p. 154. -J.P.A.]

[21] [Ed."Compensation." The passage in p. 188: "We cannot part with our friends. We cannot let our angels go. We do not see that they only go out that archangels may come in. We are idolaters of the old." - J.P.A.]

CHAPTER 21

The Birth of Tragedy

There came a time in the hospital when I was allowed to have a book, but only one. Many titles passed through my mind of things that I longed to read. There was, however, a wise doctor who advised me not to choose a new book.

"It will be best", he said, "to take something that you have read: something, in fact, that you know rather well, so that you will not be reading continuously, but rather looking here and there, just to remember passages that you like."

I chose *The Birth of Tragedy*.[1]

I was anxious to see why, years before, I had cared for it extravagantly: whether, in the meantime, my closer approach to Greek tragedy had pricked the Nietzschean bubble of fascination, or whether still I could be blown by the strong revolutionary wind of what he called "the metaphysical miracle of the Hellenic Will."[2] And again, in spite of Nietzsche's own rather just later criticism of this book, that it is "badly written, heavy, bristling with frantic, incoherent images,"[3] I found here the one European whose instinct hurled him with the impetus of a true dancer almost into the heart of Greek drama.

Nietzsche disregarded all the usual technical questions about ancient music. Whether the Greeks ever used superimposed sounds, whether they were limited altogether to heterophony, or consecutive sounds, what they meant by musical modes, were matters he did not even refer to. But he knew instinctively that they were great musicians, and with one gorgeous leap of pure intuition he threw out his wonderful statement that "tragedy sprang from the genius of music," and "was, in the origin, chorus, and *nothing but chorus*."[4]

It is now certain that the Greek chorus existed long before tragedy, and also that it sang and danced simultaneously. But no one knew it then; and it was Nietzsche who first

---

[1] [Ed. The MS gives no information about the translation the author had consulted and from which she quoted. Only the title, *The Birth of Tragedy*, is cited. I thought it best to give only the title of the work cited and the section where passages quoted may be found. In certain cases, when convenient, I also cite the page. -J.P.A.]

[2] [Ed. From *The Birth of Tragedy*, ch. 1. -J.P.A.]

[3] [Ed. From "Attempt at Self-Criticism," in the Preface of the second edition (1886) of *The Birth of Tragedy*, section 3. -J.P.A.]

[4] [Ed. In *The Birth of Tragedy*, ch. 7. Whereas Nietzsche underlines the first phrase, the author omits the italics and substitutes her own underscoring of the words "nothing but dance." Actually, she paraphrases closely Nietzsche's text. -J.P.A.]

realized the historic incontrovertibility of this fact, and also its enormous implications. This phrase was an arrow aimed unerringly by great genius, and it hit very near the centre. For it means, as he says, that tragedy sprang from the genius of music. But what music? This question Nietzsche avoids by digressions, each one fascinating in itself; about the Olympian Gods, about the Dionysian spirit, about the function of the chorus, and about the satyrs, and Euripides and Socrates; and all of these outbursts, which are like rifts in heavy clouds during a fast-moving thunder-storm, contain inspired phrases about Greek music:

> What was the force that delivered Prometheus from the vulture, and transformed the myth into a herald of Dionysian wisdom? It was the Herculean force of music, when, having reached its highest expression in tragedy, it was able to interpret the myth with new power and more profound meaning.[5]

> Singing and dancing, man manifests himself as a member of a higher order; ...now his bearing is as noble and full of ecstacy as the Gods whom he has seen in his dream. Man is no longer an artist: he has become a work of art.[6]

> The image and the idea, under the efficient influence of a truly adequate music, acquire a superior significance."[7]

But what was this adequate music? When Nietzsche comes nearer to describing it we realize that this flight of intuition concerning the priority of the Greek chorus over Greek tragedy is supported by no scholarship even distantly Greek. His enthusiasm had to fall back on what he himself knew as music: and, like all other European musicians and philosophers, the word 'music' meant to him polyphonic music.

And so we have a description of the advance of Dionysos in his chariot, covered with crowns and flowers; with panthers and tigers under his yoke; with millions prostrate and trembling in the dust at his passing; and with wild beasts of the rocks and the desert approaching peacefully. The "adequate music" which Nietzsche invokes to express this Dionysian ecstasy is simply that composition which he himself was in the habit of regarding as the supreme attainment of music. It is Beethoven's "Hymn to Joy."[8]

The medley produced in our minds in reading this passage is both comic and tragic. We are asked to visualize the passing of a god into a far country; with tigers and panthers and wild beasts of the desert in his wake; with millions of human beings prostrate in the

---

[5] [Ed. From *The Birth of Tragedy*, ch. 10. -J.P.A.]

[6] [Ed. From *The Birth of Tragedy*, ch. 1. -J.P.A.]

[7] [Ed. From *The Birth of Tragedy*, ch. 16. -J.P.A.]

[8] [Ed. The author is paraphrasing Nietzsche. The passage occurs in *The Birth of Tragedy*, ch. 1. -J.P.A.]

dust; and all this accompanied by music which requires about one hundred musicians with chairs and music-stands, about one hundred singers with books in their hands from which they read, also with chairs; and a leader on a raised platform, also with a music-stand supporting a large orchestral score.

This "adequate" music that Nietzsche imagines for his cortege was composed during a period when humanism had made great strides; when it seemed that Providence had decreed for human beings an eternity of concert halls where they could enjoy beautiful music to their heart's content, without any fear of panthers. It is as far removed as possible from any sort of actual movement, whether of gods or men or tigers. It is also, in conception, not Greek at all. For the Greeks never prostrated themselves in the dust, whether singly or by millions.

In fact this medley of Asia in Bacchic ecstacy mixed up with a gala performance of the *Ninth Symphony* in Carnegie Hall is too extravagant to hold our attention sixty years after it was written if it were not for two things. First, no progress has been made since this period to correct Nietzsche's mistake. Musicians, and scholars in general, still are suggesting various European compositions, especially oratorios, as equivalents for Greek choruses; and this passage is perhaps the only one in all Nietzsche's work which never has been challenged. And secondly, there is, in this whole book, a highly tragic content which effectively dominates any anomalies that one may choose to notice in special passages. Nietzsche was the first to realize that the Greeks were great musicians. He had nothing to go on except the historic fact that Choruses preceded Tragedy. He knew nothing about the technical side of Greek music. But this was all to the good. For research on his part, in his European surroundings, would have resulted in only negative findings, which might have discouraged him from following his own luminous intuition. Music to him, and to everybody, meant polyphonic music. And yet he attempted the impossible. With Icarian wings he flew head-on to disaster in a terrible tempest. He believed passionately in Greek tragedy; he had discovered the truth that Dionysian music really was the lover which lifted Greek art itself to its zenith. But he never guessed the Apollonian secret that the heart of it was poetry. Afterwards he felt it himself, but only in part:

> How I regret not having had the courage to employ a personal language (in *The Birth of Tragedy*) instead of trying painfully to express, with the aid of Kantian and Schopenhauerian formulas, opinions which were new and strange, and which were radically opposed to the spirit and to the feeling of Kant and Schopenhauer...But there is something else which I regret much

more: that I ruined the grandiose problem of Greece as it revealed itself to me by the intrusion of things modern, attaching myself to hopes where there was nothing to hope for, where everything indicated an end.[9]

Nietzsche repudiated Wagner and Schopenhauer and regretted deeply that he had confused "the grandiose problem of Greece" by using their formulas. But regret was not enough, and repudiation was not enough. In fact, neither repudiation nor regret was necessary. But it was vital that he understand that "the simultaneous unchaining of all the powers of man" which he imagined ideally had nothing to do with what he was used to considering as music; and that the music which he imagined, however great in itself, was entirely incompatible with Greek tragedy.

Nietzsche was in the terrible position of knowing instinctively the overwhelming musical power of Greek tragedy, of caring for it more passionately than for anything else in the world; and yet of being confined by musical formulas which are the very negation of Greek tragedy. It must have made his own vision inherently impossible. "That way madness lies."

And yet, for all that, how grand he is! "The value of a people, as also of a man, is measured precisely by this one faculty: the power to mark the events of his existence with the seal of eternity."[10]

---

[9] [Ed. The passage occurs in "Attempt at Self-Criticism," from the Preface to the second edition of *The Birth of Tragedy*. -J.P.A.]

[10] [Ed. Source unknown. The MS gives no hint. -J.P.A.]

CHAPTER 22

Greek Influence Today

The hospital windows were wide open, letting in the Spring. I was on a couch with the good sun touching me, bringing me the illusion of well-being. Ellen Chater came in and I showed her proudly that I could stand and walk. She suggested a convalescent home on Long Island, kept by some gentle-voiced protestant nuns, and I asked her to take me there.

So I was soon lying with trees above me, and lawns all about, and flower gardens to walk in quietly. And there was a chapel where the nuns seemed to pray ceaselessly, reciting long litanies on patient knees.

I like it well enough. The black-gowned ladies were kind and restful to be with, because, as Ellen had said, their voices were gently tuned. But it was only my weakness that liked it as I considered the confusion of New York to which I would soon swing back. One mode of life seemed no more intelligent than the other; in America I had never found the middle way. No wonder, in this country of hectic contrasts, some moving too fast and going nowhere, and others moving not at all, that Greek values are so far away. I tried to think of what is left of them, to find some cheer in what seemed then a cold world.

I knew that in the schools and universities the study of Greek is dying out, so that strong leaven is no longer present to raise the whole loaf; and, in the world outside the universities, the few traces that are left are lamentable indeed: railroad stations with Doric columns; gardens with plaster copies of ancient statues; young girls floating about on smooth lawns, wearing cheese-cloth dresses with meander patterns of gold paper pasted on; these and other such phenomena are today called "Greek". But there was something in me all the same which refused to be discouraged; and there were certain phenomena called "modern" that I had started to call by another name: houses which are rectangular blocks with no decoration; drawings which are only outlines; a general tendency to discard the superfluous everywhere; production in which the material used is in direct relation to the necessity which prompted its making; a healthy scorn of prettiness; a demand for usefulness on the simplest terms. This tendency, healthy because it has never been named, is really Greek.

For many ages, in European countries, and here also, much human effort has been expended in trying to copy this or that form of art invented by the Greeks. The results usually have been without excellence. But in the modern world there is a strong demand for

175

art and architecture and literature directly connected with life. The workers engaged in this have a violent detestation of the very name of Greece: so they are not in danger of falling into the age-old pitfall of imitation; they believe they are producing something new; but that is precisely what the Greeks did, and the modern world, in a way, is following in their tracks; especially in the Functional School of Architecture, often aided by what Jay Hambidge called Dynamic Symmetry, which was a restatement of fundamental laws of proportion, based on the analogy of growth in nature known and used by the Greeks, and often, since Hambidge's time, by modern architects and painters.

The moment an artist knows the rules, throws off the tyranny of useless ornament and creates from within, in accord with the human needs of himself or his client, or in direct communication with his own inspirations, he is, as Shelley said of Hassan, "Greek at heart." And often this unconscious homage produces similarities which are startling. The beautiful drawings by Picasso of children's heads are Greek both in feeling and technique, yet it is improbable that Picasso had Greek vase-painting in mind when he did them. The architectural design which took a prize in the Chicago Exhibition of 1937, as a model for an American summer residence, might have been suggested by any house on the island of Skyros today; yet it is highly improbable that the architect was copying any peasant house on any one of the Greek Islands when he designed it.

This modern effort to throw Greece out of the running is interesting because it exemplifies the real difficulty which is involved when the world tries to shake off the accomplishment of Greece. People think often that by eschewing certain outward forms which were characteristically Greek, such as using columns for temples, or plain rectangles for clothes, that they have buried the monster once for all. But the real monster they are fighting is human sincerity and intelligence and simplicity; and as soon as they assume any of these characteristics they become branded against their will; they become more Greek than the conscious imitators. Because to be Greek is an attitude of mind toward life. It means to know that man's goal is the perfection of man; to know that through his noblest efforts and aspirations man obtains a vision into still higher objectives: that art is therefore a function of life. And just as the foundation of his temples was bed-rock, with tree-trunks, which afterwards became marble columns, to hold the roof; just as man's form was his body, and not his clothes; just as man's music was his own voice and not musical instruments: so every art and every act in life were based on extreme simplicity. Every art, through elimination of the superfluous, found its own basic principles, and from these each man worked from within, to become himself a creator. They did not imitate their own works of art, for servile imitation debases the thing copied and also the soul of the copier. So, rather than fall into sentimental imitation, it is better to hate Greece, or what is called Greece, and hold fast to the effort to bring art and life into true relation with each other. But this way entails the loss of precious contributing elements which Greece holds out to us all.

Among the more conscious Greek influences in our day, there exists, of course, a survival of the sentimental attitude of the nineties, which connected Greek attainment with Matthew Arnold's idea of "sweetness and light," and for which Walter Pater, Cardinal Newman and Emerson were largely responsible. This "Greek serenity", this "childish gaiety," this "graceful lightness half sport," which made Carlyle compare them unfavourably with the "huge shadow of Odin" was not altogether detrimental to the true seeker for Greek wisdom; especially after Nietzsche had shaken the smoothness of their polished sentences with the eruption of his volcanic utterances concerning Greece. For it came to seem no small accomplishment that the most Tragedy-conscious of all peoples had nevertheless made their shadow rest lightly on the world in this latter-day impression that they were completely serene.

But in this same period of literary homage, or censure, of what was called Greek serenity and grace, which, in itself, caused no serious setback in the intelligent approach to Greek achievement, there was another theory disseminated, and rather generally accepted by the artistic circles of the period, which did strike at the very root of Greek principles: "All art is immoral" wrote Oscar Wilde; and "Art and Ethics have nothing in common." These sayings, and the attitude toward art which they fostered, and which they continue to encourage, are in direct opposition to the ideal which the Delphic Sanctuary attempted over a long period, and partly succeeded in impressing on the heart and mind of man; and they have gone far to distort any same vision of Greece which research is gradually clarifying.

For art to the Greeks was one with religion. Beauty was not an objective in itself, but a by-product of their attitude toward life. They had no aesthetic cult concerning the sacredness of their own masterpieces in art. The proof of this is: that the absolutely beautiful archaic statues (which adorned the Acropolis before the Persian wars) were used by the Greeks themselves as filling for the foundations of the new Parthenon. And by what Greeks? It was Periclean period, and Phidias, and the great architect Iktinos, were directing the work for the new temple. They had no sentimental revulsion of feeling in throwing these divine works of art out of sight as building stones; as far as we know, no hand was stretched out to save what had delighted the eyes of Athenians all their lives. And why? Because these statues had all been more or less damaged during the Persian occupation of Athens, and therefore were no longer appropriate for representing or honouring their gods. Could we ask any greater proof of the fact that art for art's sake was to the Greeks a sacrilege?

And we have another indication of this religious function of art in Greece. It is in the period of Praxiteles. He had finished a statue of Artemis, which had been ordered for the great Temple of Ephesos; and the story goes that having seen it finished, he was so entranced with its beauty that he mutilated it slightly, on purpose, somewhere at the back of the head where it would not show much, in order to keep it in his studio. This story I heard years ago, in France, in an art class, and it was cited by the professor as proof of the superior artistic sensibility of Praxiteles. I have not been able to trace it, but if true, and it has a sort of Greek swing to it, it proves two things: first that the ancient priests would not have an even slightly damaged statue in their temples; and second, that Praxiteles himself was already tainted with softness and sentimentality in his attitude toward art. Moreover this softness is evident in the only work of his which has come down to us: in the Hermes of Olympia, in which archaic virility and Phidian fervour are both lacking.

Long familiarity with the Greek language is apt, more than other branches of study, to foster a kind of intellectual independence. We can see the way it works in an incident cited by Romain Rolland in his *Life of Vivekananda*. The great Swami had arrived unknown and unheralded. It was in 1893. His object was to speak at the Congress of Religions at the first Chicago World's Fair. He had arrived with no credentials, with hardly any money, only to find that the time fixed for inscription of delegates had already passed; and that anyway, without official references, no one would be admitted. He was in despair.

> But, wrote Romain Rolland, "he trusted in fate. Instead of brooding with his remaining dollars, he spent them to visit Boston...In the train, his aspect, his answers, impress a fellow traveler, a rich lady from Massachusetts, who questions him, becomes interested, invites him to her house, presents him to the Hellenist, J. H. Wright, professor at Harvard; and he, immediately struck by the genius of the young Hindu, puts himself at his service; he insists on the participation of Vivekananda in the Parliament of Religions to represent Hinduism; he writes to the president of the committee: he offers to the pilgrim his railroad ticket to Chicago; gives him letters of recommendation to the commission on lodgings. Briefly, all obstacles are smoothed away.

Romain Rolland attributes this remarkable turn of fortune only to the personality of the Swami:

> A Vivekananda does not pass unnoticed. But after all the same Vivekananda had travelled across two continents, and had spent two weeks in Chicago entirely unrecognized. In his gorgeous Hindu clothes, still young, beautiful, and very powerful, he had been taken for a mountebank. Professor Wright, in standing so warmly by a total stranger, in insisting the he be admitted to the Parliament of Religions, without credentials, and after the allotted time for enrollment of delegates, was certainly risking his own prestige if the Swami had failed. It took

very clear judgment, and not a little spontaneous courage to champion, in so open-hearted a way, this meteor picked up in a railroad train. In fact, it took a Greek to do it.

Concerning the "rich lady from Massachusetts," whose name we do not know, one wonders if she too was a hellenist. Anyway, she had the remarkable intuition, for which the world does not seem to have thanked her, to bring India and Greece together in her house. The result was the spiritual conflagration of the great swami's whole career.

There is today, in America, a wide-spread movement which is considered Greek in origin, and this is the growing craze for sun-baths. Mr. Stuart Chase, in an article called "Confessions of a Sun-Worshipper," published in *The Nation*, and abridged in *The Reader's Digest,* from which I quote, says:

> Is it only a temporary craze? Will America strip by the millions in the next few years only to be back in its shroud in a decade? I neither know nor greatly care. If the republic wants to go native and can hold to it with any fidelity, it will probably do more than any other conceivable action to balance the inhibitions and pathological cripplings induced by the machine age in which we live.

Who will disagree with Mr. Chase's statement that the after effects of exposure to the sun are "a sense of well-being, of calmed nerves, of inner vitality?" Yet is this enough to balance the inhibitions, and pathological cripplings of the machine age? It reminds one of the claims of the Christian Scientists, who make physical health the be-all and end-all of life. No doubt, both of these methods are conducive to health. But is health, however robust, enough by itself to bring about such an important result? Can a sunburnt leg, however shapely, or a million sunburnt legs, counteract by themselves the terrible pathological cripplings to which the world is exposed today?

This matter of men going naked and feeling that there is nothing unusual about it was, of course, one of the significant innovations of Apollo. It is indicated in the fourth, and also in the third book of *The Republic*:

> Not long ago the Hellenes were of the opinion, which is still generally received by the barbarians, that the sight of a naked man was ridiculous and improper; and when the Cretans, and then when the Lacedemonians introduced the custom, the wits of the day might have ridiculed the innovation. But when experience showed that to let all things be uncovered was far better than to cover them up, the ludicrous effect vanished.[1]

And concerning the labourers in his projected Republic, Plato says: "they will work in summer commonly naked and barefoot, but in winter substantially clothed and shod."

---

[1]   [Ed. The passage occurs at *Republic*, Bk. V, 452C-D. -J.P.A.]

This attitude toward the body was possible for the Dorians only because they had already acquired a real balance between body, mind and spirit; from what Plato says, it was not a very old custom; perhaps it started with the rise of the wonderful archaic Greek civilization; and so one may infer that religion, poetry, music, dancing, architecture and sculpture had already described the whole circle of their lives. They were therefore able to disregard the feeling of the ludicrous and the improper, as Plato says, by simply getting used to it. But above all, they were occupied with too many other things in which their spirit was really absorbed to allow the besetting danger, which we have inherited from the barbarians, shame and mockery, to take a prominent place in their consciousness. With them, mind and spirit were truly in the lead, and so the body and its instincts were under normal and proper control. This Dorian purity, already relaxed in Plato's day, was in true balance for about two hundred years. After that, the conquered barbarian gradually conquered the conqueror, and we find Scopas dressing Apollo in flowing Ionian robes.

But the archaic Apollo accomplished in that time what has not been equalled since: for he produced the nearest thing to an intelligent nation of any that the world has seen, a nation which made everything they touched individual and inimitable, and which led even as cold a critic as Aristotle to say that "the public are the best judges of poetry and music."[2]

We cannot alas say the same thing today.

---

[2]   [Ed. Only the title of Aristotle's work is cited in the text. The passage the author has paraphrased is from *Politics* III, 6, 1281b 4-9. -J.P.A.]

CHAPTER 23

Isadora

Isadora, the meteor, blazed through the world of her time as the personification of Greece. But she herself disclaimed this. Toward the end of her first visit to Greece, she went one night to the Acropolis alone. She felt it was for the last time. Her dreams had burst like a glorious bubble, and the realization swept over her that she and her people were moderns, and nothing else; perhaps more nearly related to the red-Indians, or to the Scotch-Irish than to the Greeks; and the remembered chords of Isolde's death-song were what consoled her. This was at the beginning of her career. Toward the end of her book she describes her own amusement when people called her dancing Greek. She tells how, to her, the adventures of her grandparents were the origin of it when they crossed the American plains in a covered wagon, and when, in the midst of a battle with the Indians, her own father was born. This Pioneer spirit, together with the gestures of the Red-Skins, crept, she says, into the Irish jigs, and Irish songs which her grandmother taught her; and to this also, through another grandfather, was added a touch of Yankee Doodle, during the Civil War. These elements she considers the real foundation of her dance.[1]

Nevertheless, consciously or unconsciously, Isadora fooled us all. When Mrs. Pat Campbell said to me: "Oh, there's a new dancer! But I will not tell you her name because you would go off your head about her," she went on to tell me that it was like a Greek vase come to life. Mrs. Campbell said nothing, thought nothing, none of us did, about Irish jigs, or American Indian gestures, or Yankee Doodle. That was in London, shortly after Mrs. Campbell had discovered Isadora dancing one day in St. James' Park. We all saw her afterwards: Her "Narcissus" and "Ophelia", her "Water Nymphs", and her truly beautiful "Death and the Maiden"; Mendelssohn's "Spring Song", Chopin waltzes, Glück's "Orphée", etc., etc., and we all felt that the shackles of the world were loosened, that liberation was ahead of us all. But is was liberation in terms of Greek vases, not of Irish jigs. And this impression went on for years, in fact forever, while Isadora lived. What she did was always connected with Greek vases and Greek bas-reliefs; and only gradually, after a number of

---

[1] [Ed. See Isadora Duncan, *My Life*, (Liveright Publishing Corp., New York, 1955), Chapter 30, pp. 340-1. Here and in other places, when traceable, I supply the page numbers for the passages cited from Isadora Duncan's autobiography, which also seems to be the confessional "source" for Eva Palmer-Sikelianos' evaluation of Duncan's contribution. -J.P.A.]

years of unquestioning gratitude for what she brought us, one began to date the vases which were evoked by her dancing. As familiarity with these increased, it became evident that the strong invocation of Isadora's art brought to life a period which was not archaic Greece, not classic Greece, but Greece in a later decadent period. In fact, what we were seeing and raving over was Hellenistic bas-relief, or a Southern Italian vase come to life. "My arms are never still," she wrote, "but continually waving about in soft undulations."

This was true. Her arms were beautiful, and the soft undulations were infinitely charming to a world which knew only the tiresome stiffness of the ballet; but there is not a single example of any work of Greek art before the fourth century which resembles Isadora's dancing. It was always flowing. Even in powerful dances like her "Marche Slave" and her Chopin "Polonaise", the lines of her body went into curves. She always faced her audience frankly, head and chest in the same direction. There was never the powerful accent of a strong angle, and never the isolating effect of keeping the head in profile with the chest "en face" which is characteristic of archaic Greek art. Even in moving around the outside circle of the stage, it was always straight ahead, more like a child running, with none of the pause and power which are added by what I have called the Apollonian movement in the dance.

But Isadora was right. With the means at her disposal, especially with the music she had, anything else but what she actually did would have been highly inappropriate. And so the more recent schools of dancing, which are still circumscribed by the same limitations to which Isadora was subject, but which nevertheless adopted a series of strained and angular poses, give one the impression of mechanical dolls compared to the inspired creations of Isadora.

As far as I know, the type of movement I am referring to as Apollonian was used first, in modern times, by Mounet Sully in his performance of *Oedipe Roi*. Isadora has described it. Her ecstatic eulogy expresses what all Paris was feeling. She and Raymond had secured seats in the very top gallery of the huge old Trocadero, but they did not expect what was ahead of them. Up in the tribunes, they caught their breath and grew pale: never, in any country, not even antiquity, had there been such a voice. But to her, the supreme moment was when Mounet Sully danced: "the great heroic figure dancing." And she then realized that the great revelation of art had been given to her. From that moment she knew her way.

After that day, Isadora and Raymond, with the inspiration they had received from the great French actor, seem to have gone ahead in different ways. To Isadora it proved to be a powerful, fruitful, but rather indefinite influence. She caught the spirit of its greatness, and went ahead according to the way she felt it. But Raymond saw the applicability in the theatre of these ancient Greek poses, which he had himself been copying in the Louvre; and later, when he formed classes of his own, he taught angular movements copied from archaic vases. Since then many others have done this, but the results are not inspiring because, in order to manifest their full power, these highly accented movements require the inspiration and the basic rhythm of language. These innovators forget that all through *Oedipe Roi* Mounet Sully was using his gorgeous voice which, Isadora thought, had not been excelled even in the greatest days of Sophocles. And they forget his stupendous silences.

Isadora was wiser. She let the ascendancy of Mounet Sully's genius engulf her. She did not try to copy him, or to copy a Greek vase, or anything else. The path she followed was inside herself.

She has described her search for that dance which might be the divine expression of the human spirit through the medium of the body's movement: how she would stand still for hours, her hands folded between her breasts, covering the solar plexus; the alarm of her mother to see her motionless for so long, as in a trance, while she sought, and finally discovered, what she calls *the creator of power*, the unity from which all diversions of movement are born; and how, after many months, when she had learned how to concentrate all her force on this Centre, she found, in listening to music, that the rays and vibrations of the music streamed to this one fount of light within her, and how a presence of mighty power seemed to be reaching through her whole body, trying to find an outlet for this listening. And Stanislawsky quotes what she once said to visitors who had crowded to her dressing-room: that she could not dance that way, that she must have time, before going on the stage, to place a motor in her soul, and that only when that motor began to work her whole body would move independently of her will.

All this was true. Often I have seen Isadora stand quite motionless before large audiences for quite a long spell, with her hands over her solar plexus, in the manner she describes. Then, when she gave the sign for starting, she really had "placed a motor in her soul," and from then on her dancing gave the impression of being involuntary on her part. It was purely Dionysian: that was why the world was at her feet.

In the preface to the quite thrilling book called *Isadora Duncan's Russian Days* by Irma Duncan and Allen Ross MacDougall, the authors have written: "Unthinking people were confused about Isadora Duncan; so she seemed to them extraordinary and inconstant. They did not, or could not understand that, in her body, hazard had united two different people:

the woman and the artist."[2]   This is true.   But, apart from the contradictions and inconsistencies to which they here refer, there was another which, as far as I know, has not been spoken of or even noticed. One may throw light on it by a reference to the men whom she called her masters. They were Whitman, Beethoven, Wagner and Nietzsche.[3] Taking each one of these separately, it is clear that Whitman chose expression in words, and his medium was adequate; Beethoven chose expression in music, and his medium was adequate; Wagner chose a combination of these two arts which was satisfactory to himself and his followers; but Nietzsche attempted a reconstruction of ancient Greek drama in terms of Beethoven and Wagner, and the result for himself was madness, and for the world more misunderstanding of this master's purpose. Of all four of these great men, the one nearest to Isadora's spirit was Nietzsche. Both he and she were predominantly Dionysian in spirit, and both were facing the same problem which remained insoluble to both.   Nietzsche imagined millions prostrated in the dust to the music of Beethoven's "Hymn to Joy," and called it Greek drama. Isadora, following him, was passionately attached to all of Beethoven, especially to the *Ninth Symphony*.   She attempted practically, just as he had attempted imaginatively, to fuse Beethoven's music with a huge dancing chorus; and so his gallant ship and hers both foundered on the same reef.

From the moment when Walter Damrosch had the remarkable inspiration to invite her to dance with his orchestra, (and those were perhaps the happiest days of her life) to the very end in Russia, where she often nearly starved in order to have an orchestra play for her, especially when she was dancing for the very poor to whom she always strove to give the very best, to her the richest possibility in life was fulfilled in dancing with a great orchestra. Her constant dream was to get the masses in all countries to dance:

> I see America dancing, standing with one foot poised on the highest point of the Rockies, her two hands stretched out from the Atlantic to the Pacific, her fine head tossed to the sky, her forehead with a crown of a million stars.[4]

The hyperbole is at least frank, but it does express her ever dominant passion:

---

[2] [Ed. No page reference in the ms. See Duncan, Irma and Allan Ross Macdougall, *Isadora Duncan's Russian Days and Her Last Years in France*, (New York: Covici-Friede, 1929). -J.P.A.]

[3] [Ed.Compare what Isadora Duncan states in her *My Life*: "I had three great Masters, the three great precursors of the Dance of our century--Beethoven, Nietzsche and Wagner. Beethoven created the Dance in mighty rhythm, Wagner in sculptural form, Nietzsche in Spirit. Nietzsche was the first dancing philosopher" (p. 341). -J.P.A.]

[4] Isadora Duncan, *My Life*. [Ed. Only the title in the MS. The passage cited is in Chapter 30, p. 342. - J.P.A.]

I want to dance for the masses...,and I want to dance for them for nothing."⁵ From the beginning I conceived the dance as a chorus or community expression...I so ardently hoped to create an orchestra of dancers that, in my imagination, they already existed."⁶

Ever and forever in all countries, she wanted to make all the children dance. This was her truest, most constant longing. Her dream of having them all dance the *Ninth Symphony* haunted her during the whole of her life. But poor Isadora knew to her sorrow that orchestras are an expensive luxury. A very little straight reasoning would have convinced her that her two ideals do not dwell in the same promised land. Orchestras cannot play on the highest point of the Rockies, or even in fields, or in any place out of doors where workmen are apt to gather. A violin will not recover from a thunder-storm with the elasticity of a human body; it is eminently an indoor testimony of man's aspirations, and its range is properly limited to small concert halls. But workmen carry about with them the greatest of all orchestras: their human voices. Why did Isadora never discover this? She seemed always on the verge of it. Twice it was actually in her hands. Yet she died without ever looking Apollo, the Sun, in the face.

Her first chance was in the beginning of her career. She and her family were sitting in the theatre of Dionysos. They heard "a shrill boy's voice soaring into the night with that pathetic unearthly quality which only boys' voices have. Suddenly it was joined by another voice and another. They were singing some old Greek songs of the country. We sat enraptured. Raymond said:

"This must be the tone of the boys' voices of the old Greek chorus."⁷

Raymond was right. But none of them knew how this discovery could be used. After that, out of many street urchins, they collected ten; and, with the help of a Greek seminarist, they fitted, or tried to, Aeschylean words to some Greek popular, and also some ecclesiastical, songs. Penelope was there at the time, and she told me afterwards, in Neuilly, of the agonizing efforts which she and the seminarist made to square the words of *The Suppliants* to these chosen tunes. Penelope was very young at the time, but she was right in feeling that they were putting the cart before the horse: the music being the cart. None of them guessed, though Penelope knew it well later, that instead of resorting to the barbaric and completely unGreek make-shift of patching together an ancient tragic chorus and peasant tunes composed

---

⁵ *My Life.* [Ed. No reference to page in the MS. The passage is from Chapter 30, p. 342. -J.P.A.]

⁶ *Russian Days.* [Ed. No page reference in the MS. -J.P.A.]

⁷ [Ed. The passage is from Duncan's *My Life*, Chapter 13, p.129. -J.P.A.]

for other and altogether different words, they should have studied the Greek musical system still surviving in those songs which had caught their attention, and then composed music of their own. The upshot of it was that they took these unfortunate boys to Germany to form a chorus for *The Suppliants*. Isadora described these performances. In Vienna, in Munich and Berlin they received her chorus coldly, and interrupted her speeches about the reconstruction of Greek choruses, with shouts demanding the Beautiful Blue Danube, which always brought down the house. In one of these speeches which she quotes, we gather, through her truly Duncanesque medley of German and English, that the ten boys remained motionless on the stage and sang, while she herself impersonated the fifty Danaides; and she apologized to her audience: she was "furchtbar traurig" that she was only one, but "patience, gedult" and she would soon found a school and transform herself into "fifty kleine mädchen." But the cries redoubled for the Schöne Blaue Donau.

If, instead of these rather pitiful performances, Isadora had let Aeschylus alone, if she had allowed her ten Greek boys to sing the songs they knew, and had taught them to express what they were singing in movement, with herself as chorus-leader, *Koryphaios*, she would have had a true beginning for a Greek chorus; and her audiences would then not have shouted for the Blue Danube. Moreover, at that time, she had Penelope with her for about a year. But she never knew through her whole life that her sister-in-law was the personification of Greek music. Perhaps Penelope never sang for her because she sang for very few people. But if Isadora had had the slightest inkling of what Penelope really was, she would have followed, at least in sympathy, the necessary course: of learning the Method which underlies what those Greek boys were singing that night in the Theatre of Dionysos. And later Penelope herself would have been well able to show her the only possibility left us of producing *The Suppliants* or any other Greek play with approximate accuracy, at least in spirit: not by attempting to fit ancient words to existing popular songs, but by making these ancient words the basis for new Greek melodies composed in a Method which the Greeks always have used.

Isadora's second chance was in Russia, just before she left there, toward the end of her life:

> During her visits to the Sports Arena, Isadora noticed that the children, like their older comrades, the soldiers, always marched to and from the grounds to the tune or revolutionary songs sung in chorus. The thought came to her that she might compose dances to the tunes, and have the children dance to them, just as she had taught them to dance the Internationale, singing at the same time the words which their movements expressed.
>
> One afternoon, in a burst of inspiration, she accordingly composed seven dances to the

various revolutionary songs sung daily by the soldiers and children... These dances...which the girls of Isadora have since danced all over Russia, across Siberia, and in the larger towns of China, are amazing in their effect on the audience. (Of course they are!) Quite apart from their revolutionary significance, they are all imbued with real plastic beauty. Several of them... are choreographic chefs-d'oeuvres. They rank with the great dancer's greatest compositions.[8]

I never saw these Russian revolutionary dances; but I can say confidently that they were, in the method followed, the only truly Greek things which Isadora ever created; and also the only things which showed the way to a unification of her two contradictory ideals. Here, at last, after all her striving, she had a method, she had a chorus, she had what she had longed for: "an orchestra of dancers." Nevertheless, very shortly after this, in Nice, she was again dreaming of instrumental orchestras, and actually making desperate efforts to obtain a pianist for a new start for her school. The magnificent impetus which she had inspired in the very end of her stay in Russia, and almost by chance, seems to have made no impression on her at all. She slipped back again immediately to her old dependence on orchestras and pianists: Glück again, Chopin, Beethoven, Wagner, who had all forced her, quite against their own intention, back to the dance as "Thing-in-itself."

I never knew Isadora well. Once I met her in Paris in the early days: and once when she was dancing in Beyreuth. Then, later, the following incident occurred, which I record as a slight addition to the Isadoriana. It was after the loss of her children. She was passing through Athens, and I went to see her to express, or try to, what the whole world was feeling. She asked me to lunch with her, and during lunch she told me the prelude to the tragedy. She had been on tour in Russia, and all the way she kept seeing funerals, children's funerals, which often blocked her way. She arrived back in Paris, and there, on entering her bed-room, which she had left in the hands of an interior decorator to have it made over, but without giving any detailed orders, she found that he had painted all the wood-work black; and that on two doors, which were just opposite her bed, he had painted on each a white cross. On the day of the tragedy, she went out of the house to say good-bye to her children who were starting off with their governess on an excursion. They were already inside the fatal automobile, and the window-glass was closed. She went quite close, and Deirdre put her lips to the glass to kiss her; at that moment Isadora felt that the sea was between them, and that the child was drowning.

"But why," I said, "when you had so many premonitions, did you not realize that you were being warned?"

---

[8] *Russian Days.* [Ed. No page reference in the MS; only the title is given. -J.P.A.]

"Oh," she said, "I told the doctor, and he said that my nerves were unbalanced, and advised me to take some pills, which I did."

After this conversation, Isadora admired extravagantly an Indian moon-stone that I was wearing on a pendant, round my neck. It was a very large cabochon, and had, under the moonlight colour, a bright sun-ray. I had worn it for many years, and it was a gift from my mother; but I felt that at that moment, if anything could make Isadora any happier, it was right for her to have it. So I gave her my stone.

After about a year or so I received a telegram from her that she was returning to Athens specially to see me. She was wearing my stone when I saw her, but she took it off immediately and said she had come from Paris to give it back to me.

"Never," she said, "in my life have I had such terrible luck as with this stone."

I listened to this statement with a sort of shock, because I knew nothing about her life in the meantime. It was hard to imagine any worse misfortune than she had suffered in the loss of her two children before I gave her my stone. But afterwards, when I read her tragic account of the loss of her third baby, I understood what she meant.

"Your stone," she went on, "is alive. It hates me and brings me only evil. It will bring evil to everybody but you. It has forced me to bring it back to you."

"My soul was like a battle-field where Apollo, Dionysos, Christ, Nietzsche and Richard Wagner disputed the ground."[9]

Poor divided Isadora! But neither she, nor anyone else, has seen that these many ethical divergences that wrenched her in different ways all sprang from a primal split whose centre was not the often remarked inconsistency between her life and her art, but a deep-seated inconstancy in her art itself. Isadora, as artist, was completely sincere. She never deviated from the ideal which she herself had conceived as a child; and she suffered many hardships, often with heroic fortitude in the face of material temptations, to keep her ideal pure. And keep it she did until her death. There is therefore no question of conscious moral weakness in the split I am referring to. She did not know it herself, and she is therefore immune from responsibility in regard to it.

Isadora was not merely a dancer, and this she knew well herself. "What a mistake to call me a dancer!" She was a revolutionist, a reformer: not in politics, but in the specific weight of human beings; she was against the downward tendency and physical lethargy of

---

[9]*My Life.* [Ed. No reference to page in the MS. -J.P.A.]

bodies; and her dearest wish for the world was that she might bring her message, not to the few but to millions; not to the rich, but to the poor. And here was the psychic bond between Isadora and her Greek manifestation in dancing. It was fatal that her outward expression resembled a Greek bas-relief, and not an Irish jig, because Greek dancing is the upward dancing of the world; and because the Greeks alone made dancing not the specialty of a few but the universal accomplishment of a nation. That was her dream, and she could no more fail to turn toward Greece with her body, whatever her mind may have been prattling about Irish jigs, than a bird can avoid flying in the air instead of walking on the earth.

Along side of this she was passionately devoted to the vast swelling resonance of great orchestras: "I am the magnetic centre to convey the emotional expression of the orchestra. From my soul sprang fiery rays to connect me with my trembling vibrating orchestra."[10]

Here is the original clash, the primal split of which Isadora herself was unconscious. If she had been concerned primarily with her personal success as a dancer she had her chance after her first appearance with Walter Damrosch. She had created a new form of art; the world was interested; she herself was ecstatically happy in feeling herself, as she says, the magnetic centre of her vibrating orchestra. With a little clever management she could have gone on in the way as a soloist for the rest of her life; from city to city, from one orchestra to another, producing new interpretations of orchestral works. But Isadora was not a soloist: "What a mistake to call me a dancer!" She was first of all a revolutionist against the lethargy of bodies. She dreamed of schools, of nations dancing. The orchestra of musicians was not enough for her; she wanted also an orchestra of dancers: and she wanted to dance for and with the poor.

There is complete physical incompatibility between orchestras and large-scale-activity in dancing. There is first and always will be the economic obstacle from which she suffered all her life: orchestras are and will be expensive. They are cumbersome, and have to arranged for beforehand, with seats, housing facilities, with fixed dates, and what-not, thus destroying the natural spontaneity of dancing, and orchestras are normally connected with enclosed spaces, whereas the education of the masses will ultimately gravitate, in any climate, toward the open air.

> Build for them," she said, "a great Amphitheatre, the only democratic form of theatre, where everyone has an equal view, no boxes or balconies and--look at the gallery up there--do you think it is right to put human beings on the ceiling, like flies, and then ask them to appreciate

---

[10]   *My Life.* [Ed. No page reference in the MS. -J.P.A.]

Art and Music?[11]

But a true Amphitheatre precludes a place for hiding an orchestra. It asks only for human beings expressing simultaneously, with all their faculties, the meaning, the melody, and the movement. Its *raison d' être* is poetry. Everything else is out of place. Poetry, music and gymnastics, Plato's triad, with the gorgeous sound of men's voices, far surpassing any instruments ever invented, these are the foundation of the education of millions, for which Isadora so passionately longed. But she was far from it. Like Nietzsche, she was trying to make living values fit into formulas which were too small. The result, for him, was madness; and for her, it was profound inconsistency in her very essence, which was her art, and this automatically caused division in her mind and life. This is why Isadora's art was Hellenistic in character. In archaic Greece there was no such thing as dancing by itself. This only developed later, and was encouraged, not in religious functions, but rather in drinking parties, such as Plato described in the *Symposium*.

If Isadora could have seen the way to true liberation of the masses, and been able to throw into it her wonderful vitality, to see the human race caught up little by little in ever broadening melody and rhythm and movement; to see her own ideal of America come true, her own ideal of Russia come true; to see her own followers, not as what she called "[My] imitators who had all become saccharine and sweet syrup, promulgating that part of my work which they are pleased to call 'harmonious and beautiful!' but omitting anything the sterner, omitting, in fact, the mainspring and real meaning":[12] but strong supporters and inventors themselves, because their basis would have been strong: would not her personal life have assumed a noble consistency if she had walked on this rock foundation of Greek education?

And when the great tragedy was stalking her, would she not have trusted her own premonitions, and, instead of taking pills for her nerves, would she not have grasped Deirdre from the fatal death-trap when, with the child's kiss through the window-pane, she felt the sea rolling between them?

---

[11] [Ed. Only the title is cited. The passage is "copied" with slight changes from the original. I have restored the text to read as in Isadora Duncan's, *My Life*, Chapter 24, p. 253. -J.P.A.]

[12] [Ed. No reference to title or page. The passage, with slight changes, is from *My Life*, Chapter 30, p. 339. -J.P.A.]

CHAPTER 24

Men as Creators

Only leaving my Long Island retreat, I was glad to accept an invitation from Mary Hambidge to stay with her in Greenwich, and so avoid the turmoil of New York. She was living in an old rambling house built by Stanford White in the romantic Nineties, and it had so many rooms that Mary gave me a sort of palatial suite, looking out on a quiet court-yard with a huge and most beautiful copper beach beside my windows.

I settled in these pleasant surroundings with no thought of outside activities, but I was looking forward eagerly to having my time free to study music, to write more choruses for great plays. There was nothing to justify this desire: logically I might have considered these things at an end as far as I was concerned. Certainly I could not boast of the kind of strength it requires to train my kind of choruses which sing and dance simultaneously, meaning that I also had to do this, singing over the voices of the whole choir whose movements I was illustrating, and also directing the whole play. Beside that, the world around me was moving quickly. The stage and I were far from each other: there was no chance of my catching up with any of the people representing it, or, for that matter, of their catching up with me. The gulf between us was a broad one, stretching out only to the open sea. If I wrote more music for plays I could not direct them myself; no one else would ever use my manuscripts. In fact, no American would be able to decipher the Greek musical notation. Perhaps the sole thing that kept me going was my old tenacious belief in a few of the almost last words of Hamlet. "If it be now, tis not to come; if it be not to come, it will be now; if it be not now, yet it will come; the readiness is all."[1]

Readiness for death, Hamlet is talking about. But readiness for death and readiness for life are exactly the same thing. At least so I had taken this phrase when I first learned the play by heart, and then I was about twelve years old. In the meantime these words had become so much a part of me that there was no longer any conscious volition in acting on them; it was simply the only thing to do, and my only conscious excuse in going ahead and writing music for no purpose whatever was that in that way I would acquire greater facility in writing, and that seemed to be enough.

So I looked over my manuscripts to see what was already done; and over the names of Greek tragedies to choose the one I would turn to next. I had music for *The Bacchae* in

---

[1] [Ed. From *Hamlet*, Act V, Scene II, 32-34. -J.P.A.]

both French and English, which meant of course, totally different scores for each: *The Seven Against Thebes, Hippolytus, Prometheus Bound* in English, and *The Persians,* done for a translation by Jean Vanderpool; this I had written during a visit to Canada when I was staying with Harriet Rutherford, and it was this I used in the Federal Theatre. Then there was the *Peace* of Aristophanes, and the Christmas music, both done for the Federal Theatre; and that was all in the way of plays. But there were quite a number of songs also, many from Swinburne, and many of Stevenson's little songs for children; some from Whitman, and from the Prophet Isaiah, and from the Psalms. I found all these last amusing, and, as it seemed easier then to do something short than anything sustained, I decided to write all the songs of Shakespeare; and after that, if my courage did not falter, to turn again to the Greek plays that have choruses for men.

Still I was haunted, though accomplishment was evidently impossible, by my vision of men in a Tragic Chorus. Why this persistent mania? Why had I veered about so completely, when all the work I had done with girls had had such fine results? I tried to find reasons that were adequate, and I said: "Men's strength is greater," but my girls were wonderfully strong, and did not feel the strain of dancing and singing simultaneously any more than the men with whom I have worked. I said: "Men are more simple;" but my girls were simplicity itself in their direct attack. I said: "Men's voices are incomparable." But this may be merely my personal taste.

In both Delphic festivals my choruses had been beautiful beyond my own hopes; yet in spite of this, and ever since then, I had felt that there are possibilities in this form of art which have not yet been touched, and that, when a Tragic Chorus will attain its own possible excellence, it will also prove that this form of art is the basis of an intelligent approach both to the theatre and to life.

To explain why I feel that this next peak must be scaled by men will lead me back logically to a time in my life when my own concern with Greek drama was still overshadowed by my passion for Shakespeare, and the Elizabethans and the French dramatists; when the Greeks still seemed so far away from us in sheer perfection that I had not yet dared to reckon with them as possible stuff for actual theatre. It was the time when the fight for women's suffrage was in full blast. My mother was an ardent believer in the abundance of positive benefits which were to stream toward mankind when women would have obtained political power; and so she was in the advance guard of the zealots. I listened to them all and agreed with most of what they said, and I do still agree with much of it. But, irrelevantly names uncalled-for went striding through my brain: Orpheus, Homer, Pythagoras,

Aeschylus, Pindar, David, Dante, Shakespeare, Goethe, Beethoven, Bouddha, Jesus: the great creators have all been men. These names and others awakened in me then, and have since sustained, a thought which has persisted in spite of examples one may invoke to the contrary. Are not men inherently creators whenever the problem involved reaches beyond local barriers and boundaries? Women have written truly beautiful lyric poetry; but not one of them has ever formed an ideal synthesis of her own country as Shakespeare did for England, Goethe for Germany, David for the Jews, Dante for Italy. None of them has spoken to the human race of all ages and places as Jesus did, and Bouddha; and not one could be called by Pindar's title, bestowed by the Delphic Sanctuary: "Creator of all Life."

The theatre, this kind of theatre I was dreaming about, is the thing, if greatly used, which can "liberate simultaneously all the faculties of man," and also direct them to noble uses. It is essentially beyond local barriers and boundaries, and can lift us, if anything can, into that Panic of insight and love which alone can make man sane.

If then man has in his nature an inherent creative power, if he has this latent capacity for synthesis more greatly than women, or even on the chance that perhaps he has it: must it not be man who will restore this mighty form of art to the world?

Along with these thoughts a memory returned to me which seemed relevant to my longing for a great tragic chorus of men. It was the manner in which I myself first started to write music for Greek plays. Here is how it happened.

When I began to study Byzantine music, my first reaction was regret that I had given up playing the violin. I was carried away by the beauty of the thing simply as melody, and I wanted an instrument through which I could pour out these beautiful tunes which I was then learning to read. It had to be some instrument whose intervals are not fixed, in order to accommodate the differences between different musical modes. I did actually put strings on my old Amati, and tried to recover whatever technique I had had as a child; but it was very far gone: it needed hours and exercises which I diligently started to perform; but my spare time, after caring for my house and my baby, was given up soon again to deciphering these strange Byzantine signs.

My next impulse was to get some musician, violinist, violist, cellist, to learn this notation, so that I and others could hear the melodic wonders which are locked in these strange old books. I hoped to persuade a cellist to do this, because the cello responds so beautifully to slow, full-throated melodies; and the actually existing literature for this instrument has never given it sufficient change to turn its own best qualities to account. This is natural, because melody is inevitably restricted according to the theory of polyphonic music, and a sustained and varied melody cannot be written within the limits of the tempered scale. At least, no one has ever done it. One hears, in cello recitals, an occasional beautiful theme that pulls at one's heart-strings, but it is always interrupted by technical passages which do not suit this deep-toned instrument so well; and so one's longing for more and more pure melody from the cello always remains unsatisfied. I told all this to friends of mine who were cellists, and how there are books full of such melodies which would sound divinely on the cello, but which hardly anyone can read today. It required however, considerable trouble to learn the notation, and also a different technique to become accustomed to so many unfamiliar intervals. So nothing came of this effort.

But gradually I became absorbed in the Greek theory that music is dependent on words; and, from then on, melody as such attracted me no longer. Of course, then, I was headed full sail toward Greek drama.

It all dawned on me: how the word, enlarged melodically and rhythmically, was itself a dance, inviting gesture; how this would become highly individual and exciting: each member of a group expressing personal reactions to the same unifying word. And I saw how this principle of drama is not confined to the Greek language, but could throw radiance on English, French, German, or any speech of man.

From then on, more than ever, I longed for a musician who would study this strange writing, charged with positive and negative currents, waiting for the master hand to unite them and give a new splendour to the theatre. It became an obsession with me to find someone capable of using the thing, who would pay attention to my dream. But if they did not listen to me in regard to the cello, there was little chance for my notion about Greek choruses.

The first Delphic festival came and went. I have described how my Greek professor wrote the score, and how, in spite of his great erudition, he temporized and Europeanized, modernized his own music. In spite of success, I was dissatisfied. The great thing was yet to do. But I had no notion of attempting it myself. Then, after a lecture tour in America, I was again in Paris. It was before the rising of the propitious wind which carried us through the second festival. Everything had failed, and I had no reason to hope for further activity. I had settled down to work in the Bibliotheque Nationale, an excellent resort for moody idealists. I also wiled away some of my time with old friends.

Among these was a Greek girl: Maria Malandrínou, who had then become commissioned by Gémier to produce *The Libation Bearers* of Aeschylus at the Odéon. She was to direct this performance, and also act the principal role herself. I saw her quite often, and followed her growing anxiety concerning the music for her play. It had been entrusted to a French musician who naturally composed according to the way he had been taught, and had produced a score as creditable perhaps as possible under the circumstances. Maria had spent much of her life in Paris, and her own musical training had not been different from any other; but her Greek instinct was strong enough to balk at this medley of Aeschylean words corseted in harmonies of the Conservatoire; and day by day her distress mounted toward despair. One day she rushed to my house looking like an Aeschylean Fury.

"I am going to throw over the whole play," she said, "I cannot stand the music".

When she had gone I picked up Paul Mazon's translation which she was using, and turned to the first chorus, wondering how one could help this French musician to an understanding of the sort of music for which I knew Maria was longing, but which she could not describe.

I started tentatively to write, allowing the melody to follow the lilt of the French words. It soon came more easily than I had expected, and in a few hours the first chorus was finished. I had written it in European notation, which gave only a poor approximation of what I was trying to express; but my only thought had been that this might serve as a suggestion to Maria's musician, and give him an idea as to how Greek choruses should be handled. The next morning Maria was there again looking very miserable. She was on her way to the theatre to give in her resignation. I had her sit down and explained to her that if she liked the little thing I had done, she could give it to her musician in order to show him the method of approach which might produce what she wanted. He could use it, I said, simply as a suggestion, and perhaps he would write a new score in that manner. I then sang it to her and she was extremely excited.

"What suggestion!" she cried, "this is the thing itself."

After that I was leaving Paris immediately. The propitious wind had started to blow, and I was off to Greece to direct the second festival. I dined with Maria to celebrate this event, and she asked me for music for the whole of *The Libation Bearers* done in the manner of my first chorus. I told her that my attempt was without excellence; that it had been so hurried I did not know myself what I had done; and that anyway, if she were to teach it from a European score, which was all she was able to read, she would produce only a deplorable caricature. But she liked it as it was, and felt that it was the only hope for her play. So finally I told her that I would write it on the train going down, and send it back to her at once, but only on one condition: that she promise me that my name never be used in connection with it.

Maria made me this promise.[2]

I started for Greece, and wrote the rest of the score against the wobbling of the Orient Express; and on arriving in Athens I cleaned up my shaky manuscript as well as I could and sent it off to Paris. But this incident meant nothing to me. I had no faith in the dynamic power of this type of music when it has passed through the crucible of European notation; and, apart from that, my own performance, so hurried and thoughtless, did not in any way deflect toward myself my customary search for a musician. This attitude was not a reasoned decision on my part. It had never been a matter of choice; nor was there ever any notion of sacrificing for one reason or another a talent which I felt to be latent in myself. I simply felt nothing; and I had no more urge to compose music than I have today to write a sonnet, for which I knew that I have no talent at all. Therefore, if it had not been for the occurrence which I shall now relate, certainly I never would have started. So I soon became absorbed in the trials and delights of the second festival, and *The Libation Bearers* passed entirely out of my mind.

Well, the festival came and went. The world had become quiet again, and I was living alone in a little garden cottage near Athens. I had many affairs to attend to, and music was far from my thoughts.

I will prelude what follows by saying that I never have dreams (at least I have not had any since I was a child) and also by the fact that, during the period I am recording, I was completely normal. There was nothing in my life which could have caused me any emotional excitement; and night after night I went to sleep with quite ordinary thoughts or worries on my mind.

But one night in my dream there was another sleeping near me: I did not know afterwards who, but in my dream I was deeply in love, and this creature near me was in love with me, but in love as a woman loves a man. And a wave of passion swept over me as I possessed her, with a kind of physical power that my body could not have felt. Then on waking I felt a kind of weakness which, again, my body could not know. Life had gone out of me.

In this experience there is probably nothing very unusual except the fact that, on waking, this transformation did not change back to normal. Awake, and going about my ordinary occupations, in the street, or with my neighbours whom I saw every day, I was a

---

[2] But it was not kept. Years after that I learned that a performance had been given at the Salle Pleyel of *The Libation Bearers* with very lamentable choruses, which, on the program, were attributed to me.

different person. I was vividly conscious of being a man, with his physical organs, and, to a certain extent, with his muscular strength; and I was astonished that no one saw or felt that I was different. My outward appearance must have been entirely unchanged, because I saw numbers of people; I walked about; I kept appointments at various ministries; friends bowed to me in the street, and we talked and no one betrayed any surprise or constraint. But I was inwardly thinking: how dull they are not to realize that I am somebody else.

This metamorphosis, as real as the air I breathed or the food I ate, lasted for over a month. It was nothing but a projected dream: but in the glow of this new reality I wrote all the choruses of *The Bacchae* of Euripides, in a French translation by Mario Meunier. While it lasted I was conscious of a mastery of my medium which I had never felt in anything before. I was really creating music. Then, when my score was finished, this illusion faded imperceptibly, and I was conscious of it no more. In me it was a sensation that came and went: but it left me with the capacity of writing music; and also with the certainty that my vision of a tragic chorus will not come true until it is done by men.

This psychological phenomenon which I have here recorded has reminded me of a book I once heard of. I did not read it, and I do not know either the title or its author, but I remember the theme: the twelve Olympic gods represent the twelve basic qualities of MAN; that some of these qualities are predominantly masculine, and some are predominantly feminine; but that each man or woman, in the soul's spiritual ascent, must acquire and perfect them all.

Perhaps, sometimes, during one cycle of experiences, a shaft from another cycle may be thrown athwart one's house, and so confuse one's sight with excess of light.

CHAPTER 25

Ted Shawn

The Shakespeare songs were finished. I had lain in the bell of a cow-slip, and came unto the yellow sands, and borne him barefaced on the bier, and I had let the canakin clink.[1] It was fun, and I had enjoyed doing them, but almost from the start, my next venture was slated. All along I had been reading different translations of the *Agamemnon* of Aeschylus, with the whole great Trilogy set as my next goal ahead. One above all was incomparable: the one by my deeply admired friend Edith Hamilton, who has written very noble words about Greek drama:

> Only twice in literary history has there been a great period of tragedy, in the Athens of Pericles and in Elizabethan England. What these two periods had in common, two thousand years and more apart in time, that they expressed themselves in the same fashion, may give us some hint of the nature of tragedy, for far from being periods of darkness and defeat, each was a time when life was seen exalted, a time of thrilling and unfathomable possibilities. They held their heads high, these men who conquered at Marathon and Salamis, and these who fought Spain and saw the Great Armada sink. The world was a place of wonder; mankind was beauteous; life was lived on the crest of the wave. More than all, the poignant joy of heroism has stirred men's hearts. Not stuff for tragedy, would you say? But on the crest of the wave one must feel either tragically or joyously: one cannot feel tamely. The temper of mind that sees tragedy in life has not for its opposite the temper that sees joy. The opposite pole to the tragic view of life is the sordid view. When humanity is seen as devoid of dignity and significance, trivial, mean, and sunk in dreary hopelessness, then the spirit of tragedy departs."[2]

And about translations she wisely says: "Until the perfect, the final, translator comes, the plays should be perpetually retranslated for each generation," for, as she amusingly points out, translations follow the spirit of the age of the translator, and quickly become dated.[3] But perhaps her own *Agamemnon* forms the exception to this excellent rule. It is more starkly near the Greek than any other, and, at times, it is also great English poetry:

> "Drop, drop--in our sleep, upon the heart
> sorrow falls, memory's pain,

---

[1]   [Ed. The phrases from *A Midsummer Night's Dream*, Act II, Scene 1, lines 8-10 (Fairy): "..And I serve thee fairy Queen/ To dew her orbs upon the green/ The cowslips fall her pensioner be./...I must go seek some dewdrops here/ And hang a pearl in every cowslip's ear." Also line 126 (Titania): "And sat with me on Neptune's yellow sands..." -J.P.A.]

[2]   Edith Hamilton, *The Greek Way*, pp. 143-4. [Ed. Page numbers in the MS refer to the 1930 edition; see also the augmented edition of this work, printed by W.W. Norton & Co. New York, 1942, p. 232. -J.P.A.]

[3]   [Ed. No reference in the MS. I have not been able to locate the source of this quotation. -J.P.A.]

and to us, though against our very will,
even in our own despite
comes wisdom
by the awful grace of God."[4]

One night, saying these beautiful lines to the resounding house, I was wandering around rather late. It was after one o'clock, mid-winter, and I was quite alone.[5] Mary was in New York. I went down the broad old-fashioned stairway into the living-room, and suddenly the telephone started ringing. It had been ringing at intervals all the evening, but over in my part of the old house I might as well have been in the next town; and only this chance walking about to the tune of Edith's lines made me hear it. It was Peggy Murray, who, during each entr'acte of a play, and finally at an after-the-theatre supper party, had tried to get me.

"You must come to New York tomorrow to see Ted Shawn dance. Katherine Dreier has invited us both, and she wants you very much."[6]

"But darling whirlwind Peggy," I remonstrated, "I don't want to come. I have decided to go back to Greece to die there. I have seen many American dancers, and passed enjoyable evenings watching most of them; but between their feeling for the theatre and mine there is a gulf which is not spanned by any bridge. I am not in the mood for seeing any more."

"But you have never seen Ted Shawn," argued Peggy. "You cannot be so unreasonable as to allow a great dancer to pass you by unnoticed: especially if you are going away."

"But dear Peggy," I said, "I do not feel well, and the theatre tires me."

"Well or ill," insisted Peggy, "tomorrow you must come."

It was true: I felt that my last American venture had come to an end. I could just as well, I reasoned, write choruses to Edith Hamilton's *Agamemnon* in any one of my favourite villages, and breathe Greek air at the same time, as to stay for the rest of my life near Mary's friendly copper-beach; and then some day, I thought, in Greece, I might begin to dare to

---

⁴ [Ed. From *Agamemnon*, ll. 179-81:
στάζει δ' ἐν θ' ὕπνῳ πρὸ καρδίας
μνησιπήμων πόνος· καὶ παρ' ἄ-
κοντας ἦλθε σωφρονεῖν. -J.P.A.]

⁵ [Ed. The event must have taken place in January 1939, when Ted Shawn's Company performed at at the Washington Irving High School in New York. -J.P.A.]

⁶ [Ed. Katherine Dreier, an abstract painter and ardent admirer of Ted Shawn, wrote a book titled, *Shawn the Dancer*. See Walter Perry, *Ted Shawn: Father of American Dance*, (The Dial Press, New York, 1976), p. 133. -J.P.A.]

write music to Greek words instead of English.

The next night, in the crowded Washington Irving High School, I was definitely annoyed with Peggy for having broken down my resistance: or rather with myself for having let her break it down. So, when the curtain opened on the "Dance of the Ages,"[7] I was wondering how soon I would be able to slip out from the stifling jam of students. But presently I was standing up and shouting more fervently than any of the youthful fans around me. Here at last were men who were not afraid of being beautiful; who, with no trace of sentimentality or effeminacy, actually were beautiful.

After the play, when Shawn heard my name, he said:

"But I have been looking for you for years; where have you been?"

"There are things," I said, "that I want to talk about with you, but they cannot be said over a tea-cup; when can we have an hour or so straight ahead, with nothing to interrupt us?"

"Tomorrow," he said, "at dawn, I am going West. It will have to be next May."[8]

At that Katherine Dreier suggested that we each come half way on his return: that he come down from Lee, and I come up from Greenwich, and that we spend a day together at her house near Danbury. We both accepted. And so, for the time, the copper-beach gained the day.

Four months after this, on a bright Connecticut morning, Katherine's car came to fetch me. A friendly welcome from Barton Mumaw at her door, and from Katherine and Shawn within; a pleasant lunch with recollections of mutual friends, of where we might have met and didn't; and then, on a bench in the garden, I soon was trying to say a dozen things in one, and yet keep my words clear: that dancers alone can restore great theatre; they alone have the physical power, and when their minds see the true goal ahead, their bodies will not be afraid; that all the clap-trap paraphernalia of the theatre must be scrapped, and architecture restored; that music must rediscover melody, the human voice must be freed to convey great poetry to men without the drag of heavy static accompaniments; that the rhythm of human feet must take the place of these. And thus the dancer, with all his faculties liberated, will be the true interpreter of man's own inner vision of himself.

Shawn's answer was immediate. He had seen many attempts by others at singing and dancing, or reciting and dancing simultaneously. He had done it himself in his "Penitentes" and the "Maori War Haka"; but he had always observed that in such art forms the attention

---

[7]   [Ed. Comp. W. Perry, *Ted Shawn*, pp. 18, 19. -J.P.A.]

[8]   [Ed. The time intended for the meeting would have been May, 1939. -J.P.A.]

of the audience is not centered; that there is no possibility of producing an effect which is direct, because people must either listen to the meaning of the words, or watch the movement of the dancing; they cannot do both at the same time, and therefore the result is inevitably blurred and unsatisfactory. I said that I had not seen the performances he referred to, but I believed that in all these cases the words and the movements had not been coordinated organically. The words may have been only descriptive, or, even if they awakened dramatic emotion in the reader or hearer, they did not coincide with the only vaguely related movement of the dancer. They lacked, in short, what I called "dramatic immediacy."

Up to that moment Shawn had listened with flawless courtesy but with no inner response. But these two words: "dramatic immediacy", broke down the wall between us. From that moment we were speaking the same language. I tried to explain the function of Greek music in this other kind of theatre. I sang a few short songs: from Whitman, the Psalms, the Prophet Isaiah, and two little war dances from Aristophanes. Shawn said: "I should like to try it." But he went on to explain that his company of men was a corporation, that therefore no decision could be taken concerning any joint activity without a general vote; but on returning home he would consult them at once, and, in case they agreed with him, would I come up to Lee for a trial? He also said that he had been thinking of composing a dance for a poem by Witter Binner: "Dance for Rain at Cochiti." Would I see what could be made of it from my point of view if he sent it to me?

After that we went to the house, and Katherine presented to me a beautiful book bound in vellum. It was the tribute to Shawn which she had published, containing pictures of him, and her own appreciation of his genius. She wrote in the date: May 15th, 1939, and she and Shawn both inscribed most gracious words about our meeting. And so this memorable visit came to an end.

Memorable indeed. I had spent a day with one whose gifts and experience were equal to the great new race to be run; whose mind was not fixed in a groove in spite of most varied activities, of which he had always been the centre; who was able to consider intelligently an aspect of his own art which he had never thought of before. For the first time a great dancer had listened to what I was longing to say.

Very shortly after this a letter came from him fixing a date, May 29th, for my coming to Lee. His group were "genuinely enthusiastic" and "honestly looking forward to the new experience." And the little book arrived with Witter Binner's poems. Shawn had sent it hastily on first returning home, but he wrote that "in the light of our talk" he realized that I would reject it. Almost the whole poem is a description of what the eye takes in at a glance, and therefore words are superfluous: how the bodies of the Indians are painted, what their costumes are like, and so forth. There was hardly a word coming straight from the consciousness of those dancing. It was a poem which could have inspired Jess Meeker to write one of his remarkable dance-conscious compositions:[9] but it had no place in that other kingdom where "poetry, music and gymnastics are one."

I had hardly arrived in Lee, when I found myself in the studio with all of Shawn's group around me. Some were sitting on benches, but most of them on the floor. Shawn had asked me to teach the Isaiah: "Awake, awake, put on thy strength, O Zion,"[10] the two Pyrrhic dances from Aristophanes, and two short poems of Whitman's. I was teaching these things orally, fascinated by the trained attention I was receiving which made the work go fast. Shawn was sitting near, listening, but not taking part. Suddenly, after a few repetitions of one of the little war dances, and before the group knew it well, Shawn got up with an exclamation:

"I can't stand it any longer: I must see how it works."

And with that he taught the choreography of this dance which had sprung from his mind, fully armed, as it were by merely hearing the music. So there were the men singing and dancing in an hour's time as if they had done it all their lives.

About a week after this Shawn was leaving to teach at a Summer School in Peabody College Tennessee. I had expected to return to Greenwich. But one day he said:

"After I go, students for my Summer School will be arriving. Certain members of my group will stay to teach them for the first two weeks, and then I will take them on my return. But in the meantime, would you like to stay and take these boys who are coming? And would you teach them a Greek chorus? And could you have the words and music ready by the time I return?"

For such a request I did not need persuasion. I started at once to revise my first chorus of *The Persians* of Aeschylus, feeling, through this short experience with Shawn, and through certain very intelligent remarks of his, that I had already learned how to write music better. It was an ambitious choice. This chorus is enormously long, but I felt that it is immensely interesting choreographically, and I was anxious to try it.

Shawn left, and the Summer School arrived about a week after. As soon as they were settled, they were told that they were all to gather at five o'clock for a lesson with me, and

---

[9]   [Ed. See W. Perry, *op. cit.*, pp. 5, 54, 144, 153, 155-7. -J.P.A.]

[10]   [Ed. From *Isaiah*, Ch. 52, verse 1. -J.P.A.]

that from five to six every day I would teach them. So there were these boys who had come to study dancing, and Shawn not there to tell them anything about it. However, their manners pulled them through the first ordeal satisfactorily. That is to say, they did gather together, and they did listen, which was a great relief, remembering my first hours in the Federal Theatre; and during that first hour I got them singing, and then all was easy. The time in which we had to do it was so short that it needed lots of pushing ahead: leaving what they had barely begun to understand for other passages entirely new, and again abandoning these for other new ones, and so on till we reached the end of the great chorus. The boys were doubtful about this method. They wanted to learn each part well, and then go on to the next. They were afraid they would forget. But they were surprised on going back to what had before been very shaky to find that they almost knew it; and on a second and third complete revision to find that the beginning seemed to grow by itself as they learned the end. And so when Shawn arrived, they sang the whole thing to him by heart. Soon those of his own group who had been absent also knew it, and then, in all, there were thirty men singing.

Shawn's task was no less arduous than mine had been: for he also had two weeks to compose and teach the choreography for this monstrous thing, because he wanted to have it ready for one of his Friday Teas, which have long been an institution in the Berkshires. He did not let me come to his rehearsals. So when his part was ready it burst on me as something completely new, with every emotion of this great chorus expressed in appropriate gesture. It was a very thrilling moment when Shawn called me in to see it.

At the Tea, when this chorus and several other things of mine were given, I heard people asking the boys afterwards how they felt about singing and dancing simultaneously, were they not out of breath, didn't they feel tired? And their answer amazed even me: they were not conscious of singing: it made dancing easier.

After this first performance another was asked for, and this was fixed for the last Friday Tea, in the beginning of September. Thus, the few days I had expected to spend in Lee were lengthening into months. Meantime, some boy in the Summer School, then a few more, and finally the whole Shawn establishment wanted to learn to make sandals. So I started classes of cobblers, as many as I could take at a time, and before long, tennis shoes and sneakers had disappeared, and nice looking feet were walking about with quite becoming straps. These boys had grown fond of our work together, and when there was to be a rehearsal or a performance of the Chorus they would say: "Today we have our dear Persians." Altogether, the atmosphere at Jacob's Pillow was unusual and delightful. In this machine age Shawn had succeeded in founding a community in which there was nothing mechanical. In spite of very strict discipline in his classes which no one ever infringed, and an iron-bound routine in his dancing technique which seemed to be the same for all, he had produced a group of dancers who were highly individual, and each one totally different from the other. In their group movements, in Shawn's fascinating choreographic creations, these men could and did fuse their very different personalities for a common objective, and produce a perfectly harmonized general effect; but when they started dancing solos something came out of each in which they were unlike Shawn and also unlike each other, and, often, very attractive, showing that Shawn's method in teaching, beside making people work well together, had also made each one free to express himself. Beside these marked differences in their solo dancing, each one of these men had a trade of his own, and, like an ancient monastery, this place was kept up with hardly any outside help. Wilbur McCormack, in spite of his beautiful leaps, was a carpenter, Frank Overlees a mechanic and electrician, the Delmar twins were gardeners, but I have also seen them build a very good house. Johnny Schubert was a costumer, and Fred Hearn, although he sat with perfect ease in midair with nothing to support him, could also sit at a large table and make out complicated tax reports. Each one of these men could do one or several things well, beside being excellent dancers, and they were always busy about something useful.

In the midst of this, Shawn, indefatigable, worked much harder than anyone else. What with a boy's Summer School, and a girl's Summer School, and his own group with whom he was preparing a new program for the winter, and also the choreography of my choruses, his teaching schedule was nine hours a day. He also took entire care of his very large correspondence, and, beside all this, everyone's personal troubles, and whatever mishaps occurred on the farm all went to him. During all this time we never said more than a passing greeting. He was far too busy. Although he had written from Nashville that he was returning by plane which would give him two extra days at the farm: "there is so much to talk to you about," and that would give us a little time before the summer schedule began, this conversation never came off.

He had also written asking me to think up a solo for him which the boys could sing while he danced, to make part of the program with my choruses. This was no easy matter, as I had realized before in searching for words for possible dances; for, in spite of the enormous and impressive body of English literature, there is astonishingly little that has the quality of almost any Greek chorus. Measured by this test, English poets are obviously scribes writing beautiful words: they are not dancers.

I finally chose, rather reluctantly, nine verses from the 4th act of Shelley's *Prometheus*

Unbound. It was not what I wanted, but Shawn made it beautiful, wearing as he did the dress I had woven for Okeanos in *Prometheus Bound;* and in dancing he made me realize why I had taken so much trouble to weave these costumes for the plays I produced. At last my material and my floating embroideries were responding to noble movement in the way I had imagined.

During these Teas I saw many of Shawn's great dances; and, looking over the lists of those I had not seen, I realized how constant he had been in the kind of subjects he has used for his art. Of course in his eclecticism he has many branching capacities, but on the whole, the thing that has drawn him has been the religious aspect of dancing: "Prometheus Bound," the "Mevlevi Dervish," "The Cosmic Dance of Shiva," "Ramadan Dance" (also a dance of cosmic union), "The Divine Idiot, Saint Francis". All these are spiritual heroes, and Shawn has also done the whole Christian Ritual in dancing. All this goes back to his own youth when he chose to enter a theological school to become a Christian minister. Subsequently this choice proved too narrow for his spirit, and he gave up the ministry, not because his inward ideal had changed, it has never changed, but because he saw in dancing a truer way of approaching it.

During my recent years I have often thought: "Where are the American pioneers?" Did the mighty spiritual eagerness which settled America feel satisfied: had it gained its only goal when material plenty was acquired? Are there no sons and grandsons to carry on the struggle for objectives which are better than the search for gold? Well, here was a pioneer! A man who could cut down forests and let in sunlight, and then move on into more impenetrable wildernesses, leaving the clearing behind him for those who were looking for ease. Shawn had done it over and over again. Every phase of his career had been a grapple with impossible difficulties until he had tamed them; but for gathering in the fruits of his own planting he had always been indifferent. His gifts, his acquired techniques, his ceaseless labours, his ever-new outlook on life were an answer to my formulated hope; the *Koryphaios* who could and would restore great theatre in America, and make it a mirror to reflect the true Spirit of the American people.

One Sunday afternoon we gathered in Mac's cabin secretly so that no one would find Shawn, and I read for the whole company *The Dithyramb of the Rose.* That evening Shawn said to me:

"I cannot bear that this poem should remain unknown; if I could give it even to a few people I should be happy."

Some days after this he had found his plan: instead of giving many little presents at

Christmas, books to some, candy or fruit or flowers to others, he would publish *The Dithyramb:* and so at least his own friends would possess it.[11] I had read this poem very often during all these years in America: in fact I have read it to anyone who cared to listen, and there had always followed the usual vociferous utterances of praise, real or false; but only two people have grasped it as a hungry man siezes food, or as one parched draws in long draughts of clear water. The other one is beloved Elsa Barker, to whom I have read all the few things of Anghelos' which have been translated into English. Her eagerness and understanding have been purely Greek. What more can one say?

The second performance of our choruses had passed, and I was again preparing to go. But Shawn said one day at table that the Company had a proposal to make to me. They had to buy stuff to replace old costumes; would I like to bring my loom and weave it for them, and so they got better material, and we could all stay together a little longer?

So Frank Overlees drove me down to Greenwich in one of the station wagons into which we piled my loom, and any threads I happened to have. I had enough for one good warp, and we ordered more at once. For the threading of my first warp the weather was beautiful, so after making my long silk braid I hung it over a tree, tied my reed and heddles to one of the branches, and did my threading under the spreading boughs. To the unskilled, my warp at that stage must have presented a complicated appearance, for Fred Hearn came walking by, and he said:

"Eva darling, do you really think you know what you are doing?"

Presently, however, my loom was the envy of all. There wasn't a boy who didn't want to learn; "Eva, won't you please teach me?" And another voice: "Can't I try too?" and, as far as throwing the shuttle was concerned, most of them did learn; and many were most helpful in winding for me quantities of bobbins.

For about a month my loom was working in Lee, and in that time I made three warps amounting to ninety-six yards in all. I also dyed this stuff in three different colours. This weaving was a new problem, for the stuff had not only to hang well, but it had to stand the

---

[11] [Ed. This dramatic poem was in fact translated. See Anghelos Sikelianos, *The Dithyranb of the Rose,* (Translated by Frances Sikelianos. Privately printed for Ted Shawn. A limited edition of five hundred copies. Christmas, 1939. Copyright 1939 by Eva Sikelianou). The translator was Glafkos Sikelianos' first wife. I have in my collection copy 496, with Anghelos Sikelianos' signature and also Ted Shawn's signature at the bottom of the page of his own "Introduction." Attached to the first page is a note he wrote from Eustis, Florida, on February 20, 1950, to Mary (Hambidge?): "Dear Mary: Finally I located a copy of The Dithyramb of the Rose (sic), which I promised you--so here it is. Will be back in New York from March fifteenth on for six weeks and hope to see you then. Yours, Ted". Eva Palmer-Sikelianos entrusted this copy to me before departing for what proved to be her last visit to Greece. -J.P.A.]

kind of wear which the Shawn Group clothes are subject to: so violent that often they had to have new costumes after three or four performances. But evidently I managed it, for here is a hurried note from Shawn, written in Terre Haute, Indiana: "We all adore the Malpai pants: they are heavenly in every way. Color is too beautiful: like the most expensive suede leather, and a sort of mist like on grapes. And they fit so well, hang so marvelously, and feel more comfortable and right than ever before." So I had acquired a new technique, making stuff that would not only look well: for these costumes, after a whole winter on tour with the Shawn Company, now broken up and scattered, are all washed and put away, and still as good as new.

The weather was growing cold, and this time I really was going back to Greenwich. But we wanted costumes for the *Isaiah* which Shawn thought of taking on tour, with a few things of Whitman, etc. I felt a little nervous about this, and regretted losing our good work in the Aeschylean chorus with his fine summer group of thirty men. After this, the company of eight, fine as they are in dancing together, were meager for singing, especially as only one of them had a fine voice, and that one is the only one who had a perfect ear. All the others could follow along well enough when I was singing, but when alone they would slump back into the tempered scale, which took the edge off the effectiveness of my tunes. Yet it seemed a pity to give it up, for they were beautiful anyway; so I consoled myself with the thought of effective costumes which I would embroider in the loom. And Shawn said:

"How about Florida? We shall all be there before Christmas; we could then have more rehearsals, and you could get some sunshine in the meantime?"

I was met by the parents of Barton Mumaw who drove me to their lovely home in central Florida.[12] Their house is under tall southern pines and very grand live oaks, in grounds facing two small lakes, and right next to Shawn's. For a while I stayed in their hospitable home, and then they offered me a little two-room cottage, ideal for whoever really likes to be alone. There I set up my loom, and started my eight embroidered costumes for the *Isaiah.*

While these were still under way, Shawn and his whole group arrived. He asked me if I would think up another solo to replace the Shelley: he was afraid that the singing of the *Prometheus Unbound* would be too difficult, that the flute interludes would be impractical in travelling, and that, anyway, neither of us liked it much from the start, and it would be fun to try something new. So there I was again facing this problem: in the mass of English

---

[12]   [Ed. In Eustis, Florida. -J.P.A.]

literature is there anything which the poet himself, in writing it, had visualized as movement? They, our poets, often give us the impression of movement, and one turns to long-remembered poems with the idea: "that will be it." But on rereading, disappointment is almost inevitable. It was awkward, at that moment, that my own books were scattered to the four winds, the few I had with me were mostly ecclesiastical music. Shawn's books were almost all at Lee, and there was no public library anywhere near. With this dearth of books, I did what I could. Remembering a certain dramatic quality in the short lyrics by Eugene O'Neill in *Lazarus Laughed,* I sent to New York for this, and when it came I found that in attaching these short poems together, in their actual order in the play, they produced a very effective miniature drama, almost an epitome of the play itself. So I wrote this, and I liked the result; but the difficulties ahead in learning Mr. O'Neill's whereabouts, in obtaining permission to disconnect these poems from their context, for reasons with which he would be entirely unfamiliar, to produce with them a sort of dance drama, all seemed too complicated.

Shawn telegraphed to New York, and ordered by air mail *Man With the Bull-tongue Plow,* by Jesse Stuart, feeling that American earth is alive in these sonnets. I felt so too, and I wrote a song to one of them: "The call of earth is pounding on my head", but it was not what I wanted. I turned to the Psalms and wrote "By the waters of Babylon", and this had the quality I was searching for (quite naturally, because David was a dancer, and perhaps Isaiah was too) but it was melancholy and biblical, and I agreed with Shawn that one thing of that sort on the program was enough. So from that, at least to effect a contrast, I turned to the Chorus of Initiates in *The Frogs* of Aristophanes; but Shawn read the words first, and was upset by the meadows and berries and myrtle crowns, and did not even hear my music. He wanted something American: why didn't I take Whitman? Obediently I turned to *When Lilacs Last in the Dooryard Bloomed,* and wrote perhaps the best thing I have ever done, but it was too long and not appropriate for a sort of solo wind-up to choruses. It had to be something shorter and much snappier.

In the midst of our dilemma Katherine Drier came to spend the day. She suggested "Merlin and the Gleam" by Tennyson, as a sort of good old stand-by. We obtained this from the little library in Eustis, and I wrote it the following day. But the result would have been excellent for a young ladies "Finishing School" about fifty years ago. The music simply emphasized the meaning and the manner of the poem, it can do nothing else, and here, in Tennyson's "Gleam", the meaning is all right: but the manner is dated to say the least. I reread *Leaves of Grass* more diligently, and finally stopped over the "Song of the Open

Road", sure that that was what we wanted. I wrote it, and liked it, Shawn liked it, and the men got together to learn a new song.

Christmas came, and, with Shawn's sweet old-fashioned way of keeping everyone's Christmas, and everyone's birthday, we had a tree. Each had his own pile under the tree, but Shawn's pile had become so preposterous that his Christmas-morning ceremony, with and excellent egg-nog made by himself, lasted four hours before he could finish opening his own presents which had been collecting for weeks from all over the United States.

Shortly after New Year's he was to open his new ballet, "The Dame" in Miami. I did not go, fortunately, because they encountered sub-zero weather in a theatre built of cement which possessed no heating apparatus, not even an oil stove.

Afterwards I saw "The Dame" in St. Augustine, and I was delighted that Shawn had won the day and kept my pieces on the program. The *Isaiah* was beautiful, so was the Pyrrhic Dance, and I loved Shawn's "Song of the Open Road." At this performance I realized that Barton Mumaw is a very great dancer. Up at the farm, in the studio, I had been carried away by the few solo dances he had done, and had even compared his with the great Nijinsky, but throwing the greater praise on Barton's side. His acrobatic feats, I said, are as breath-taking as Nijinsky's, but he has an inner spiritual quality and a dramatic quality that Nijinsky lacked. In St. Augustine, however, I saw something else. It was in the quite thrilling Jacob's Pillow Concerts, where the whole company is on the stage most of the time, which involved, for each, waiting about in various attitudes while the others danced. This waiting about was attractive in all of them because Shawn had arranged it well. But what Barton did was not a matter of arrangement. He had an ease in doing nothing on the stage which could not have been exceeded if he had been alone in his own pleasant drawing-room in Florida. There was no apparent consciousness of "Here am I, and there is the audience." Whether he happened to be facing them or turning his back made no difference. In fact, though he never had been in one, he might as well have acted all his life in a real theatre instead of in the puppet shows which modern theatres are. He had that most rare thing on the stage: an all-round-consciousness.

After St. Augustine they went their usual way, dancing in far-separated towns for single nights, themselves chauffeurs, stage-hands, electricians, mechanics, beside racing along with blizzards that year all the way. In Boston, in May, they danced together for the last time. Shawn had accomplished what he had set out to do. He had made dancing an honourable profession for men, and he felt that that special task was finished. After that, the summer and autumn and early winter passed for him in various activities, and toward

Christmas, 1940, he and Barton came again to Florida, where, in the meantime, I had remained.

When Shawn and I first met in the Washington Irving High School, and I asked him to appoint a time when we could talk together for an hour or so, his first answer was: "You don't know what you're asking"; and when Katherine proposed that we both spend a day at her house on his return from the West, he said that he had not had a single holiday in twenty-eight years. It seemed exaggerated when he said it; but after having watched his activities for over a year and a half, I believed it was true. In fact, by that time, I had acquired a general impression that Shawn does speak the truth; and that the little minor vice of prevarication which artists often allow themselves was not part of his make up. From day to day I had seen him carrying on regardless of outside difficulties, and of minor hurts and ills, and I remembered a boast I had made once that I had not yet found anyone who could work with me in double harness when I once got started, that I had to take people always by relays and allow to each periods of rest while I went on working. It was true that in directing a play, or a Delphic festival, or whatnot, and weaving costumes at the same time, I had more than once carried through a schedule of eighteen hours a day for long periods at a time. But I certainly could not boast of swinging such work as a steady regime for twenty-eight years, and evidently Shawn could.

As a result of this, our day at West Redding had remained the only time we had talked together peacefully. But this second holiday period in Florida moved at a more leisurely pace, and conversation seemed a permissible way of spending one's time.

One day Shawn had been reading something I had written about the priority of poetry over the other arts, which was to him insufferable heresy. How could I say such a thing? How can words be a source of anything since they are merely a tool of the intellect, and are the one thing about which people never agree? Words mean one thing to one person and another thing to another. Over words and differences of opinion as to their meaning religious wars have been fought, schisms have occurred to split churches asunder, and it is the fight over the meaning of words which had made of Christianity a collection of warring sects, whereas the living Christ would draw all men to him in one single congregation. There is no great mystic in the world's history who has not complained bitterly about the inadequacy of words to say what they had to say. Whereas dancing, he said, is the root and trunk of all the other arts; it is the very staff of life itself; it is the only thing which can express the ultimate: and so Orpheus, Apollo and Dionysos were dancers, and they "danced out the mysteries", which meant that the highest, deepest, and most sacred emotions of mankind are beyond the possibility of words to express.

I also believed, I said, that dancing was the first of all the arts. Children dance before they talk, and should be encouraged to dance freely and expressively, and let that be their first experience in education, which would be vastly better than being made to sit at desks and learn words which they do not understand. But I remembered how he himself had complained once that as dancing perfects itself in subtlety of expression the great public is less and less able to follow the meaning, and that they lose the most important things which the dancer is expressing. Both of these arts can misfire in their isolated efforts to carry meaning to minds only partly trained; but it is precisely those people who should be enlightened by art. There is not the slightest doubt that word and movement together, if they can say the same thing at the same time, are an immense help to the slower comprehension of the majority of men, and it is at this point that the priority of poetry becomes incontrovertible. Probably all primitive people used word, melody and movement spontaneously as a single expression, and separation into specialized art forms came later. But on reaching the stage where artistic creation becomes conscious, one nation alone preserved and mightily developed this union of the arts, but they knew well that the way to accomplish this is to give priority to poetry. For in this combined art-form music must express the meaning of the word, and dancing must follow both word and music if the three are to be simultaneous. Therefore at this stage of art, that is to say, where drama becomes preeminent in uniting all the arts, dancing is no longer first but becomes the last of the triad; and so it becomes possible for *meaning,* the luminous meaning which great poets convey, to be infused organically into the mind and heart of a whole people.

Shawn agreed with me that in all arts there is only one objective, which is to convey *meaning,* and that without that any art is horrible. He also agreed that the fusion of word, melody, rhythm and movement, if it can ever again be attained, is the perfect medium for this end. And so our crossing of swords about the priority of the arts ended on common ground where we agreed.

But there existed a difference between us which could not be brushed aside so easily. I had noticed in Lee, when I first stated teaching his group, that when I corrected their pronunciation and insisted on certain changes, Shawn's leaning was with them, and not with me. He did not say anything, he just stiffened a little, and let it be. Also, in his own way of speaking, though much less noticeably than in theirs, there was a trace of the same sound which I was trying to get rid of in the others. In him it was barely noticeable, because his habit of speaking in public, which he does well, and also of reading out loud, which he does delightfully, and, in general, of carrying off everything he does with a manner, made this a very minor flaw which one could forget. But in Florida he had leisure for a thing he had wanted to do from the start, and he fixed a time every afternoon to study a certain role in Greek tragedy with me. Words started to assume a new value and importance, and then this latent difference between us became open disagreement. Our bone of contention was the letter R which he pronounced in the guttural manner of the Middle West, which is the grave-yard of beautiful English. He said that my idea that the musical quality of the language is ruined by this sound had no basis in reality; that I felt that way merely because I had been brought up that way, and had heard either English or New English speech all my life: that after living many years abroad I was not near enough to American feeling to appreciate their kind of speech, which is stronger, more masculine, and altogether finer than the sissified manner which I was upholding. (I did not interrupt him here to say that he was reminding me of my derelicts in the Federal Theatre who thought it sissified to act in a Greek play). He went on to say that I could produce no argument based on reason to show that my preference was anything but prejudice. In answer to this I asked him to hold his own larynx between two fingers and go on talking slowly, and note that for every word in which a guttural R occurs there is a downward stiffening of the throat which does not happen for any other letter. He did this and admitted that this stiffening does occur.

"But," he said, "that is very fine: it is like a stiffening of the muscles before a leap in dancing; it is an obstacle which has to be overcome, and adds power to one's speech."

It was evident, at that moment, that Shawn was talking patriotism rather than art, and that his own manner of speech was not only an ingrained habit, but also, a point of view which had become confused with his ardent love of America.

It was very disappointing. During the months in which we had collaborated on small things my imagination had built up a plan of great magnitude for work that I would some day do with him. Everything about him had fitted into a preconceived picture of the rebirth of drama, drama greater than the Greek, on American soil. But in me, this vision had always been bound up with my passion for the English language. My long effort in America to produce one great play in such a way that its inherent Bacchic vigour would be released, had had, as one of its main incentives, the conviction that the beauty and vitality of the English language has never been fully revealed, and that its finer qualities will become evident only when it will be linked to the Greek theory of music.

In fact, during this nine year period, whenever complete discouragement pushed my face to the earth, it was my dream of what English might become, a torch for spiritual awakening, which had somehow held me separated from my Greek mountains and seas. Even my ultimate hope of presenting Greek tragedies worthily, especially *The Sibyl, Daidalos, Asklepios,* and *Ariadne,* by Sikelianos, had always somehow depended on a belief that the thing must first be done in English, although I myself could find no logical reason for this belief. Therefore, waiting as I did for Shawn's return from the West after I first met him, I had been waiting, of course, for a great dancer, but I had also been waiting finally to hear the musicality of English as it had long been projected in my own consciousness. Yet here was Shawn defending the very sounds which make English insufferable, and which destroy it as a medium for lyrical and dramatic fervour. In listening to him my whole edifice again seemed to crumble. I told him that the dream I had built up around him had come to an end: that I had no heart in working toward a result which had already deviated from its true direction, and that we might as well give it all up. Shawn laughed:

"Your dream," he said, "is so definitely a fabric of the land of dreams, with no hope of realization that either of us can foresee, that it need not disturb us for the moment: so let's go on working."

And we did. But the zest was gone.

CHAPTER 26

American Drama

It was Shawn's Americanism which blurred my picture of him as animator of a new and great Theatre, and his defence of Middle Western English as a proper dramatic medium had left me disheartened. Nevertheless, it had also been his Americanism which had awakened his interest in what I said to him at West Redding. He had referred then to the chasm which separates the modern world from anything Greek, however fine it may be in itself; and he thought it would be difficult to mount a Greek drama with the tide of opinion running as strongly against it as it has during the last few years.

But I said that to me the study of Greek Drama was only a step on the way we were heading. The world must recover a medium which can speak powerfully and quickly to great masses of men. If they are not moved by Greek mythology, let them use their own American stories to stir their hearts. All that matters is that the principles of Greek drama are eternal and will never be superseded, and these principles must be recovered and used in a context which has direct bearing on the consciousness of men as they are; and in that way we shall be much more Greek in spirit than with any stereotyped representation we might produce of the fragments that have come down to us. We have in American history, and in American legend, subjects which are unsurpassed in their dramatic and ethical import. We also have poets who possess a broad vision of America's destiny, and adequate technique to express it. But they must no longer be hampered by a lame theatrical form which deprives man of most of his faculties of expression. They must use the great American legends in a way which can let our own ethical concepts shine with their true inner light.

Shawn was on fire with the idea that the compete dramatic liberation we had been discussing could be applied here and now to new and great drama; and at once he illustrated what I had been saying by describing the beautiful story of Johnny Appleseed which he had been thinking of for years as a possible dance drama. And poets, I said, must learn enough about the theory of Greek music to know that their lyrics will no longer be buried in libraries as a pastime for leisurely intellectuals, but they will become bread and wine for a whole people, nourishing all their truer instincts which are now dormant, and running through their arteries with the throb of warm understanding and joy. Actors must learn that they can no longer stalk about the stage with pompous gestures, nor yet move mincingly with no gestures at all; but their whole body and soul and spirit must be so balanced that simultaneously as dancers and singers and actors they can transmit God's truths to men. What we need for great theatre is not a slavish reproduction of what has once inspired a certain race, however great, but to seize in their fullness the principles which that race understood, and use them, in the way they used them, as the only quickly effective means towards making a whole people intelligent and beautiful and aware.

CHAPTER 27

Architecture

Again I remained in Florida, in my little house under the tall pine trees and near the clear lake, ideal for any kind of work that one can do alone. With a good deal of patience I acquired a vegetable garden, my loom was working again, there was time to study music, and study Greek, there was even time to write a book. My passion for great drama had not much to do with these bucolic occupations, and remained a silent spectator of whatever else I might undertake, reminding me always that drama is a social action, and cannot be fostered in solitude. There were moments when I envied my sister, who likes being alone as well as I do, but whose art does not call for collaboration with others; and my brother, who had concentrated his music entirely in himself, seemed wise.

In all the years that had passed, I had never written to him a word about the Elysian fields I had entered through following another musical theory. I had not written at first because I was embarrassed and somewhat afraid of having thoughts about music which were different from his. Then later, when I felt more sure of myself, I still had not written because I like to guard the illusion, which might always be the truth, that if he once opened this door he would go along with me wherever it leads. In this way I have kept him apart from all the other musicians I know who consider my dream for restoring great drama sheer nonsense. To them Greek music is as dead as the proverbial door-nail, and has been for over two thousand years. This loss does not concern them much, because they are convinced that since the Greeks knew nothing about superimposed sounds, music with them was barely in its infancy, and therefore could not be interesting to us from the point of view of art. One even hears that it could have been nothing but a "monotonous bellowing;[1] and, they believe, there

---

[1] In writing about modal music, it is somewhat frightening to realize the overwhelming weight of contrary opinion which is securely established against it. There is not such thing as discussion concerning it. To everyone, musicians and laymen alike, the idea of music without harmony is simply a joke. A striking example of this may be found in Mr. Hendrik Willem van Loon's book called *The Arts*. Its title page announces that this book includes "everything that has been done within the realm of painting and architecture, and music and sculpture and the theatre, and most of the so-called minor arts, from the beginning of time until..." One could hardly expect a single human life to suffice for a reasoned opinion concerning all the branches of all the arts during the whole history of the human race. Mr. van Loon admits this is what he writes concerning the Greek theatre: "being lamentably ignorant about the stage in general, I do not indulge in any theories of my own, but I shall do what I always do under such circumstances, I shall make for the nearest dictionary."
About polyphonic music Mr. van Loon writes with the kind of fluency which makes one infer personal familiarity on his part with this subject. But concerning prepolyphonic music one wonders what dictionary he has consulted. He says, for instance, that among the Greeks there is a complete lack of any system of notation. (But the Greeks have invented three systems of musical notation, one of them being very highly developed.) "We know so little about Greek music," he says, "that we dare not even guess." (He might have made several guesses if he had read Plato, Aristotle, Aristoxenos, Alypios, Euclid, Plutarch, etc.,) He describes the Greek chorus as "a slowly chanted eulogy or lamentation a little like the sort of thing you hear when you attend Bach's *Passion according to St. Matthew*, or Haydn's *Creation*, or any other modern oratorio." (But Greek choruses

is no hope of recovering even a notion of what this "bellowing" really was, because the musical inscriptions found in the excavations are so few and so inadequate. As to the relation of Greek ecclesiastical music to it, no one seems to have thought this worthy of serious study, and no musician has followed up an analogy I have suggested between the mastery by Scholars of Egyptian hieroglyphics after centuries of total loss, and the possible reemergence of Greek music in our consciousness.

The discovery of the Rosetta Stone, in 1779, during Napoleon's expedition to Egypt, gave the first impetus in the deciphering of ancient Egyptian writing through the juxtaposed translations on this stone of one phrase in three languages, including ancient hieroglyphics and Greek: so that, through the known, scholars mastered part of the unknown. In the same way, when the Hymn of Apollo was discovered in the Delphic excavations, scholars were able to decipher its alphabetical notation through the key which we possess in the *Introduction to Music* by Alypios. But the words on the Rosetta Stone were too few to insure further progress in the Egyptian art of writing, just as the musical fragments were too few to permit a more exhaustive study of Greek music. Both of these investigations came to a standstill through lack of further data from ancient monuments; and in both cases scholars decided that any effort to gain a clearer understanding was hopeless. But in the case of Egyptian hieroglyphics, after about a quarter of a century of scholastic despair, the French scholar, Champollion, thought of studying modern Coptic. Having mastered this, he began a comparative study of ancient remains with the rich traditions of a spoken language; and, little by little, he was able to throw light on the ancient writing that, in a few years, a complete mastery of ancient hieroglyphics was the result.

My own musical thesis is in no way a plea for the actual antiquity of any song existing in Greece today, either in or out of the church. It is not possible that any ecclesiastical or traditional tune be exactly like any ancient tune because the words have

---

were fast or slow, lamenting or rejoicing or making fun, according to the context: compare the choruses of Aristophanes, with Aristotle's *Poetics;* and the one thing we know quite certainly about them is that they were never in the least like the *Passion according to St. Matthew,* or *The Creation,* or any other modern oratorio.) Mr. van Loon tells us that polyphonic music did away with the "monotony and bellowing" which preceded it; and he speaks of early ecclesiastical music as "a most regrettable chaos of cacophonous sound."

I believe that this book really is representative, in all cases where Mr. van Loon has not an opinion of his own, of the accepted opinions of most people on all artistic subjects: and therefore that the general idea about music before the development of harmony is that, in all nations and in all periods, there was nothing but a "monotonous bellowing" and "a regrettable chaos of cacophonous sound." So it seems somewhat adventurous to suggest that the musical instinct of the human race is older than polyphonic music.

changed more or less, and Greek melody, then and now, depends on the meaning and emphasis of words. That is to say that when the Greeks became Christians they used their ancient musical method to express another context which necessitated a different musical expression. For this reason the analogy between the recovery of hieroglyphics and that of ancient Greek music will always be partial.

The "anadromic method", that is the going-backward, or the remounting-the-current method which was used by Champollion led Egyptologists to complete mastery of hieroglyphics; whereas the use of this same anadromic method will lead musicians, not to a recovery of exact tunes, but to the recovery of a musical theory different from that familiar today, and closely resembling what the Greeks themselves wrote about music. But in no case has the question of exact sameness to ancient tunes any relevance to my general thesis: which is that we possess, in the musical method of the Greek Orthodox Church, a way of relating music to words which is approximately the one described by Plato, Aristotle, Aristoxenos, Euclid, Alypios, Nikomachos, Quintilian, Aristides, Claudian Ptolemy, Plutarch, Lucian, and others,[2] and fulfills the conditions concerning music which they considered essential.

If this be true, we have in our hands a medium for original creation in all the artistic forms used by the Greeks: notably in religious ceremonies, in tragedy, comedy and pageants, regardless of the comparatively few written tunes which have come down to us from antiquity, and regardless even of the Greek language. It is a method which can be applied to any language, and which would add life to any kind of drama or ceremony.

There is very little hope that excavations will uncover the actual songs of Aeschylus and Sophocles, and still less for the songs of their predecessors, e.g., Thespis, Pherecydes, Phrynichos, and the other poets and dramatists. But as long as we know the manner, or approximately the manner in which they composed, we can enhance their words, or any words of our own, in melody suggesting motion, and so recover the emotion, or an analogous emotion to the one they experienced in their theatres and festivals.

In short, with these new building materials, we shall not be able to reconstruct a lost art in an archaeological manner; but we should be able to reerect the Platonic triad of poetry,

---

[2] Whoever cares to seek further details concerning these ancient musical critics will encounter certain differences of opinion between them concerning musical intervals: especially the famous feud between the followers of Pythagoras, called the canonical, and those of Aristoxenos called the harmonious. These differences need not trouble us until we become able to hear the intervals about which they were arguing. This will take us some time, considering that on both sides of the discussion these Greek musicians distinguished several hundred intervals in the octave. Meantime, the system accepted by the Orthodox Church mercifully gives us a method which we can understand and apply practically.

music and gymnastics which has been lost for about two thousand years; and it will not be a slavish imitation, but a new creation of our own on the same old rock foundation. For without this musical method, all the talk, and all the effort in the world to recover the Platonic triad results in nonsense. There is no such thing as a Platonic triad as long as melody is limited to the tempered scale, and as long as dancers are forced to follow the rhythms of orchestras or pianos, instead of being themselves the leaders of melody and rhythm. Then indeed dramatists can write plays if they have anything they wish to express to the people; and musicians can enlarge and glorify their words; and dancers, with all their faculties: diction, song, movement, intelligence, feeling, can show what the Greeks meant by making their gods men, and their men gods.

The impact of any true product of art is direct. It requires personal contact through the eye or the ear of the receiver. It cannot be reproduced in a plaster copy or a photograph, and a description deprives it of all the qualities which make it excellent. With music this is particularly true, and the human mind can gain no conception of what music might be without actually hearing it. Therefore Greek music should be heard: how otherwise can people become aware of it? But it is almost impossible to hear Greek music. It is properly not a sole performance. It requires many voices, preferably fifty, to make its true beauty evident; and it is necessary, in the beginning at least, in order to manifest its essential power, that these be men's voices and not women's. Again, Greek music is not a thing in itself, and therefore it cannot be exemplified by the process of putting fifty men, sitting on fifty chairs, on a platform, and having them sing together before an audience which is staring at them head-on.

The essence of Greek music is to convey the word through perfect diction, pure melody, and through gesture expressive of the meaning of the word. But these combined necessities throw light on another obstacle in regard to the application of this theory today. Apart from the obvious difficulty of finding fifty men who would consider this effort worthwhile (and, be it said in passing, this could be accomplished more easily with men who have not acquired a training in any existing school of music) there is the further and much greater difficulty that even if an American poet were to write for us a most beautiful and thrilling drama; even if fifty men were to get together and perfect themselves in singing and dancing the choruses of this American play, or of any Greek play; even if they had hand-weavers working on the costumes, and the most gifted actors collaborating with them in the principle parts, when all was ready their effort would prove useless because they would have no place to perform.

So here we are facing the most essential of all necessities for the reconstruction of great drama: ARCHITECTURE.

Because the theatre as it is today is not only the fundamental hindrance to the representation of any Greek play, it is also actually disintegrating to all higher forms of theatrical and musical art. No doubt very few will accept this statement, so I shall try to evoke from their own inner consciousness a different kind of structure to which the name "theatre" rightly belongs: because I believe that this prodigious instrument which the Greeks projected into human experience still exists subconsciously, almost like a living organism, at least as an undefined craving, in the "sea of oblivion" which is not far from the surface in all great artists, and that through them mankind in general will again become conscious of the huge potentialities which this instrument holds within itself for the eventual liberation of the world.

It was at first a circle and nothing more. A place where at harvest the wheat was spread even, as high as the bellies of the horses that galloped around and around, as in a circus ring, four abreast, driven by a youth who balanced precariously on a wooden float, studded beneath with prongs to trample and crush the straw, and free the wheat from its tight straw wrappings. Then, when all the straw was broken, they would sweep it to the centre, along with the hard, strong wheat, and the villagers would throw it high in the air with their winnowing fans, and watch the straw float away in the wind, while the heavy wheat fell straight and clean in the centre. These various stages of the harvest were all animated by songs: songs to urge on the horse; songs to give strength to the driver at their heels; songs to bring the favouring wind for the straw; songs to encourage the winnowers.

But here, at other seasons, the poets would gather the people: old men, young men, boys, usually by fifties. Here they would teach them their own words brought back from the abyss of Being, and their own melodies which exalted and intensified these words. Then, the participants were taught, sometimes together, sometimes antiphonally or even in smaller groups according to the requirements of the text, to sing, and to express in movement the full meaning of the poetical phrase. Sometimes the poet would create and teach these movements; but, as his students grew more aware, they would be able to convey, each his own reaction to what the words signified. This fact, that the participants were not all bound to be alike in their movements, but rather to be related among themselves because they were expressing personal reactions to the same thought, gave a chance to each actor to develop his own capacity from within. They had of course to be conscious of each other, and not disturb the general harmony of the whole, but within these limits each participant was an individual. In short this art of the chorus, as it developed, came to be the highest type of art: because it became a personification of ideal society.

Is man an eagle or an insect? Is he destined to be free of his fellows and fly where he likes and how he likes, seizing what he desires with beak and claw: or must he become eternally similar to his fellow-ants, secure in unchanging ugliness forever? Through the history of mankind these two types have fought each other with ever-changing fortunes. Some men have believed in, and seized their right to fly, and others have been doomed to mass ugliness and monotony. But Apollo alone dared to say that all men are, and must be, both ant and eagle. For he, calling on the other god, created with him that type of art which forced men to be at the same time members of a harmonious group, and individual creators.

During the lessons in the threshing floors, the villagers would gather round the circle to look on. Seats were erected later, with the first row placed sufficiently high for the audience to see above the heads of the dancers, and so obtain a view of the whole orchestra, which is otherwise obscured by the dancers who happen to be in front. Then a low stage was erected in the centre, on which the leader of the chorus, impersonating Dionysos (and later any god or hero) was placed, to distinguish him from his followers, who were the chorus. This was the Dithyrambic stage. Later, probably by Thespis, the audience were deprived of about a quarter, and afterwards of a third of the circle, when they erected a platform tangent to the circle, on which two, and afterwards three actors performed. But the circle remained intact; and this, with the audience gathered around it, was always the essence of the theatre; and today, Professor Doerpfeld and other archaeologists believe that, even in the classical period, much of the acting was performed in the circle, and that the stage was used only occasionally. The implications of these facts are not immediately apparent to those who know only the modern theatre; so I will try to show some of the intrinsic excellences of the Greek theatre which differ fundamentally from what the world is accustomed to at present.

In this circular arrangement, the actors were separated personally from the audience in three ways: they were well below the level of the spectators; and, as it is natural, in acting, to look at one's fellow performers, they would not have seen the audience except by expressly raising their eyes to look at them; and even then, they would have seen only a small portion of an audience which extended all around them; and if, in a moment of exultation, they lifted their eyes as it were to heaven, it would have been to a great circular heaven of attention expanding on all sides, and, beyond that, the sky. And this huge attention would be directed, not on them, but on the Idea which they were representing, on the Word: and thus would be attained the true unity between actors and audience, in a reaching-out, on the part of both, to a harmony beyond themselves.

This psychological phenomenon of unity realized outside of themselves was accentuated also by the use of masks.

Again, because the orchestra was circular, and many of the dance figures moved around the outside of the circle, the performers were taught what I have called the Apollonian movement, in which the right arm moves forward with the left foot, or the left arm with the right foot, while the head and feet are in profile, and the chest or back in full view. This type of movement requires perfect balance, gives great freedom to the spine, is adaptable to an enormous variety of poses, and allows powerful springs in rhythmic passages, starting from bent knees, and culminating in the full long sweep of the body; and it also sustains very majestic bearing in tragic passages. But the most excellent attribute of this type of movement was moral even more than physical: the fact that the head was habitually in profile, looking either forward or back, separated the actor in a way from his audience: because if he turned to see them his attitude was ruined, so that when he was moving properly he could not see those who were looking at him. This had the effect of isolating him, almost as if he were by himself, and entirely obliterated the theatrical self-consciousness to which actors are otherwise subject. He was alone with what he was expressing. One might almost say there existed nothing for each individual actor but himself and the god he was worshipping, and thus his whole being was absorbed in adequately expressing the emotion which the poet's words evoked in him.

Considering all these obstacles to the exploitation of personality, it was as if the Greeks had consciously raised barriers against all the usual theatrical tricks which are devised to turn personality to account: it is as if some strong religious purpose had fixed conditions in which many human defects were automatically eliminated, in which silly embarrassment and self-consciousness starve for lack of fodder, in which personal aggrandizement also finds no food. In the ancient theatre an actor could not if he would smirk and look pretty, because, even without a mask, he never could be sure that anyone was looking at him. His only sure spectator was his own inner conscience, and whatever god he believed in. And it is significant that the acclamations of the audience, in the end, were for the play, and not for the actors.

From the point of view of the audience, this architectural arrangement had tremendous consequences. The fact of looking down on the performance from a vantage ground, which was equally good in any seat among an audience of twenty to thirty thousand, so vast that, as Nietzsche says, it was like being in a solitary valley, gives to each person a complete view of the whole stage. All movement, backwards, forwards, sideways are equally visible. The ancient spectator never saw actors moving as in a flat silhouette, (except when such effects were produced on purpose by the actors on a raised stage) whereas the modern stage differs little from the photographic screen of a moving picture; he never had to crane his head upwards from the best seats; and he never saw his favourite actor with the bottom of his legs cut off. In fact the ancient spectator saw the play in three dimensions, whereas today people always see it in two.

Beside this three-dimensional view, due to the fact that the audience sat around the play and above it, there was the further fact that the actions and attention of actors, chorus and audience were all centered round the same point, which was the centre of the circle. It will be difficult to make modern theatre-goers believe, until they have actually experienced it, that this concentration of attention in a circular form, around action which includes meaning, melody and rhythm, generates magnetic currents which are totally unknown wherever the audience is spatially divided from the stage.

Finally in the acoustic properties of all Greek theatres they again made use of physical laws. And here it is strange that modern engineers, or architects, appear to know nothing about these laws. They must have heard and seen the disagreeable instrument called a loud-speaker which is nothing more than a device for carrying sound from a point over an enlarging circumference. But it has not occurred to them that the Greek theatre is itself a loud-speaker which carries sound to thousands, by the same physical law, but with no gadgets.

These, I believe, are the principal differences between the Greek theatre and any other: and it will be evident that all are due to observance of physical laws which have since been disregarded. They are the moral isolation of actors within their circle, eliminating self-consciousness and histrionic vulgarity, the three-dimensional view obtained by spectators, the magnetic current generated by the circular relation of actors, chorus and audience and finally the flawless acoustics which never have been equalled or even approached.

This living organism received its death-blow when the Romans cut off half of the Greek Circle. In this one Vandalic act they destroyed the fundamental conditions which made the Greek Theater a proper extension of the Greek Temple: a place essentially religious in its activities. From then on, the complete spatial separation of actors and audience, and all the related changes were inevitable because, as a spiritual entity, the Theatre had already ceased to exist. And now, after two thousand years, it is only a dream that a theatre has existed once, and might exist again, whose organic structure was sufficiently noble to hold up an ideal solution of the problem of MAN IN SOCIETY, a beacon for the final conquest of brutality and greed, a star for the victory of Man-the-Creator, which is the TRAGIC CHORUS.

Perhaps it is because I have once worked in such a theatre, and have seen and felt the regenerating spirit which moves in its Circle when the Chorus moves, that I have no faith in any measures toward reconstruction of the Drama which do not include, which do not in fact give predominant importance, to architecture.

Today the feeling is widespread that the spiritual unity of actors and audience must somehow be recovered; and many are the devices which are planned to bring this about. We have seen stages built with what they call "aprons" projecting into the audience; we have heard informal conversations over the foot-lights during performances; we even have seen actors appearing from any point in the auditorium, sauntering around casually, and sitting down anywhere to mix in a friendly way with the lookers-on: but this does not recover the unity they are seeking, it rather destroys the little there is left. For Unity, in the Drama, does not consist in the temporary intimacy of Jim and Jack, actors, with Bill and Bobbie, spectators. It consists in the mutual absorption, through Representation, of all four, in an Idea which is beyond themselves.

We also cannot recover this Unity in any of the so-called Greek theatres, built in the open air, of which there are now over fifty in the United States, the one in Berkeley, California being the best, but that also a mere makeshift. In none of them have the physical laws I have enumerated been observed with proper care. Especially can we not recover it in those theatres which have a sheet of water dividing audience and actors. This may be useful for reflecting pretty girls in still water, but it is not useful for anything else.

There is in fact no apparent effort, over the whole United States, to produce even an example of this admirable architectural achievement which can, as Nietzsche said, liberate simultaneously all the faculties of man. And without it, our hands are tied. Not all choruses, or the dancing and singing and acting we could dream of, not the ancient Greeks themselves if we were to put them on a modern stage, could accomplish the miracle which is nevertheless a normal consequence of the mere shape of a Greek theatre. Something happens in this great magnetic circle which does not and cannot happen anywhere else, something which is the very be-all and end-all of Theatre: a sweeping emotion which does overcome enmities and misunderstandings, which makes hatred and fear fall inert in the great rotating wind of beauty which Aristotle called Purgation, and which actually is Upward Panic.

And for this, architecture is the indispensable foundation. It is so important that without it all efforts will fail: in fact such efforts should never begin, for they will not succeed in imposing this true and magnificent function of the Theatre: but they can present to the stage as it is a new and powerful instrument which can be used for indifferent or unworthy ends. At present this instrument is unknown. Rather than allow it to become trivial or corrupted it had better be left where it is now, in the hospitable land of theory.

All this sounds hopeless enough, but I believe that it is not. We do not need a building of Pentelic marble, or even cement. The shape and proportions are all that are essential, and these could be had quite well in a wooden theatre. In fact, the three great tragedians, and all their predecessors, had nothing better. It does not need to be very large because it could always be added to from the back if multitudes began to clamour for entrance. It does not even need land of its own: for it had better, at first, be a movable structure which could travel from place to place, and be set up in any vacant lot which was quiet; and it could have a tent of its own, and so be used in rainy weather. The initial expense would not be comparable to any of the so-called Greek theatres, or even to any ordinary theatre. And once done, and with one or two plays already rehearsed, it could travel north in summer, and south in winter to all University towns, and perhaps to even smaller places. Once launched, it would take care of itself.

But if it did not, it would be exciting to use it for other, in fact for all the higher forms of music and drama to see what would happen.

Symphony concerts would be heard for the first time in their full beauty owing to the perfection of the acoustics: and the modern orchestra would occupy the place which the Greeks called an Orchestra.

Oratorios would be immensely enhanced and for the same reason.

All plays of Shakespeare, returning to approximately the original condition of the early Elizabethan theatre, when the audience saw from all round, through the windows, or from the balconies of inn yards where plays were then acted, would take on an impressiveness and a vivacity which is not dreamed of at present. For few know that it is not necessary to see an actor's mouth in order to hear what he says: it is merely a matter of proper acoustics. Therefore actors can be placed naturally in speaking, and need not stand in false positions towards each other so that the audience may hear them. This is, of all theatrical conventions, the most subversive of the great art of acting, and also the most corrupting of the true nobility of the actor: for it keeps him constantly aware of the audience: what they are thinking of him, how he looks to them: whereas his whole being should be absorbed in the play.

Operas also would be improved, especially those with large choruses, such as

Lohengrin and *Die Meistersinger*. But Mozart also would be incredibly fascinating performed in this way.

Dancers have suffered enough from the misery of small stages circumscribing and mutilating a great art![3]

But if this theatre once got built, and with one or two plays ready for the road, none of these partial dramatic arts would have any chance for a try-out. For it would then be evident that Great Theatre is true to its origin: a threshing-floor providing wheat for men: and when men had once tasted this kind of bread, multitudes would come to be fed.

---

[3][Ed. This paragraph begins with the phrase, "And, as for dancing!" in the original. -J.P.A.]

CHAPTER 28

Greece

One little country in all Europe dared to stand up when all the others, large and small, had been devastated. With no money, no clothes, hardly any military equipment, a handful of men went to war with their meagre supplies carried by donkeys, or merely with saddle-bags hung from their own shoulders for whatever ammunition they had, and a little bread, and cheese, and olives. And their women went with them, carrying food on their backs, and shovelling snow for the men to pass. In this way they went to fight mechanized armies, immensely more numerous and powerful than they. They fought on mountain peaks in blinding snow-storms, and charged into fortified battalions with no arms but their bayonets. Gaining in this way a few guns and stores, they scaled new peaks, and conquered new valleys, with nothing to encourage them but their own spirit. Their only ally was far away, and sore pressed, with the scales, at the time, apparently turning against her. There was no human consideration that made the action of Greece reasonable from any point of view. Yet she won the first victory of the war.

"At last," wrote Mary Hambidge, "Greece will come into her own." And from one day to another the whole world was crying out what one had long ceased to dare to whisper, because others had grown weary of listening: Greece has never changed: today the race has all the qualities that made her great. American head-lines, American editorials and magazines all over the country were ecstatically praising her: "The stuff that myths are made of has been spun out recently in Greece. The Greeks have spoken and acted like a race of giants twenty feet tall, hurler of thunder-bolts, crushers of men."[1]

The little shopkeepers in Eustis were babbling about the blood of heroes of Marathon and Salamis; one's own long-masked belief was shining on everyone's face. Suddenly one felt the total rapture of having the whole world know what one knows, love what one loves.

On this rising tide of enthusiasm I too wrote: "Greece is repaying a debt to Rome which dates from 146 B.C., when Mummius destroyed Corinth, and therewith the freedom of Greece." My lovely daughter-in-law, Frances, took exception to this: she called my outburst picturesque and heroic, but far from accurate. She reminded me how Greeks and Italians, in the meantime, had befriended and died for each other, and she felt I was going far afield in calling the present battle a throwback to ancient Greece and ancient Rome. All

---

[1] *Time,* March 17th, 1941.

that she said is true: nevertheless, I meant what I said. Greece is clearing an account of over two thousand years, and, as usual, when Greece does such things, it is an account in which the whole world is concerned. We have all grown so accustomed to the death-grip that Rome hold over the world that we do not even know any longer that we are shackled: we are like the prisoner of Chillon who, after long years of confinement, did not wish to leave his cell when freedom finally came to him. We do not even feel the heavy irons that impede our movements, because we now possess callouses hundreds of years old that make these chains seem a normal part of our anatomy. We do not know that our greatest medium for the enlightenment of the people is now a purely secular, often a profane display, because Rome so mutilated the true plan of the Theatre as to preclude its use from then on for any themes of religious import.

Our music is Roman. Jay Hambidge said about what he called Dynamic Symmetry that either the Romans were too dull to understand it, or the Greeks never told them their secret. In architecture, [this] means that they never applied the inner law of organic structure by which leaves and sea-shells grow, natural laws of proportion, which the Greeks correlated and used to obtain a control of areas which became the basis for the glowing vitality of their design in architecture and sculpture, and which the Romans and all succeeding civilizations ignored. So in music, the Greeks either kept the secret of their infinite melodic sequences and varieties, or the Romans were too dull to understand them. Undoubtedly, through Guide d'Arezzo, then Palestrina, and finally the whole beautiful Italian school of music, they were the originators of modern harmony, and this is the greatest legacy that Italy has given to the world. Nevertheless, in so doing they destroyed the very memory of pure melody, and even made the world believe that, as musicians, the Greeks were morons. In this way another art of music, magnificent in itself, has been developed: but with the result that music has been separated from life's greatest symbol: the Theatre.

Our laws are Roman. We have forgotten that originally they were established, "not that good people live among bad, but that rich people live among poor."

The education of our children is Roman. If they obtain knowledge of any ancient language they are always forced to learn Latin first, and hit or miss if they ever reach Greek. They are brought up on Roman history, and made to study the lives of the Roman emperors, the most furious, vicious and loathsome distortions of human dignity that have ever disfigured the earth. This imperial display of the meanest crimes was a fitting product of the deeds sown by a band of brigands who at first did not even have any women, but had to steal them from a neighbouring town, and who chose a wolf as symbol of their city because their leaders actually had been nourished by a wolf.

How different from the founding of Athens by the goddess of heavenly wisdom, whose gift to the city was an olive-tree, and who left them as a symbol the owl: the large-eyed bird who sees in the night.

The "Greco-Roman period" which historians write about is wicked deception. There has never been a Greco-Roman period. There has been Greece, and there has been a detestable parody of Greece and that is all.

The Romans had a creative period in the Renaissance when humanism shone through in an original way. But shortly before this awakening, hordes of Greek refugees poured into Italy after the fall of Constantinople, and they left their mark on Italian performance for several generations.[2]

Roman literary works are often very fine, but they dwindle to insignificance when compared to the master works which were their models. We have had enough of this second-hand culture. It is time we recovered direct contact with the Greek language again. And in this connection let us remember a legend of early India. It is recorded that two travellers came to the door of a monastery and asked to be admitted. They were received, and treated merely as strangers to whom hospitality was extended. But presently, some one of the higher priests of the order discovered that these strangers were speaking Greek, and immediately they were advanced to the highest grade of initiation. Mere knowledge of the Greek language was considered adequate training to prepare man's soul for the deepest mysteries.

May Greek heroism in Albania so open our eyes! And if it does, may America be the mighty transmitter of one of the beacons that Greece first lit for the world!

But is that enough? Has it been enough for America? Along with this "best" that we shall be giving them, how shall we avoid leading Europe to the precarious blessedness of our own present outlook on life. In the land rich enough to supply the world with food we cannot insure to our own coming generation any hope of decent means of merely keeping alive. We cannot give gifts that we do not possess; we can only give what we've got; and we ourselves do not know the cause of this terrible anomaly which we are offering to other nations who would emulate our prosperity. But one of our own poets told us the cause:

> Alas for the Man, so stealthily betrayed,
> Bearing the bad cell in him from the start,

---

[2] For instance, the works of Cimabue and Giotto, fathers of Italian painting, are definitely extensions of Byzantine art: so are the mosaics in Ravenna: and, in the little Museum of the Acropolis, the lovely "Maidens" excavated from under the Parthenon, and therefore antedating the Persian wars, all have Florentine faces.

Pumping and feeding from his healthy heart
That wild disorder never to be stayed
When once established, destined to invade
With angry hordes the true and proper part,
Till Reason joggles in the headsman's cart,
And Mania spits from every balustrade.
Would he had searched his closet for his bane,
Where lurked the trusted ancient of his soul,
Obsequious Greed, and seen that visage plain;
Would he had whittled treason from his side
In his stout youth and bled his body whole,
Then had he died a king, or never died.[3]

But Edna St. Vincent Millay has not told us the cure. With a poet's vision which "turns the world to glass", she has shown us what we and all the world at last should know: the nature of the "bad cell" which has been in man from the start: obsequious Greed. It ought by now to be clear that no form of government, however stringent, or however benevolent, has ever rooted out this cancerous growth. America is riddled with it. Greece, which invented democracy, was consumed by it. In our private lives among neighbours, outwardly as cut-throat nations, the world is forever betrayed by this "wild disorder." No government has ever controlled it. Monarchy, democracy, socialism, all have been tried, and all have failed, and they all will fail forever, because governments are like human faces, which may be well constructed and yet conceal a malevolent nature, or may be outwardly mis-shapen and yet show a generous spirit shining through the eyes, because the disease is in the heart of man, and neither outward force nor outward persuasion has ever touched anyone's heart.

In Europe there is not a single country that has not, at one time or another, increased its own area at the expense of its neighbours. There is also no one that does not believe in its heart that the farthest boundaries it has ever attained in history are its own proper limits. Any normal American can imagine his own chagrin if his own back-yard were to be seized by violent means, and occupied by the owner of the adjoining yard; but it is very difficult for him to imagine a situation where whole nations, in fact all nations, are in this predicament. For at some time, past or present, everybody has owned land beyond his normal borders. Also, experiencing in America the constant blessedness of having one language from ocean to ocean, and that language the greatest and with the greatest literature, barring Greek, that has been created by man, we cannot easily imagine the dreadful annoyance of hearing

---

[3] *Wine From These Grapes.*

incomprehensible and barbaric sounds spoken by people who are living on lands that we consider our own. And along with these languages go customs and points of view that are the very breath of life to those who cherish them. All these differences in Europe have roots that are very old: and changing, often foreign and hostile governments have had no effect in eradicating them, even though they have often resorted to most violent means to level these people down to a common denominator.

During the Turkish ascendancy in Greece, the Turks cut out people's tongues to make them stop speaking Greek; and the grandmother of a friend of mine remembered being shut up, as a child, in a large armoire with her mother, who taught her Greek grammar on the sly in this way. This situation lasted for over four hundred years, yet today all Greeks speak Greek. There is no outward force which can level these anomalies, and the very fact that all European nations, at one time or another, have fought and suffered for these cherished manners and customs makes them extremely tenacious of the very characteristics which their governments often try to crush and eliminate altogether.

The history of Europe is old enough now for us to realize that all these leveling-down processes, instigated at various times, and enforced by one or another form of government, have had uniformly only one result: they have made the bright coals of racial habits burn more brightly under the ashes that have covered them periodically, only to flare up with renewed vigour whenever a propitious wind blew them clean.

There are, roughly, three ways of settling this problem of races: one is the way of Attila and Genghis Khan, who both wished to kill the whole human race. But they did not succeed, and neither have their more adept and more vicious heirs of today succeeded, neither will anyone else ever succeed. Then there is the American way of teaching English to everybody, and allowing everyone to speak any language he pleases. This is a good way, and really produces a feeling of common patriotism among widely differing peoples; it also would not injure the integrity of the English language if only the language were properly taught. But unfortunately the American way also reduces these people to a sort of chain-store uniformity which is not the best they are capable of, and, in the second generation, it makes them ashamed of their parent languages (even when that language happens to be Greek) and so it gradually obliterates racial characteristics which could have contributed much power and originality to American life. The third way, the only one which could guard the precious uniqueness that all of these nations have struggled to preserve, exists at present only in the infinitely deep "sea of oblivion" which is the sub-conscious fathomless ocean of Greek wisdom. Its essence may be found in a single word, one which, like many Greek words of noble import, has been debased beyond recognition. In fact, has become a by-word in all nations, expressing the accumulated meanness and despicable self-seeking at the expense of their constituencies in all countries, of many public men, so that the word "Politics" not only connotes, it actually denotes in common parlance, the ignoble machinations of public office-holders to retain their place in power, or unlawfully to squander public funds.

Yet here, according to Dorian Orthodoxy, and expressed in the 5th Delphic principle, is what that word really meant:[4]

> The basic autonomy of every soul, individual or of a people, united with the knowledge of its own infinite sociability, thanks to which it can find itself in continuous and beneficial relations with all other souls, and with all the Apollonian and harmonious elements of the world, aiding thus, each one, his own separate development, and also the elevation of the psychic and civilizing Apollonian Rhythm of humanity in general.

And here are some of the results of the application of this Principle to actual life by the colossal Delphic Educational Organization in the past:

> First Council, obliged vigilantly to follow and overlook all the contemporary historical currents of all peoples then known in the world, and to concentrate these above obscure fanaticisms toward a Hearth of Knowledge of the Universe, and Knowledge of Oneself, without the slightest trace of dogmatic slavery, and this was called the Council of the Guardians of the Sacred Archives. Second Council, obliged to represent Greece from end to end, and called the Amphictyonic Council. Third, local Council, which was a Court of Justice. Fourth, communications with various secular initiates, Greeks and foreigners, with an aim of cultural action. Fifth, very broad councils of arbitration for the spiritual encounter of all peoples of the earth, and similar extensive institutions for Greece: such as spiritual and athletic contests, the equality of political rights for men and women, the emancipation of slaves, and so forth. Sixth, festivals, which embraced, in a spirit of One-Godliness the whole terrestrial Myth, and hospitably received all the currents of the earth, in order to unite them.[5]

These are some of the results of the application of this Delphic Principle to life, and these concepts are still sub-consciously flowing in the blood of the Greek race, making them potentially the people who can blaze the path that must be trodden by humanity itself, if humanity is to avoid hopeless deterioration. For the Greek race is the only one that has a deep-seated capacity for the understanding of super-national ideas: not the kind which tries to super-impose the ideas of one nation on another by violence; but the kind that recognizes "the basic autonomy of every soul, individual or of a people, and knows that the only way for them all, not only to survive, but to develop infinitely, is through the genius "of infinite

---

[4]　[Ed. For this, and other Delphic Principles, see *Proanakrousma,* by Anghelos Sikelianos. [The translation of the passage from the Greek text is Eva Palmer-Sikelianos' own. The Greek text in Anghelos Sikelianos, *Collected Prose Works,* vol. 2, "Delphika", ed. G. Savidis (Athens: Ikaros, 1980), p. 359. -J.P.A.]

[5]　[Ed. The Greek text, *op. cit.,* pp. 359-60. -J.P.A.]

sociability, thanks to which each one can find himself in continuous and beneficial relations with all other souls, and with all the Apollonian and harmonious elements of the world."

Greece alone can teach this kind of Politics. America cannot do it because she is too young. All other nations cannot do it because they are too old. But we know today that Greece balances youth and age in immortal equilibrium. We know it from the few words spoken by Mr. George Vlachos, on a day when the future seemed completely black: "Greece," he said, "has shown the world how to fight; she will show it how to die." This perfectly clean Greek tradition:

> Tell them in Lakedaimon, passer-by,
> That here obedient to their word we lie.

Repeatedly, during over four thousand years, Greece has sent us such messages. We have heard so many that it is as if Greece herself inwardly must know why she is so lavish with her own life: why, in fact, she never plays safe. It is as if she foresaw the ultimate danger which it is her destiny to face, and had been practicing for this great performance during all the ages.

For indeed it would require this age-long preparation of the race through temporal and spiritual victory, then hopeless defeat, rising again to other victories only to know the bitterness of slavery through hundreds of years, and again rising, renewed and young, to teach the world how to fight and how to die. Dionysos, god of joy, and god of sorrow, torn by the Titans, and again reborn: Osiris dismembered, his limbs scattered to the ends of the earth, and again reassembled and renewed: Christ crucified and resurrected; Greece has lived it all. And in her heart, in her great subconscious wisdom, Greece knows her own destiny, knows the ultimate danger that is ahead. She knows that her victory of today over tyranny, whenever it may be completely consummated, and however more glorious it will be than all other mortal victories, will be only another preliminary test of her strength to enter the lists and tilt for the final trophy to be won by man.

To muster courage for this coming contest, it would require such venerable age, such reckless youth. For only age can know its true nature, and only youth has spirit to run such a race. The age of Greece knows through ever-recurring life, death, and resurrection, that certain phrases we are in the habit of saying are not mere words; that values about which we often prattle like children become intoxicating as strong wine when we inject them into our veins: "Seek ye first the kingdom, and all these things shall be added unto you." All things shall be added unto us then, because then there will be something else that we shall desire more passionately than the baubles we are fighting for now, and only then shall we deserve to have the baubles also when we know of something better that we care for more. This something better is the kingdom that is ours for the asking, for we are all king-makers by a mere change of mind. "Become what thou art," say the Hindus: and "The kingdom of heaven is within," said Christ. These two phrases are saying the same thing, and Emerson also is saying the same thing: "The simplest person who in his integrity worships God, is God."

All great initiates and prophets and saviours are saying the same thing, and the Christian Church will become what it has always claimed to be, but never has been, a universal church, when it too knows and proclaims that Christ was speaking the truth, and that the kingdom of heaven actually is inside of every man and woman in the world, and that whoever seeks it in himself will find it. The ancient Greeks also knew this, and here we possess an unexpected testimony with no less a witness than St. Paul himself: "That they should seek the Lord, if haply they might feel after him and find him, though he be not far from everyone of us: for in him we live and move and have our being." This beautiful text, this very foundation of all true religion, which has been quoted and requoted in the Christian Church as the essence of its doctrine, is not Christian at all, at least it is not originally Christian. It is Greek. For St. Paul adds immediately after these words: "as certain also of your own poets have said." There the words stand in the *Acts of the Apostles,* 17, 28: "For in him we live and move and have our being: as certain also of your own poets have said." We do not know from whom St. Paul was quoting; from some of those, perhaps, who are to us merely names, or from others whose very names are lost to us, but it is certain that here we have the source of what is called Greek beauty, Greek balance. The ancient Greeks were not exclusively or even especially concerned with physical beauty. If they had been they never would have created such beauty as they did.

Often they have "felt after him and found him", and so they know that at that moment a strange thing happens: suddenly, as one may fall in love with a woman, by an inner revolution in one's blood that can in no way be controlled, one falls in love with God. It is a thing that others laugh at, as first love is laughed at by one's elders; but to the boy, consumed and shaken with emotion, nothing else is real.

And to whomever this happens another emotion equally overwhelming suddenly sweeps him away: he also loves his neighbour. For through this first illumination his own immense potentialities and his own shortcomings are seen clearly, and so he sees the true destiny of others, and longs only to pour out this wine for the whole earth.

There is no other way of loving one's neighbour. He is mean and ugly and cruel and vicious, and any love one may profess for him through a sense of duty or what not, is hypocritical nonsense. But when one has seen his generosity and his beauty streaming from the source of one's own potential generosity and beauty, one actually does love one's neighbour as one's self.

And so the age of Greece will say to its youth: "Move toward this neighbour in ardent beneficent Rhythm, and this is the second Delphic Principle." And age will say: "The whole of you will be 'Radiance' the first Delphic Principle, which signifies communion with the sun."

On that day Greek youth will know what it means for "Greece to come into her own", for such knowledge is the very marrow of Greek bones. They will see around them a world caught in the grip of horrible events, transfixed as in a nightmare, while a raging fire sweeps nearer to them, burning their faces, singeing their hair. Men will be praying in terror for Salvation from without to come and deliver them, and they will not know that their immense longing is itself the power that can overcome destruction. No one will tell them that man has in himself the great Liberator which is stronger than all the forces armed with bombs and poisonous gases. This force is in each man, and it multiplies with overwhelming speed when many use it together. It's name is RHYTHM. Rhythm, more than any other human faculty, has been abandoned and forgotten by the present human race; they have substituted for it mechanical noises; but it is the one faculty which cannot be eradicated until man will have renounced all his latent excellence, and it will always spring new in man's soul whenever his mind longs for it. Today it is the only force which can carry man in triumph over hostile frontiers, certain again that they are god's anointed.

This will be the final trophy to be won by mankind on a field of battle, and the call will be sounded to Greece to come and seize this trophy. On that day they will not advance with the deafening din of drums and fifes, cunningly contrived to stupefy all man's faculties of reason. But their Rhythm will be their own heart's beating, and the beat of their hearts will not be the excitement of the coming slaughter of enemies, their faith will not be in their bombs and bayonets and bullets. They will have cast away these hideous toys impeding the noble movement of men and with the mighty breath of their whole life, with all the strength that their race has gathered for thousands of years, they will advance in a very wind of beauty, singing to their enemies that they cannot kill the men they love.

This is the only military strategy which has never been tried in the world and there is more than an even chance that such an advance into battle would encounter, not destructive cannon fire, but passionate brotherly embraces. But also its failure would be a death worth dying in a world of hideous and useless carnage. To give such an advance a real hope of success, the men would have been taught, not military tactics, but the language of the enemy: and MUSIC would be their Saviour. Not the music of closed concert halls which cannot reach beyond the walls that enclose it, nor yet that of brass bands which is only another mechanized noise, but the music that can carry truth from heart to heart, the truth that quivering lips hardly dare to articulate now, but which could, like God's thunder, strike across earthly battle-fields, with men's voices singing what each man knows: that love is stronger than hate: man's love of God: man's love of man.

This is UPWARD PANIC, which alone can carry man beyond their own fear, into the heart of their love of each other.

This kind of spiritual victory must precede all else. Man must pass through the flame of such a trial to be worthy of the goal that is ahead of him. Only after such a proof in the flesh that faith and courage are still real, and even greater than they have ever yet been, can his own grandest visions materialize into human excellence. Then, if men choose to debate their differences, they will find them already more than half solved, for then they will be holding each other's hands, and each will see himself in the eyes of the other.

In this battle there will have been only one murder. Man will have killed the "trusted ancient of his soul, Obsequious Greed", killed him and buried him forever. In this final heroic dance he will at last have "whittled treason from his side": for when he cannot kill the man he loves, he also cannot cheat them.

It was this that we dreamed of in Delphi. A place where Beauty, Rhythm and Spontaneity; where Education, Economy and Justice would not be jostled as intruders; where not Tolerance but Love should lead to that other side of the Mountain whose near side is Fear and Distrust; and where those whose vision foresees man's true destiny would have their home. Not for all an actual material home. For who knows then how large this place would have to be. Perhaps almost the size of the earth: but a place, however small, whose outlook should have, not a local and limited range, but would, in spirit, really embrace the earth. In such a beginning, size is unimportant because quickly do men and women of great heart and clear vision reach out toward each other; and very quickly indeed would the pent up emotions and generosities know where the heroes are, in however distant localities, and quickly would they draw strength from each other. It is perhaps this fact, subconsciously realized by those who prefer the world as a battle-field for hostile armies, which makes it so difficult to find a plot of ground for such an end.

At all events it was right that this first impetus should have chosen Greece, and especially Delphi as its cradle, for no other place in history has gone so far toward establishing a true basis for the friendly meeting of man with man, and of peoples with peoples; and toward raising the vision of man himself above petty cults and prejudices.

And we dreamed of bringing together there those men in the world of today who are again worthy of being called Guardians of the Sacred Archives: which means Guardians of the spiritual attainments of the Human Race. That they, working as the ancient Sanctuary worked, and adding thereto all the experience and knowledge that humanity has since gained, would gradually found a University of Human Sympathy. The fact that a signal so small as ours evoked so great a response, and also elicited so much official antagonism, is sufficient proof of the vitality of the Delphic Idea.

But if, for one reason or another, it still prove impossible for Delphi, the cradle of intelligence, to shelter the grown man, what matter? There are Greeks all over the world, men who dwell in the Greek spirit wherever they were born, and the Delphic Idea is not confined to one point in space. Somewhere in the world the Greeks will get together, and some one of the existing democracies will give us Sanctuary; and so Greece itself, later on, will perhaps come in second or third in the race toward sanity. However this be, and wherever and by whomever this work be continued, this new impetus will carry on the immemorial Delphic method, and make use of the only medium which can move quickly, and infuse intelligence into masses of men: DRAMA.

Drama, worthy of its own great mission, must act in the only way which can succeed. It will transmit to a living poet the command which the Sanctuary of Eleusis once imposed on Aeschylus: "Write tragedies." This chosen poet will be imbued with the noblest aspirations of his own country. He will infuse into the local traditions of his race the broad certainty of Apollonian harmony, and through the clarity of this thought, with his mastery of poetic rhythms, he will carry his actors and his audience into the very Presence of human sympathy. If also he be a musician his rhythms will turn into song, and if he be a dancer he will himself be the *Koryphaios* of these new crusaders; but if he be not, he will find the best musician and the greatest dancer to transmit the contagion of his poetic vision to ever-increasing masses of men. If he believed that renunciation of all human desires be the solution of human suffering, he will reincarnate the beautiful Hindu god. If he believed that Apollo is he who can again create harmony, he will renew the Sun's radiance in his play; or if he believed that Christ is he who can best restore man's heart and mind, he will throw new life into the Christian legend. But whatever god he choose, he will represent him in his universal aspect, and this means that he will follow a command both older and younger than

Apollo. For Krishna said: "They who love me with dear love, they are in me and I in them." And Christ said: "That ye love one another."

In any bit of earth the world over, this work can take root. It needs only two or three to gather together. But it will be well if Greece retain in this her age-old leadership. For there the air and the mountains, the sea and the sky, nourish their own children well. And there they have a poet who knows the way: who

> "nourished by the Inevitable,
> Who lives with Necessity, and gives Birth
> To pure Destiny."[6]

---

[6] Anghelos Sikelianos, *The Dithyramb of the Rose*. [Ed. The last paragraph and lines 532-4 from Sikelianos' poem are missing in one of the MS copies in the Benaki Museum. Eva Palmer-Sikelianos added these lines when she made her revisions in the original MS (from which copy #1 was made) and were inserted in manuscript number #2 (=p. 338). Actually, lines 532-4 paraphrase *Frag. Orph.* 110 (Abel). -J.P.A.]

INDEX